Human Relations: Principles and Practices

Third Edition

Barry L. Reece
Virginia Polytechnic Institute and State University

Rhonda Brandt
Phillips Junior College

Houghton Mifflin Company   Boston   New York

Sponsoring Editor: *Jennifer B. Speer*
Senior Associate Editor: *Susan M. Kahn*
Project Editor: *Elizabeth G. Napolitano*
Senior Production/Design Coordinator: *Jill Haber*
Senior Manufacturing Coordinator: *Marie Barnes*
Marketing Manager: *Michael B. Mercier*

Cover Design: Peter M. Blaiwas—Vernon Press
Cover Image: Schlemmer, Oskar
     Bauhaus Stairway. (1932)
     Oil on canvas, 63⅞ × 45″
     The Museum of Modern Art, New York. Gift of Phillip Johnson.
     Photograph © 1996 The Museum of Modern Art, New York.

Page 142: Lotus Operating Principles, © Lotus Development Corporation. Used with permission. Lotus is a registered trademark of Lotus Development Corporation.

Printed in the U.S.A.

Library of Congress Catalog Card Number: 96-76949

Student Text ISBN: 0-395-79609-1

123456789-DH-00-99-98-97-96

To Vera, Lynne, Mark, Monique, Michelle, and Colleen

BARRY L. REECE

To Matthew and Patrick

RHONDA BRANDT

Contents

2 Improving Interpersonal Communications   27

6   Personal Values Influence Ethical Choices

9   A Life Plan for Effective Human Relations

About the Authors

The strength of *Human Relations: Principles and Practices* reflects the diverse backgrounds of its authors, who bring together a wealth of experience to ensure the currency, accuracy, and effectiveness of this text.

BARRY L. REECE *Virginia Polytechnic Institute and State University*

Dr. Barry L. Reece is Professor at Virginia Polytechnic Institute and State University. He received his Ed.D. from the University of Nebraska. Dr. Reece has been actively involved in teaching, research, consulting, and designing training programs throughout the past three decades. He has conducted more than 500 workshops and seminars devoted to leadership, human relations, communications, sales, customer service and small business operations. Prior to joining the faculty at Virginia Tech he taught at Ellsworth Community College and the University of Northern Iowa. He has received the Excellence in Teaching Award for classroom teaching at Virginia Tech and the Trainer of the Year Award presented by the Valleys of Virginia Chapter of the American Society for Training and Development.

Dr. Reece has contributed to numerous journals and is author or coauthor of twenty books including *Business, Effective Human Relations in Organizations, Supervision and Leadership in Action,* and *Selling Today—Building Quality Partnerships.* He has served as a consultant to Lowe's Companies, Inc., First Union, WLR Foods, Kinney Shoe Corporation, and numerous other for-profit and not-for-profit organizations.

RHONDA BRANDT *Phillips Junior College*

Rhonda Brandt received her M.Ed. from the University of Missouri—Columbia. She is currently Chair of the Administrative Support Department of Phillips Junior College in Springfield, Missouri, and serves as a member of the Faculty Senate. Prior to joining Phillips Junior College, she served for ten years as the human relations instructor at the Hawkeye Institute of Technology in Waterloo, Iowa. Professor Brandt has been active in the training and consulting industry for over fifteen years, specializing in human relations and self-esteem programs for small businesses, large corporations, and educational institutions. She was a member of the National Council on Vocational Education's working committee for the Presidential White Paper *Building Positive Self-Esteem and a Strong Work Ethic.* Professor Brandt is also coauthor of *Effective Human Relations in Organizations.*

Preface

As businesses struggle to remain competitive in a global environment characterized by change, it is becoming increasingly evident that human relations has achieved a new level of importance in the lives of most people. We have seen the evolution of a work environment that is characterized by greater cultural diversity, more work performed by teams, and greater awareness that quality relationships are just as important as quality products. Employers want to hire persons who can work effectively with fellow employees, clients, customers, and members of the public. The third edition of *Human Relations: Principles and Practices* focuses on the skills a person needs in order to function effectively while working with people. These skills represent an important category of the "basic" or "transferable" skills that employers value so much today.

This edition, like all previous editions, provides the reader with an in-depth presentation of seven major themes of effective human relations: Communication, Self-Awareness, Self-Acceptance, Motivation, Trust, Self-Disclosure, and Conflict Management. These broad themes serve as the foundation for contemporary human relations courses and training programs. They also reflect the current concern in human relations with achieving personal growth and career success.

DEVELOPING THE TOTAL PERSON

The "total person" approach to human relations continues to be a very popular feature of *Human Relations: Principles and Practices*. We strongly support the premise that human behavior at work is influenced by many interdependent traits such as self-esteem, emotional control, values orientation, physical fitness, healthy spirituality, and self-awareness—to name a few. This approach focuses on those human relations skills people need to be well-rounded and thoroughly prepared for a work environment characterized by economic volatility, constant change, and new levels of competitiveness. We continue to believe that if the whole person can be improved, significant benefits occur for the employer because the employee will be able to make wiser choices when human relations problems arise.

IMPROVEMENTS IN THE THIRD EDITION

The third edition of *Human Relations: Principles and Practices* reflects suggestions from current adopters and reviewers, interviews with human resource development professionals, and a thorough review of the current literature. It is a practical text that includes many new real-world examples obtained from a wide range of progressive organizations (large or small) such as Ben & Jerry's Homemade, Inc., Federal Express, Tom's of Maine, Hewlett-Packard Company, and Marriott Corporation. Several important improvements appear in this edition. The most significant changes include:

- **Greater emphasis on transferable job skills.** This change is the result of new content and new learning activities. Some of the new skills-related topics added to this edition include integrity as an element of career success, high-tech communications strategies, negotiating gender-specific language barriers, achieving balance between work life and family life, and assuming leadership roles as an employee. Other new topics include self-efficacy as a dimension of self-esteem, strategies for achieving emotional control, and the corporate casual look.
- **Valuing Work Force Diversity.** A growing number of employers recognize the need to identify, respect, and enhance individual differences in order to remain competitive. The changing demographics of our work force is becoming a vital economic issue today. This new chapter, Chapter 7, introduces the primary and secondary dimensions of diversity, describes how prejudiced attitudes are formed, and identifies ways individuals and organizations can enhance work force diversity. Sexual harassment is also discussed in this chapter.
- **Strategies for Resolving Conflict and Achieving Emotional Control.** Chapter 8 has been extensively revised and includes new material that recognizes that emotions play a critical role in both our work and family life. Some people experience emotional imbalance because they learn to inhibit the expression of certain emotions and overemphasize the expression of others. The emotion of anger is given considerable attention in this chapter.
- **Career Corner Added.** The Career Corner is a new learning activity featured at the end of each chapter. Through its inviting question and answer format, students will be able to obtain answers to important work-related questions.

FEATURES THAT ENHANCE LEARNING

Human Relations: Principles and Practices (third edition) includes several special features that enhance the learning process.

- Each chapter begins with an **opening vignette** that builds reader interest.
- Several **Thinking/Learning Starters** in each chapter give readers the chance to reflect on the material and relate to the concepts discussed.
- **Total Person Insights**—a series of thought-provoking quotations from a variety of authors, business leaders, and scholars—appear in every chapter.
- Each chapter ends with a **summary, Career Corner,** list of **key terms,** and **review questions** designed to reinforce readers' understanding of important ideas.
- Following the review questions are **application exercises,** which enable readers to apply newly learned concepts and practices, as well as to draw on their own experiences.
- A **self-assessment exercise** appears at the end of each chapter with the exception of Chapter 1. These assessment activities provide readers with increased awareness of their strengths and a better understanding of those abilities they may want to improve.
- Each chapter features a **case problem** based on a real-world situation. The majority of these cases deal with current situations in actual organizations.

INSTRUCTOR'S RESOURCES

The Instructor's Resource Manual is a complete teaching guide for the third edition of *Human Relations: Principles and Practices.* The introduction provides a review of the most important teaching and learning principles that facilitate human relations training, a review of several teaching methods, and a description of suggested term projects.

Part I provides a chapter preview, chapter purpose and perspective, a presentation outline, and suggested responses to the Thinking/Learning Starters, review questions, and case problem questions for every chapter in the text. Answers, when applicable, are provided for the application exercises. Additional application exercises are included as well.

Part II contains the test items and answers. True/False, multiple-choice, fill-in-the-blank, and short-answer questions are provided.

Part III provides information regarding videos and supplemental teaching aids.

A set of color transparencies is also available for use with this text. The program consists of figures and key concepts in the text, as well as pieces that are exclusive to the program.

ACKNOWLEDGMENTS

Many people have made contributions to the three editions of *Human Relations: Principles and Practices.* The text has been strengthened as a result of numerous helpful comments and recommendations. We extend special appreciation to:

James Aldrich, *North Dakota State School of Science*
Lois Anderson, *Central Texas College*
Garland Ashbacher, *Kirkwood Community College*
Susan M. Avila, *South Hills Business School*
Rhonda Barry, *American Institute of Commerce*
C. Winston Borgen, *Sacramento Community College*
Charles Busch, *Lee College*
Professor Charles Capps, *Sam Houston State University*
Lawrence Carter, *Jamestown Community College*
Cathy Chew, *Milwaukee Area Technical College*
Dale Dean, *Athens Area Technical Institute*
Ruth Dixon, *Diablo Valley College*
Michael Dzik, *North Dakota State School of Science*
John Elias, *University of Missouri*
Mike Fernsted, *Bryant & Stratton Business Institute*
Dave Fewins, *Neosho County Community College*
Dean Flowers, *Waukesha County Technical College*
George G. Francis, *New York Institute of Business Technology*
M. Camille Garrett, *Tarrant County Junior College*
Roberta Greene, *Central Piedmont Community College*
Sue Hahn, *South Hills Business School*
Ralph Hall, *Community College of Southern Nevada*
Sally Hanna-Jones, *Hocking Technical College*
Carolyn K. Hayes, *Polk Community College*
Stephen Hiatt, *Catawba College*
Bill Hurd, *Lowe's Companies, Inc.*
Marlene Katz, *Canada College*
Robert Kegel, Jr., *Cypress College*
Vance A. Kennedy, *College of Mateo*
Grace Klinefelter, *Ft. Lauderdale College*
Deborah Lineweaver, *New River Community College*
Roger Lynch, *Inver Hills Community College*
Russ Moorhead, *Des Moines Area Community College*
Marilyn Mueller, *Simpson College*
Erv. J. Napier, *Kent State University*
Barbara Ollhoff, *Waukesha County Technical College*
Jean Ostrander, *Hamilton Business College*
Leonard L. Palumbo, *Northern Virginia Community College*
James Patton, *Mississippi State University*
C. Richard Paulson, *Mankato State University*
Naomi W. Peralta, *The Institute of Financial Education*
William Price, *Virginia Polytechnic Institute and State University*

Linda Pulliam, *Pulliam Associates, Chapel Hill, N.C.*
Jack C. Reed, *University of Northern Iowa*
Lynne Shanklin, *Rockwell International*
Mary R. Shannon, *Wenatchee Valley College*
J. Douglas Shatto, *Muskingum Area Technical College*
Cindy Stewart, *Des Moines Area Community College*
Rahmat O. Tavallali, *Wooster Business College*
V.S. Thakur, *Community College of Rhode Island*
Linda Truesdale, *Midlands Technical College*
Wendy Bletz Turner, *New River Community College*
Marc Wayner, *Hocking Technical College*
Steven Whipple, *St. Cloud Technical College*
Burl Worley, *Allan Hancock College*

We would also like to thank Dr. Denis Waitley and Mr. Charles Haefner for helping us develop a fuller understanding of human relations.

Over 100 business organizations, government agencies, and nonprofit institutions provided us with the real-world examples that appear throughout the text. We are grateful to organizations that allowed us to conduct interviews, observe workplace environments, and use special photographs and material.

BARRY L. REECE
RHONDA BRANDT

Chapter 1

Introduction to Human Relations

Chapter Preview

After studying this chapter, you will be able to

1. Understand how the study of human relations will help you succeed in your chosen career.

2. Explain the nature, purpose, and importance of human relations in an organizational setting.

3. Identify the reasons human relations is receiving more attention in the workplace.

4. Identify the major forces influencing human behavior at work.

5. Review the historical development of the human relations movement.

6. Identify the seven basic themes that serve as the foundation for effective human relations.

MANY JOB APPLICANTS AT Southwest Airlines Co. are surprised to learn that a sense of humor is an important employment requirement. The company wants to hire people who work well in a collegial environment and feel that work should be an enjoyable experience. The result of this hiring practice is a group of employees who often go out of their way to amuse, surprise, and entertain the customer. Veteran Southwest fliers expect to have a few laughs on every flight. The customary no-smoking announcement on one flight was replaced by this effort: "Good morning, ladies and gentlemen. Those of you who wish to smoke will please file out to our lounge on the wing, where you can enjoy our feature film, *Gone with the Wind*." An attendant on another flight hid in the overhead luggage bin and then popped out when passengers started filing on board.[1]

Herb Kelleher, Southwest's zany chief executive officer, says people are the most important company asset. He sees a strong connection between workplace satisfaction and company success. Kelleher's dedication to employees has earned his company recognition as a leader in good employee-management relations. Although Southwest has grown from 198 employees in 1971 to 12,000 people today, the company has been able to maintain a close-knit family atmosphere. He has proven that a large company with a unionized work force can be a place where kindness, cooperation, and human spirit abound.

Can a company that emphasizes fun as a way of life operate efficiently and earn good profits? Apparently so. By almost every measure of efficiency in the airline industry, Southwest is at the top of the charts. Profitable every year since 1972, it was recently recognized as the major airline with the fewest consumer complaints.[2] ■

Southwest Airlines' emphasis on relationships is not an isolated case. A growing number of U.S. organizations, from hospitals to hotels, are discovering and rediscovering the benefits of work environments that emphasize employee growth and development opportunities and the human side of enterprise. Most organizations that survive and prosper over a long period of time maintain a balance between concern for production and concern for people.

THE NATURE, PURPOSE, AND IMPORTANCE OF HUMAN RELATIONS

Many of America's best-managed organizations are not simply being "nice to people"; they are genuinely helping employees come alive through their work. Managers have learned that the goals of worker and workplace need not conflict.[3] This chapter focuses on the nature of human relations, its development, and its importance to the achievement of individual and organizational goals.

Training helped this Motorola team win top honors in the company's annual quality contest. (Michael L. Abramson)

Human Relations Defined

The term **human relations** in its broadest sense covers all types of interactions among people — their conflicts, cooperative efforts, and group relationships. It is the study of *why* our beliefs, attitudes, and behaviors sometimes cause interpersonal conflict in our personal lives and in work-related situations. The study of human relations emphasizes the analysis of human behavior, prevention strategies, and resolution of behavioral problems.

Knowledge of human relations does not, of course, begin in the classroom. Although this may be your first formal course in the subject, your "education" in human relations actually began with your family, friends, and early employment experiences. You learned what was acceptable and what was not. You tested your behavior against that of others, formed close relationships, experienced conflict, developed perceptions of yourself, and discovered how to get most of your needs met. By the time you completed high school, you had probably formed a fairly complex network of relationships and had a pretty good idea of who you were.

The Importance of Human Relations

One of the most significant developments in recent years has been the increased importance of interpersonal skills in almost every type of work setting. In the minds of many employers, interpersonal skills represent an important category of "basic" or "transferable" skills a worker is expected to bring to the job. Technical ability is often not enough to achieve career success. Studies indicate that many of the people who have difficulty in obtaining or holding a job, or advancing to positions of greater responsibility, possess the needed technical competence but lack interpersonal competence.

Several important trends in the workplace have given new importance to human relations. Each of the following trends provides support for the development of competence in human relations:

• *The labor market has become a place of churning dislocation caused by the heavy volume of mergers, buyouts, and business closings.* These activities have been accompanied by thousands of layoffs and the elimination of hundreds of product lines. Even industries noted for job security have recently engaged in massive layoffs. A million U.S. defense workers have lost their jobs since the end of the Cold War. The wave of consolidations in the nation's banking industry set the stage for more than 100,000 job losses in the early 1990s. And more than 100,000 AT&T workers have been cut since the family breakup began. At International Business Machines Corp. (IBM), where a job once meant good pay, great benefits, and job security, 170,000 jobs have been cut worldwide in recent years. Even when the economy is strong, many companies continue to eliminate jobs.[4] Massive downsizing has created another phenomenon in the workplace — the large-scale use of temporary workers. More than 2,000 firms nationwide are now involved in employee leasing. Some estimates indicate that one of every four employees is a part-time worker, a freelancer, an independent professional, or a leased employee. The temporary work force is expected to grow steadily to the year 2000.[5] As people attempt to cope with rapid technological change and a radically changed job market, there is every reason to believe we will see more, not less, volatility in the labor force. For large numbers of workers, whether full-time or temporary, interpersonal skills represent the critical "transferable skills" needed in an ever-changing labor market.

• *Organizations are increasingly oriented toward service to clients, patients, and customers.* As the authors of *Service America* note, we now live in a service economy, which means that relationships are becoming more important than physical products.[6] Restaurants, hospitals, banks, public utilities, colleges, airlines, and retail stores all must now gain and retain the patronage of their clients and customers. In any service-type firm, there are thousands of "moments of truth," those critical incidents in which customers come into contact with the organization and form their impressions of its quality and service. Employees must not only be able to get along with customers; they must also project a favorable image of the organization they represent. Constant contact with the public requires a high degree of patience, versatility, and sensitivity to the needs of a diverse population.

• *A growing number of organizations are recognizing improved quality as the key to survival.* The notion of quality as a competitive tool has been around for

THE **IBM** UNIFORM:

BLACK EYEGLASSES
WHITE SHIRT
BLUE POLKA-DOT TIE
BLUE SUIT
PINK SLIP

LAYOFF

many years, but today it is receiving much more attention. In a period of fierce competition, a consumer does not have to tolerate poor-quality products or services. Stephen Shepard, editor-in-chief of *Business Week*, states that quality "may be the biggest competitive issue of the late 20th and early 21st centuries."[7] People are at the heart of every quality-improvement program. Well-trained workers who are given authority and responsibility can do the most to improve quality.[8]

• *Many companies are organizing their workers into teams in which each specialized employee plays a part.* Organizations eager to improve quality, improve job satisfaction, increase worker participation in decision making and problem solving, and improve customer service are turning to teams. Typical of the team approach is the Hewlett-Packard Co. service center in Mountain View, California, where employees answer phones and respond to customers' questions. This self-regulated team is given a great deal of autonomy, including the selection of their own supervisor.[9]

Although some organizations have successfully harnessed the power of teams, others have encountered problems. One barrier to productivity is the team member who is uncooperative and hinders teamwork. Another barrier is the poorly prepared team leader. The use of teams is increasing, but most organizations experience growing pains as human problems interfere with team development.[10]

• *Diversity has become a prominent characteristic of today's work force.* In the years ahead, a large majority of those entering the work force will be women and people of color. Passage of the Americans with Disabilities Act in 1990 opened the employment door to more people with physical or mental impairments. And in the future, we will see increased employment of the over–sixty-five population. Within this heterogeneous work force we will find a multitude of values, expectations, and work habits. Today, the new buzz words are "valuing differences" and "managing diversity." There is a need to develop increased tolerance for persons who differ in terms of age, gender, race, physical traits, and sexual orientation. Work force diversity is the major theme of Chapter 7.

• *A new type of leader is needed among the ranks of supervisory-management personnel.* The current generation of workers is frequently referred to as Generation X. Members of this group, sometimes labeled Twentysomethings, grew up in the 1970s and 1980s. They entered a fickle job market offering less job security than that available to the Baby Boomers, the previous generation. Although generalizations are dangerous, it seems likely that Generation X workers may bring to the job less company loyalty, less desire to work long hours, and less optimism about the future. Many members of Generation X believe that nearly all jobs are temporary, so they are less likely to be motivated by a pension plan or some other benefit that has a long-term payoff.[11] These attitudes further increase the need for leaders who can assume the role of teacher, mentor, and resource person. Leaders who can shift from manager-as-order-giver to manager-as-facilitator are more likely to bring out the best in the people they supervise. James Baughman, head of management development at General Electric Co., sees leadership as simply common sense: "It's just treating people with dignity and making them feel like part of a team."[12]

It is safe to say that no line of work, organization, or industry will enjoy immunity from these trends. Today's employee must be adaptable and flexible to achieve success within a climate of change and uncertainty. It is important for everyone to develop those interpersonal skills that are valued by all employers.

The Challenge of Human Relations

To develop and apply the wide range of interpersonal skills needed in today's workplace can be extremely challenging. You will be working with clients, customers, patients, and other workers who vary greatly in terms of age, work background, communications style, values, cultural background, gender, and work ethic. When you make contact with these persons, you present yourself as a multifaceted being with a complex array of values, experiences, and perceptions. The authors of *Workforce America!* point out that "human beings are complex systems and [that] each dimension of diversity adds another element of complexity to the overall functioning of the system."[13] Because every person you come in contact with is unique, each encounter offers a new challenge.

Human relations is further complicated by the fact that we must manage three types of relationships. The first relationship is the one with ourselves. Many people carry around a set of ideas and feelings about themselves that are quite negative and in most cases quite inaccurate. In fact, many people reserve the very harshest criticism for themselves. People who have negative feelings about their abilities and accomplishments, and who engage in constant self-criticism, must struggle to maintain a good relationship with themselves. The importance of high self-esteem will be addressed in Chapter 4.

The second type of relationship we must learn to manage consists of the one-to-one relationships we face in our personal and work lives. People in the health-care field, sales, food service, and a host of other occupations face this challenge many times each day. A nurse, for example, must build one-to-one relationships with patients. In some cases, racial, age, or gender bias serves as a barrier to good human relations.

The third challenge we face is the management of relationships with members of a group. As already noted, many workers are assigned to a team on either a full-time or part-time basis. At General Motors Corp.'s Saturn plant in Spring Hill, Tennessee, cars move along the line on wooden pallets, and teams of workers travel with them.[14] Lack of cooperation among team members can result in quality problems or a slowdown in production.

The Influence of the Behavioral Sciences

The field of human relations draws on the behavioral sciences — psychology, sociology, and anthropology. Basically, these sciences focus on the *why* of human behavior. Psychology attempts to find out why *individuals* act as they do, and sociology and anthropology concentrate primarily on *group* dynamics and social interaction. Human relations differs from the behavioral sciences in one important respect. Although also interested in the why of human behavior, human relations goes further and looks at what can be done to anticipate problems, resolve them, or even prevent them from happening. In other words, this field emphasizes knowledge that can be *applied* in practical ways to problems of interpersonal relations at work or in our personal life.

Human Relations and the "Total Person"

The material in this book will focus on human relations as the study of *how people satisfy both personal growth needs and organizational goals in their careers.* We believe, as do most authors in the field of human relations, that such human traits as physical fitness, emotional control, self-awareness, self-esteem, and values orientation are interdependent. Although some organizations may occasionally wish they could employ only a person's skill or brain, all that can be employed is the **total person.**[15] A person's separate characteristics are part

Total Person Insight

"To me, there's no essential difference between the way we spend time in work and the way we spend the rest of our lives. Time is time; our working life adds up — in a few short decades — to be our life itself."

MARSHA SINETAR

Author, *Do What You Love . . . The Money Will Follow*

of a single system making up that whole person. Work life is not totally separate from home life, and emotional conditions are not separate from physical conditions. The quality of a person's work, for example, is often related to physical fitness and nutrition.

Many organizations are beginning to recognize that when the whole person is improved, significant benefits accrue to the firm. These organizations are establishing employee development programs that address the total person, not just the employee skills needed to perform the job. These programs include such topics as stress management, assertiveness training, physical fitness, problem solving, and values clarification. A few examples follow:

Item: Com-Corp Industries, a 100-employee metal-stamping shop in Cleveland, Ohio, recognizes that money-management problems add stress to the lives of many employees. Workers are given personal money-management lessons on such subjects as structuring a household budget; calculating the advantages of buying a house compared with renting an apartment; and buying a car by paying cash instead of taking out a loan.[16]

Item: Patagonia Inc., a designer and distributor of outdoor wear, offers new fathers in its employ eight weeks of paid paternity leave. The company also provides several special programs for working mothers. These family-friendly workplace initiatives earned Patagonia a spot on *Working Mother* magazine's roster of the country's best companies for working moms.[17]

Item: Lands' End, Inc., the Wisconsin-based mail order company, is working hard to encourage physical fitness. Employees have been provided with a $9 million state-of-the-art fitness and recreation complex. Computers were installed so that employees could record progress toward individual fitness goals.[18]

Some of the results of these programs may be difficult to assess in terms of profit and loss. For example, does the person in good physical health contribute more? If an employee is under considerable stress, does this mean he or she will have more accidents on the job? Specific answers vary, but most human resource management experts agree that an employee's physical condition and mental state have a definite impact on job performance and productivity.

The Need for a Supportive Environment

John W. Humphrey, chief executive officer of the Forum Corporation, says, "These days, the only sustainable competitive advantage in any business is people, not product."[19] Unfortunately, not every CEO or manager attributes the same importance to people or people problems. Some managers do not believe that total person training, job enrichment, motivation techniques, or career development will help increase productivity or strengthen worker commitment to the job. It is true that when such practices are tried without full commitment or without full management support, there is a good chance they will fail. Such failures often have a demoralizing effect on employees and management alike. "Human relations" may take the blame, and management will be reluctant to try other human relations methods or approaches in the future.

A basic assumption of this book is that human relations, when applied in a positive and supportive environment, can help individuals achieve greater personal satisfaction from their careers and help increase an organization's productivity and efficiency.

Myths and Misconceptions

Now that you know what human relations *is*, it may be helpful to explore what it is *not*. It is not concerned with giving you information on personality or character development that will enable you to manipulate people. Nor does the study of human relations offer the ultimate formula for solving the people problems you are likely to encounter. In dealing with others, you will find that there is seldom a clear-cut "right" or "wrong" way to handle problem situations. In one plant, for example, the night superintendent found that workers on the first shift settled their disputes themselves. They viewed his efforts to arbitrate as an interference. Workers on the second shift, however, expected their superintendent to settle disagreements and brought him all their disputes. Their view of a good manager was someone who knew how to arbitrate.

Nevertheless, the study of human relations *can* help you develop appropriate solutions to problems by giving you a good grasp of behavioral concepts that apply to your own behavior and that of others. Texts such as this one can provide a good grounding in the fundamentals of human relations and offer guidelines and suggestions for modifying behavior and enhancing group interaction. Each chapter in this book will provide you with some tools that will help you to be more effective in managing relationships with yourself and others.

Thinking / Learning Starters

1. How important will human relationship skills be in your future career(s)?

2. Do you believe the trends in the workplace described in this chapter will continue throughout the 1990s? What new trends might develop?

THE FORCES INFLUENCING BEHAVIOR AT WORK

A major purpose of this text is to increase your knowledge of factors that influence human behavior in a variety of work settings. An understanding of human behavior at work begins with a review of the six major forces that affect every employee, regardless of the size of the organization. As Figure 1.1 indicates, these are organizational culture, supervisory-management influence, work group influence, job influence, personal characteristics of the worker, and family influence.

Organizational Culture

Every organization, whether a manufacturing plant, retail store, hospital, or government agency, is unique. Each has its own culture. **Organizational culture** is influenced by the mission, vision, beliefs, and values of the firm. Most organizations over a period of time tend to take on distinct norms and practices. At Maytag Company, for example, a commitment to high-quality products has been instilled in every member of the work force. Maytag machines rank at the top in industry comparisons, and this fact builds pride in the workers. The American Honda Motor Car Company has made the same commitment to quality.

An organization's culture is an outgrowth of the beliefs, values, goals, and aspirations of those who join together to create it. For several decades IBM was guided by three basic beliefs expressed by Thomas J. Watson, Jr., son of IBM's founder: Pursue excellence; provide the best customer service; and show employees "respect for the individual."[20] Many companies have given direction to their employees by preparing written mission, credo, or vision statements. A mission statement often frames the firm's guiding philosophy. Part of the Ford Motor Co. mission statement reads as follows: "Our mission is to improve

FIGURE 1.1

Major Forces Influencing Worker Behavior

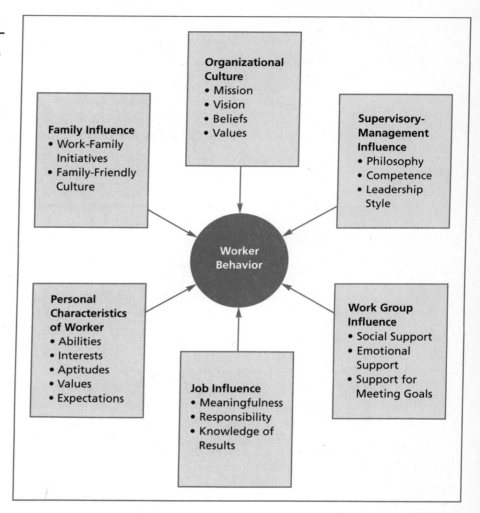

continually our products and services to meet our customer's needs, allowing us to prosper as a business and to provide a reasonable return for our stockholders, the owners of our business."[21] Ford's mission statement is supported by several basic values. The first value focuses on employees: "Our people are the source of our strength. They provide our corporate intelligence and determine our reputation and vitality. Involvement and teamwork are our core human values."[22] A growing number of organizations are creating vision statements that direct the energies of the company and inspire employees to achieve greater heights.

Total Person Insight

"Jobs do a lot more than merely provide income. They provide the opportunity to learn and enhance skills, to have some control over one's fate and, perhaps most important, to gain a sense of self-worth, a sense of carrying one's own weight."

WILLIAM RASPBERRY

Syndicated Columnist

Supervisory-Management Influence

Supervisory-management personnel are in a key position to influence employee behavior. It is no exaggeration to say that supervisors and managers are the spokespersons for the organization. Their philosophy, competence, and leadership style establish the organization's image in the eyes of employees. Each employee develops certain perceptions about the organization's concern for his or her welfare. These perceptions, in turn, influence such important factors as productivity, customer relations, safety consciousness, and loyalty to the firm. Effective leaders are aware of the organization's basic purposes, why it exists, and its general direction. They are able to communicate this information to workers in a clear and positive manner.

Supervisory-management personnel hold the key to both outlook and performance. They are in a unique position to unlock the internal forces of motivation and help employees channel their energies toward achieving the goals of the organization. Today, managers need to use both logic and intuition, recognize both facts and feelings, and be both technically competent and emotionally caring.[23]

Work Group Influence

In recent years, behavioral scientists have devoted considerable research to determining the influence of group affiliation on the individual worker. They are particularly interested in group influence within the formal structure of the organization. This research has identified three functions of group membership.[24] First, it can satisfy *social needs*. Many people find the hours spent at work enjoyable because coworkers provide needed social support. Second, the work group can provide the *emotional support* needed to deal with pressures and problems on or off the job. Finally, the group provides *assistance in solving problems and meeting goals*. A cohesive work group lends support and provides the resources we need to be productive workers. The potential value of work group influence helps explain why so many organizations are using various types of teams to improve productivity.

Job Influence

Work in modern societies does more than fulfill economic needs. A job can provide a sense of meaning, a sense of community, and self-esteem.[25] As one organizational consultant noted, work has taken center stage in the lives of many people: "We spend most of our working hours doing our jobs, thinking about work, and getting to and from our workplaces. When we feel good about our work, we tend to feel good about our lives. When we find our work unsatisfying and unrewarding, we don't feel good."[26] Unfortunately, many people hold jobs that do not make them feel good. Many workers perceive their jobs to be meaningless and boring because there is little variety to the work. Some factory workers complain that their work is noisy, dirty, and monotonous. Many operators of electronic data-processing terminals say the tedious work causes them physical and mental anguish.

Job satisfaction tends to increase when there is compatibility between the wants and needs of the employee and the characteristics of the job. To be completely satisfying, a job must provide three experiences for a worker: meaningfulness, responsibility, and knowledge of results.[27] To enhance both meaningfulness and responsibility, some organizations encourage employees to acquire the training needed to perform a wide range of tasks. Many secretaries do research on the Internet, purchase large-scale office technology, and give presentations at business meetings.[28]

Personal Characteristics of the Worker

Every worker brings to the job a combination of abilities, interests, aptitudes, values, and expectations. Worker behavior on the job is most frequently a reflection of how well the work environment accommodates the unique characteristics of each worker. For more than half a century, work researchers and theorists have attempted to define the ideal working conditions that would maximize worker productivity. These efforts have met with some success, but unanswered questions remain.

Identifying the ideal work environment is difficult because today's work force is characterized by much greater diversity. A single parent may greatly value a flexible work schedule and child care. The recipient of a new master of business administration (MBA) degree may value challenging work and career advancement opportunities above other benefits. Other workers may desire more leisure time.

Coming into the workplace today is a new generation of workers with value systems and expectations about work that differ from those of the previous

Patience and a caring attitude are two of the important personal characteristics needed by Marcia Baynes, a teacher at Longfellow School in Cambridge. (David L. Ryan/The Boston Globe)

generation. Today's better-educated and better-informed workers value identity and achievement. They also have a heightened sense of their rights.

Family Influence

There is general agreement that people need to establish a balance between work life and family life. Balance implies an interconnection among many areas of work and the family.[29] We are just beginning to understand some of these strong linkages. For example, a study of blue-collar fathers in dual-earner households found a powerful tie between conditions at work and treatment of children. Fathers who experienced autonomy at work and worked for supportive bosses tended to have higher self-esteem and to treat their children with greater acceptance and warmth. The same researchers found that families often bear the brunt of job stress.[30]

Many organizations have found that family problems are linked to employee problems such as tardiness, absenteeism, and turnover. The discovery has led many companies to develop work-family programs and policies that help employees juggle the demands of children, spouses, and elderly parents. Lancaster Laboratories Inc., a small firm in Lancaster, Pennsylvania, offers its employees on-site elder care, on-site child-care, and on-site sick care.[31] Marriott International, Inc., introduced a number of work-family initiatives after learning that family and personal problems fuel turnover as high as 300 percent at some of its hotels.[32] Johnson & Johnson, the New Jersey–based maker of health-care products, is considered to have one of the most family-friendly cultures in America. The company maintains four on-site child-care facilities, offers up to $3,000 help to workers who are adopting children, and supports a one-year parental leave program. The company credo includes this sentence: "We must be mindful of ways to help our employees fulfill their family responsibilities."[33] Johnson & Johnson has established a family-friendly culture by recognizing that employees need help in balancing their work lives and their home lives.

In recent years the field of psychology has given greater recognition to the powerful influence of the family on individual behavior. Family behavior is patterned, and these patterns influence the behavior of individual members. In some families, for example, affection is not expressed openly. Individuals who grow up in such families may have difficulty expressing warmth and affection outside of the family setting. **Family therapy** is an approach to treating human problems by bringing together the members of a family to help them work out conflicts and other problems at their source. Unfortunately, many families turn to family therapists only after a crisis.[34]

THE DEVELOPMENT OF THE HUMAN RELATIONS MOVEMENT

Problems in human relations are not new. All cooperative efforts carry the potential for people-oriented conflicts. But it is only within the past few decades that management, behavioral science researchers, and industry experts have recognized that human relations problems can have considerable impact on organizational productivity. During this period, the human relations movement has matured into a distinct and important field of study.

The Hawthorne Studies

Researchers became more aware of the complex nature of human behavior as a result of studies conducted in the 1920s. A Harvard University research team headed by Elton Mayo initiated a series of experiments to determine relationships between changes in physical working conditions and employee productivity. Their research became known as the **Hawthorne studies** and has become a landmark in the human relations field.

For one part of their research, Mayo and his colleagues selected two groups of employees doing similar work under similar conditions and kept output records for each group. After a time, the researchers began to vary the intensity of light for one group while keeping it constant for the other. Each time they increased the light, productivity rose. To determine if better illumination was responsible for the higher outputs, they began to dim the light. *Productivity continued to rise.* In fact, one of the highest levels of output was recorded when the light was scarcely brighter than the full moon! The researchers realized some other influence was at work.

Mayo made several important discoveries. One of them was that all the attention focused on the test group made these individuals feel important and appreciated. For the first time, they were getting feedback on their job performance. In addition, test conditions allowed them greater freedom from supervisory control. Under these circumstances, morale and motivation increased and productivity rose.

Although some observers have criticized the Hawthorne studies for flawed research methodology,[35] this research can be credited with helping change the way management viewed workers.

From the Great Depression to the 1990s

During the Great Depression, interest in human relations research waned as other ways of humanizing the workplace gained momentum. During that period, unions increased their militant campaigns to organize workers and force employers to pay attention to such issues as working conditions, higher pay, shorter hours, and protection for child laborers. With the passage of the Wagner Act in 1935, businesses were required by law to negotiate contracts with union representatives. Other labor laws passed in the 1930s outlawed child labor, reduced the hours women worked, and instituted a minimum wage for many industries.

During World War II and the years of postwar economic expansion, interest in the human relations field was revived. Countless papers and research studies

---

Total Person Insight

"You can only get so much more productivity out of reorganization and automation. Where you really get productivity leaps is in the minds and hearts of people."

JAMES BAUGHMAN

Director of Management Development, General Electric Co.

Persons who enter the world championship sled-dog races in Alaska are highly motivated to win. The drive to satisfy human needs can be very strong. (Danny Daniels/The Picture Cube, Inc.)

on worker efficiency, group dynamics, organization, and motivational methods were published. Douglas McGregor introduced his Theory X, a rather pessimistic, authoritarian view of human behavior, and Theory Y, a more positive, optimistic view. Abraham Maslow, a noted psychologist, devised a "hierarchy of needs," stating that people satisfied their needs in a particular order. Each theory had considerable influence on the study of human behavior at work.

Since the 1950s, theories and concepts regarding human behavior have focused more and more on an understanding of human interaction. Eric Berne in the 1960s revolutionized the way people think about interpersonal communication when he introduced transactional analysis, with its "Parent-Adult-Child" model. At about the same time, Carl Rogers published his work on personality development, interpersonal communication, and group dynamics. In the early 1980s, William Ouchi introduced the Theory Z style of management, which is based on the belief that worker involvement is the key to increased productivity. Two books published by Jay Hall during the 1980s, *The Competence Process* and *The Competence Connection*, reminded management of the vast reserve of talent and the desire to perform embodied in most workers. Organizations must determine how to tap this reserve of competence.

There is no doubt that management consultants Tom Peters and Robert Waterman also influenced management thinking regarding the importance of people in organizations. Their best-selling book *In Search of Excellence,* published in 1982, describes eight attributes of excellence found in America's best-run companies.[36] One of these attributes, "productivity through people," emphasizes that excellent companies treat the worker as the root source of quality and productivity.

In 1989 Stephen Covey authored a powerful book on leadership and human relations entitled *The Seven Habits of Highly Effective People.* He describes the principles of fairness, integrity, honesty, patience, and humility as essential ingredients in what he describes as the *character ethic.* Covey believes that character is the foundation for true success and happiness in life.

Thinking / Learning Starters

1. What do you personally find to be the basic rewards of work?

2. The book *In Search of Excellence* cites "productivity through people" as an attribute of excellent companies. Do you agree or disagree with this view?

3. What degree of worker involvement have you experienced in places where you have worked?

MAJOR THEMES IN HUMAN RELATIONS

Seven broad themes emerge from the study of human relations. They are communication, self-awareness, self-acceptance, motivation, trust, self-disclosure, and conflict management. These themes reflect the current concern in human relations with the twin goals of personal growth development and the satisfaction of organizational objectives. To some degree, these themes are interrelated (see Figure 1.2) and most will be discussed in more than one chapter of this book.

Communication

It is not an exaggeration to describe communication as the "heart and soul" of human relations. **Communication** is the means by which we come to an understanding of ourselves and others. To grow and develop as persons, we must communicate. John Diekman, author of *Human Connections,* says that "if we are going to do anything constructive and helping with one another, it must be through our communication."[37] Communication is the *human* connection. That is why the subject is covered in more than one section of this book. In

FIGURE 1.2

Major Themes in
Human Relations

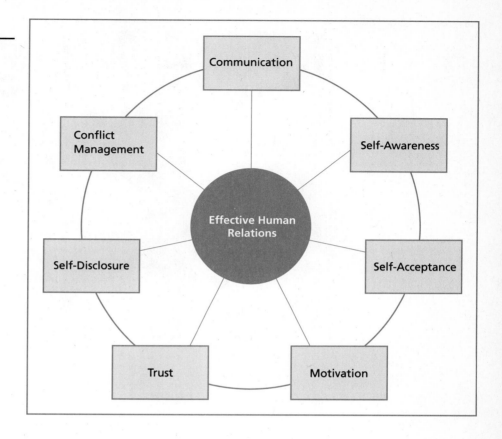

Chapter 2 we will explore the fundamentals of both personal and organizational communication. It is these fundamentals that provide the foundation for all efforts to improve communication. Suggestions on how to improve communication will appear in other chapters.

Self-Awareness

One of the most important ways to develop improved relationships with others is to develop a better understanding of ourselves. With increased **self-awareness** comes a greater understanding of how our behavior influences others. Stephen Covey says that self-awareness enables us to stand apart and examine the way we "see" ourselves. He states that self-awareness "affects not only our attitudes and behaviors, but also how we see other people."[38]

The importance of self-awareness is being recognized by an increasing number of professional trainers and educators. Recently, the University of

Good communication and trust enhance the quality of music played by the Boston Symphony Orchestra. (Miro Vintoniv/The Picture Cube, Inc.)

Pennsylvania's Wharton School overhauled its MBA program. A major goal of this overhaul is to place greater emphasis on people skills. Now during the entire first year, students get involved in a variety of group-interaction exercises and complete a series of personality instruments. Student character traits determined by test instrument scores are transformed into video vignettes and are shown in class. Students see themselves and listen to analysis from classmates. The goal is to help students learn how others perceive them.[39] Accurate self-knowledge is essential for developing positive personal relationships, managing others effectively, and setting appropriate life goals and career paths.[40]

Self-Acceptance

The degree to which you like and accept yourself is the degree to which you can genuinely like and accept other people. **Self-acceptance** is the foundation of successful interaction with others. In a work setting, people with positive self-concepts tend to cope better with change, accept responsibility more readily, tolerate differences, and generally work well as team members. A negative self-concept, however, can create barriers to good interpersonal relations. Self-acceptance is crucial not only for building relationships with others but also for setting and achieving goals. The more you believe you can do, the more you are likely to accomplish. Chapter 4 will explain why high self-esteem (complete self-acceptance) is essential for effective human relations. That chapter will also help you identify ways to achieve greater self-acceptance.

Motivation

Human behavior researchers no longer talk about **motivation** in terms of reward and punishment; rather, they now view it as a drive to satisfy needs. Most employees tend to work best when they feel the organization is meeting their needs for growth and development. As a result, motivation is likely to be high where employees and managers support and influence one another in positive ways. Chapter 6 will help you identify the priorities and values that motivate you.

Trust

Good relationships, whether among coworkers or between employer and employee, are based on **trust**. Without trust, most human relationships will degenerate into conflict. William Ouchi, author of *Theory Z*, a popular book about how American business can meet the Japanese challenge, recognizes trust as a key to long-term personal and organizational success. He says, "To trust another is to know that the two of you share basic goals in the long-run so that left to your own devices, each will behave in ways that are not harmful to the other."[41]

When a lack of trust exists in an organization, a decline in the flow of information almost always results. Employees communicate less information to their supervisors, express opinions reluctantly, and avoid discussions. Cooperation, so necessary in a modern work setting, deteriorates. When a climate of trust is present, frank discussion of problems and a free exchange of ideas and information are encouraged. The concept of trust will be discussed in several chapters.

Self-Disclosure

Self-disclosure and trust are two halves of a whole. The more open you are with people, the more trust you build up. The more trust there is in a relationship, the safer you feel to disclose who you are. Self-disclosure is also part of good communication and helps eliminate unnecessary guessing games. Managers who let their subordinates know what is expected of them help those employees fulfill their responsibilities. Chapter 2 will emphasize the need of individuals to verbalize the thoughts and feelings they carry within them and will provide many practical suggestions on how to use constructive self-disclosure.

Conflict Management

Conflict management in human relations refers primarily to conflicts among people *within* the organization, although the term can also mean disputes among organizations or between an organization and the public. It is true that whenever people work together, some conflict is inevitable. But unresolved disputes, personal clashes, and disagreements can hurt an organization's operations and reduce its effectiveness. Conflict tends to obstruct cooperative action, create suspicion and distrust, and decrease productivity. The ability to anticipate or resolve conflict can be an invaluable skill. Although Chapter 8 will deal specifically with the topic of conflict management, suggestions on how conflict can be handled constructively appear in other chapters.

Thinking / Learning Starter

Now that you have had an opportunity to read about the seven themes of human relations, what do you consider your strongest areas? In which areas do you feel you need improvement? Why?

HUMAN RELATIONS: BENEFITS TO YOU

As previously noted, the work force is currently characterized by downsizing, mergers, buyouts, and business closings. We are seeing more emphasis on quality products and quality services. In addition, diversity has become a more prominent characteristic of today's work force. These conditions will very likely continue throughout the 1990s. One of the best ways to cope with these changes is to develop and apply the interpersonal skills needed for success in today's working world.

A basic course in human relations cannot give you a foolproof set of techniques for solving every people-related problem that might arise. It can, however, give you a better understanding of human behavior in groups, help you become more sensitive to yourself and others, and enable you to act more wisely when problems occur. You may even be able to anticipate conflicts or prevent small problems from escalating into major ones.

Many leaders feel that courses in human relations are important because very few workers are responsible to themselves alone. These leaders point out that most jobs today are interdependent. If people in these jobs cannot work effectively as a team, the efficiency of the organization will suffer.

Summary

The study of human relations helps us understand how people fulfill both personal growth needs and organizational goals in their careers. Many organizations are beginning to realize that an employee's life outside the job can have a significant impact on work performance, and some are developing training programs in human relations that address the total person. Increasingly, organizations are discovering that many forces influence the behavior of people at work.

Human relations is not a set of foolproof techniques for solving people-related problems. Rather, it gives people an understanding of basic behavior concepts that may enable them to make wiser choices when problems arise, to anticipate or prevent conflicts, and to keep minor problems from escalating into major ones.

The development of the human relations movement involved a redefinition of the nature of work and the gradual perception of managers and workers as complex human beings. Elton Mayo's Hawthorne studies represent a landmark study of motivation and worker needs. Many industry leaders predict an increased emphasis on human relations research and application. The reasons for this trend include greater awareness that human relations problems serve as a major barrier to the efficient operation of an organization, the employment of workers who expect more from their jobs, and worker organizations and government agencies pressing for attention to employee concerns.

Seven major themes emerge from a study of human relations: communication, self-awareness, self-acceptance, motivation, trust, self-disclosure, and conflict management. These themes reflect the current concern in human relations with personal growth and satisfaction of organizational objectives.

Career Corner

Q. The daily newspapers and television news shows are constantly reporting on mergers, business closings, and downsizing efforts. With so much uncertainty in the job market, how can I best prepare for a career?

A. You are already doing one thing that is very important — keeping an eye on labor market trends. During a period of rapid change and little job security, you must continuously study workplace trends and assess your career preparation. Louis S. Richman, in a *Fortune* magazine article entitled "How to Get Ahead in America," said, "Climbing in your career calls for being clear about your personal goals, learning how to add value, and developing skills you can take anywhere." After you clarify the type of work that would be rewarding for you, be sure you have the skills necessary to be competitive in that employment area. Keep in mind that today's employers demand more, so be prepared to add value to the company from day one. Search for your employer's toughest problems and make yourself part of the solutions.

The skills you can take anywhere are those transferable skills required by a wide range of employers. These are important because there are no jobs for life. Be prepared to work for several organizations.

Key Terms

human relations
total person
organizational culture
family therapy
Hawthorne studies
communication

self-awareness
self-acceptance
motivation
trust
self-disclosure
conflict management

Review Questions

1. Given the information provided in this chapter, define *human relations*.
2. List and briefly describe the major trends that have given new importance to human relations.
3. Describe the total-person approach to human relations. Why is this approach becoming more popular?
4. List and describe the six major forces influencing human behavior at work.
5. In what ways can training in human relations benefit an organization?
6. What are some of the reasons why people need to establish a balance between work and family life?
7. Mayo's research indicated that workers could influence the rate of production in an organization. What discoveries did he make that led to this conclusion?
8. Com-Corp Industries offers its employees personal money-management lessons, and Lands' End, Inc., provides employees with a state-of-the-art fitness and recreation complex. Do these two programs represent a good use of company funds? Explain your answer.
9. What seven themes emerge from a study of human relations? Describe each one briefly.
10. Reread the Total Person Insight that quotes Marsha Sinetar and then indicate what you feel is the meaning of this quotation.

Application Exercises

1. Throughout this book you will be given many opportunities to engage in self-assessment activities. Self-assessment involves taking a careful look at those human relations skills you need to be well rounded and thoroughly prepared for success in your work life and fulfillment in your personal life. To assess your human relations skills, complete the self-assessment exercise at the ends of Chapters 2 through 9. These assessment exercises will provide

you with increased awareness of your strengths and a better understanding of those abilities you may want to improve.

2. The seven broad themes that emerge from the study of human relations were discussed in this chapter. Although these themes are interrelated, there is value in examining each one separately before reading the rest of the book. Review the description of each theme and then answer these questions:

   a. When you take into consideration the human relations problems that you have observed or experienced at work, school, and home, which themes represent the most important areas of study? Explain your answer.

   b. In which of these areas do you feel the greatest need for improvement? Why?

Case Problem **In Search of Family-Friendly Firms**

A growing number of workers are searching for an employer that will help them manage the conflicting demands of home and work. Some are even willing to accept a somewhat smaller paycheck in return for such work-family benefits as child care, elder care, parental leave, and flexible scheduling.

Demographic trends indicate that conflict between family and work will likely increase in the years ahead. Sixty percent of all mothers are employed, and that figure is expected to increase steadily to the year 2000. Two-income marriages are now the norm — a dramatic departure from an earlier era when the husband provided most of the family income. And, as half of marriages end in divorce, single parenting is increasing. Single parents sometimes face special problems balancing work and family responsibilities.

Each year *Working Mother* magazine publishes a list of the 100 best companies for working moms. Companies on the most recent list ranged from tiny G. T. Water Products, Inc. (24 employees) to General Motors Corp. On-site child-care facilities and flexible work schedules helped Lucasfilm Ltd. (maker of the *Star Wars* trilogy) win a place on the list. The authors of *The 100 Best Companies to Work for in America* recognize many companies that have displayed sensitivity to work-family issues.

The success of family-friendly programs often depends on the attitudes of supervisory-management personnel. Even when employers offer leave for new parents and flexible scheduling, some managers exert subtle pressure to discourage employees from using them. And some companies with the best family-oriented benefits have the worst records for promoting women. Research conducted by Work/Family Directions, a Boston consulting group, found that many women feel that use of family-friendly programs will seriously hamper their career advancement. Deborah Donovan, a lawyer and new mother who works for E. I. du Pont de Nemours & Co., expressed the frustration felt by many other working mothers: "The pressures of middle management are such that flextime means you don't have to work Saturday afternoon. My pet peeve was the occasional Sunday morning meeting."

Questions

1. If you were searching for a new job, would you try to find work with a company that offers family-oriented benefits? Explain your answer.
2. Family-oriented programs such as flexible scheduling and parental leave are not used by some employees because they fear their manager will disapprove of their behavior. What can companies do to resolve this problem?
3. In some cases family-friendly policies breed resentment among employees who must step in when someone leaves work early to pick up a child at day care or takes leave time to care for an elderly parent. How would you respond to such a complaint?

Chapter 2

Improving Interpersonal Communications

Chapter Preview

After studying this chapter, you will be able to

1. Differentiate impersonal from interpersonal communication.

2. Understand the communication process and the filters that affect communication.

3. Identify some ways to improve personal communication, including developing listening skills.

4. Describe formal and informal channels of communication in an organization.

5. Understand how our global economy and advanced technology are changing the way we communicate.

I N 1983, INTERNATIONAL HARVESTER CO. sold its failing Springfield, Missouri, plant to Jack Stack, the factory manager, and twelve other employees, who formed a new company, Springfield ReManufacturing Corp. (SRC). SRC buys worn-out engines and parts, fixes them to work like new, and sells them to companies such as Sears, Roebuck & Co., Chrysler Corp., Mercedes-Benz AG, and General Motors Corp. Although SRC lost $60,000 in its first year, it recently showed profits of $1.3 million on sales of $65 million and employed over 650 people.

One reason for SRC's dramatic success is its open communication climate, which includes opening its financial records to employees. Strategic planning director Dave LaHay explains, "We don't keep any secrets. We get each person to understand the financial statement so they understand why we make the decisions we do."[1]

All employees learn the meaning of such terms as *income statements, balance sheets, cash flow, equity,* and *retained earnings.* Then, on Wednesday afternoons, forty to fifty representatives from different parts of the company meet to play "The Great Game of Business." An exciting exchange of information takes place as some individuals shout out figures while everyone else busily writes them down. After the meeting, each representative reports the companywide results to coworkers in his or her department.

Cindy Jacobs, an employee in the fuel-injection department, explains her response to the weekly departmental meetings: "They show us the sales and profits, what they ship; they go through every item. If you are not working up to standard, it's going to show up on that paper."[2] Another employee comments, "With my prior company, . . . they would come down and say, 'You lost $200,000 this quarter.' [But we didn't] know where it was lost. Here you have a total view of everything that is going on."[3]

SRC employees want to see where money is being lost so they can take action to save it. If the company reaches its profit targets at the end of the year, employees are rewarded with a cash bonus of up to 13 percent of their salary. SRC management knows its open communication philosophy directly affects the company's bottom line. ∎

Good communication, which is essential for the smooth functioning of any organization, depends on the orderly exchange of information. Managers need clear lines of communication to transmit orders and policies, build cooperation, and unify group behavior. Employees must be able to convey their complaints or suggestions and to feel that management has heard what they have to say. Clear communication among coworkers is vital to high productivity, teamwork, problem solving, and conflict management. In short, effective human relations is founded on good communication.

When people in organizations want to send messages, conduct meetings, or communicate person to person, they have many options. With increased use of voice mail, electronic mail, fax machines, and satellite video-conferencing, it is a wonder they have time to read all the incoming information, let alone interpret and respond to it.

Costly communication breakdowns are a prime factor in organizational problems ranging from employee turnover to low productivity. Poor communication also takes its toll in employee injuries and deaths, particularly in industries where workers operate heavy machinery or handle hazardous materials.

Although some communication breakdowns are inevitable, many can be avoided. Leaders like Jack Stack who are candid when sharing information avoid the communication problems so common in organizations across America. Employees who are treated with respect, who are empowered to think for themselves, and who feel a sense of responsibility are more apt to communicate openly with other workers and leaders throughout the organization.

THE COMMUNICATION PROCESS

Most people take communication for granted. When they speak or listen to others, they assume that the message given or received is being understood. In reality, most messages are distorted, incomplete, or lost on their way from one person to another. It is estimated that 80 percent of a message gets distorted or lost as it travels through an organization.[4] Therefore, it is important to understand something about the process of communication.

Impersonal Versus Interpersonal Communication

In a typical organization the types of communication used to exchange information can be placed on a continuum ranging from "impersonal" on one end to "interpersonal" on the other.[5] When we use such words as *transmit* or *transfer,* we are talking about a one-way information-giving process. This impersonal, one-way communication process can be used to give basic information such as company policies, instructions, or facts. Generally, organizations use memos, letters, electronic mail, fax machines, computer printouts, voice mail, manuals, and/or bulletin boards as quick, easy ways to "get the word out." The major limitation of these forms of **impersonal communication** is that people receiving the information usually have no opportunity to ask the sender any questions or clarify vague or confusing wording. Despite these limitations, some organizations are discovering creative ways to keep employees informed using impersonal communication methods. Bob Cummins, president of Fargo Electronics, uses a daily "electronic newsletter" to keep his twenty-eight employees informed. At the end of each day, department heads put messages into the company's electronic mail system. The next morning, the messages are printed out and copies of the "newsletter" are put in the employees' break room.[6] Organizations often depend heavily on the one-way, impersonal methods of electronic mail and fax machines.

The term **interpersonal communication** describes a type or quality of communication that occurs "when the people involved talk and listen in ways that maximize their own and the other person's humanness."[7] Interpersonal communication is more than just a way to share information. One goal of interpersonal communication may be to build a stronger, more trusting relationship with another person or group of people.

Tom Chappell, owner of Tom's of Maine, which makes and sells natural toothpaste, shampoos, and deodorants, relies on face-to-face communication to cope with rumor mills, downturns in morale, and other communication problems. Several times each year Chappell gets together with his employees and talks about company performance and future plans. He says the best way to deal with employee communication needs is to be honest, be informational, and tell it like it is.[8]

For true communication to take place, the message must be understood by the person receiving the information in the same way the person sending it intended. Such words as *share, exchange, interact,* and *interchange* reflect two-way communication, as opposed to one-way information giving. In two-way communication, some type of **feedback**, or response, is necessary to make sure the message has been understood. Interpersonal communication is a dialogue during which people can share their thoughts and feelings. In an organization, dialogues can take place in meetings, over the phone, in face-to-face interviews, and in discussions.

Palmer Reynolds, CEO of Phoenix Textile Corporation, hosts monthly breakfasts with employees to build camaraderie and avoid communication mix-ups. Each month she invites five different employees, one from each department, to join her at a local restaurant. Reynolds notes that people get to know her and she gets to know them. These face-to-face meetings also uncover some communication problems.[9]

But interpersonal communication takes time, and because it does, many companies use the faster, impersonal means of conveying information. Indeed, the speed of information giving has increased tenfold through the use of computers

Total Person Insight

" 'Communication breakdown' has just about taken the place of original sin as an explanation for the ills of the world — and perhaps with good cause. As our world becomes more complex and we spend more time in organized activities, the need for interpersonal understanding has never been greater. And just as important, the cost of failure has never been higher."

PAUL R. TIMM

Educator; author, "The Way We Word"

and other technology. Stephen Roach, senior economist with Morgan Stanley, says, "The computer, if left to its own devices, is dangerously productive."[10]

Computers and other forms of technology can be invaluable when it comes to impersonal information giving, but they cannot replace the two-way, interpersonal communication process when feedback and discussion are necessary. When organizations realize that it takes people relating effectively with one another to get the job done, they also realize that impersonal communication is not enough and that interpersonal communication is the basis for success in every organization.

Sender — Message — Receiver

Effective communication is composed of three basic elements: a sender, a receiver, and an understood message.[11] To illustrate, suppose you are a clerk in a purchasing department ordering parts from a manufacturer. You phone in the order to the warehouse clerk, who repeats it to you to make sure all the details are correct. Later, the warehouse sends you a document confirming the order, indicating number, price, and delivery date. A simplified diagram of this process would look like Figure 2.1.

FIGURE 2.1

Diagram of Simple
Communication
Process

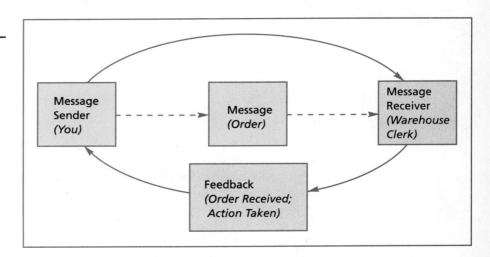

Now suppose you are explaining to your supervisor why a new procedure she wants to try will not work. The communication process becomes much more complicated, as shown in Figure 2.2. As your message travels from you to your supervisor, it must pass through several "filters," each of which can alter the way your message is understood. Most communication processes are of the complex type shown in Figure 2.2. Because these filters are so important, let's examine them in greater detail.

FIGURE 2.2

Diagram of
More Complex
Communication
Process

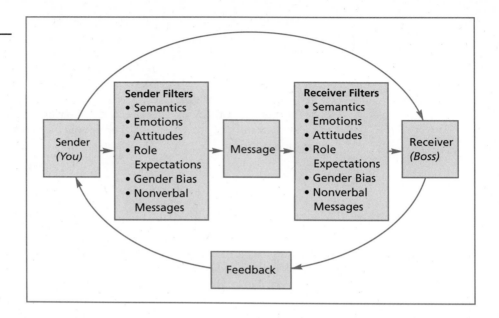

COMMUNICATION FILTERS

Interpersonal communication is filtered through semantics, emotions, attitudes, role expectations, gender bias, and nonverbal messages. When the sender is influenced by any of these filters, the message relayed may be distorted. At the same time, the receiver's filters may further distort the message.

Semantics

We naturally assume that the words we use mean the same things to others, but this can create problems. Words are not things; they are labels that stand for something. The meanings of words — or semantics — lie within us. We have agreed that particular words will have associated meanings and usage. We can easily understand what words like *typewriter, computer,* or *envelope* mean. But more abstract terms, such as *job satisfaction, downsizing, upward mobility,* or *word processing,* have less precise meanings and will be interpreted by different people in different ways. The more abstract the term, the less likely it is that people will agree on its meaning. Some professionals have been strongly criticized for using abstract words:

Item: Lawyers have been accused of using abstract words and "legalese" to confuse persons who turn to them for help. David Mellinkoff, a law school professor, says that lawyers' writing resembles a foreign language.[12]

Item: Corporate employees often use important-sounding jargon that is almost incomprehensible. In some high-tech companies you discover that the phrase *six sigma quality* simply means "good" and *enterprise environment* means "office."[13] Terms such as *megabyte, RAM, graphics mode,* or *font* may be confusing if not totally meaningless to workers who are not yet computer literate.

People's attitudes, background, experiences, and culture also affect how they interpret the words and phrases they hear. For example, one Midwestern executive sent the following message to his manager who was born and raised in Peru: "Send me factory and office headcount broken down by sex." The Peruvian manager replied, "249 in factory, 30 in office, 3 on sick leave, none broken down by sex — our problem is with alcohol."[14]

Emotions

Emotions are perhaps the most powerful communication filter. Ironically, they are also the filter over which our control is the most limited. Strong emotions can either prevent people from hearing what a speaker has to say or make them too susceptible to the speaker's point of view. If they become angry or allow themselves to be carried away by the speaker's eloquence, they may "think" with their emotions and make decisions or take action they regret later. They have shifted their attention from the content of the message to their feelings about it.

You may have had the experience of being called by an angry customer who demands to know why the wrong order was delivered. If you allow the customer's anger to trigger your own, the call quickly deteriorates into an argument. The real issue — what happened to the order and what is to be done about it — is lost in the shouting match. Detaching yourself from another's feelings and responding to the content of the message is often difficult. Yet many jobs require that employees remain calm and courteous regardless of a customer's emotional state. Emotional control will be discussed in Chapter 8.

Attitudes

Attitudes are beliefs backed up by emotions. They can be a barrier to communication in much the same way emotions can — by altering the way people hear a message. The listener may not like the speaker's voice, accent, gestures, mannerisms, dress, or delivery. Perhaps the listener has preconceived ideas about the speaker's topic. For instance, a person who is strongly opposed to abortion will most likely find it difficult to listen with objectivity to a pro-choice speaker. Negative attitudes create resistance to the message and can lead to a breakdown in communication. Overly positive attitudes can also be a barrier to communication because the listener may hear only what he or she wants to hear. Biased in favor of the message, the listener may fail to evaluate it effectively.

Attitudes can also facilitate communication. If listeners are impressed by a speaker's expertise, character, and good will, they are likely to be more receptive to the message. The quality of communication between supervisor and employee, for example, is heavily influenced by the level of openness and trust between them. More will be said about acquiring and forming attitudes in Chapter 3.

Role Expectations

Role expectations control how people expect themselves, and others, to act on the basis of the roles they play, such as boss, customer, or employee. These expectations can distort communication in two ways. First, if people identify others too closely with their roles, they may discount what the other person has to say: "It's just the boss again, saying the same old thing." A variation of this distortion occurs when we do not allow others to change their roles and take on new ones. This often happens to employees who are promoted from within the ranks of an organization to management positions. Others may still see the new manager as a secretary instead of a supervisor, as "old Chuck" from accounting rather than as the new department head. Other employees may not take them seriously in their new roles or listen to what they have to say.

Second, role expectations can affect good communication when people use their roles to alter the way they relate to others. This is often referred to as "position power." For example, managers may expect employees to accept what they say simply because of the authority invested in the position. Employees are not allowed to question decisions or make suggestions of their own, and communication becomes one-way information giving. A manager who is called on to relate to others outside the role may find it difficult to establish effective communication.

Gender Bias

Men and women tend to color the messages they receive from people of the opposite gender strictly *because* of the other person's gender. This tendency is a form of **gender bias.**

Men no longer dominate the workplace because women are entering the workplace in greater numbers than ever before and are making major strides in achieving management positions within organizations. Women business owners now employ more people than all the Fortune 500 companies combined.[15] As these changing demographics have placed men and women side by side on work teams, one consequence has been a realization that men and women tend to speak in distinctively different "genderlects," just as people from various cultures speak different dialects.[16] Psychologists and researchers are publishing their findings in books such as *You Just Don't Understand,* by Deborah Tannen; *Men Are from Mars, Women Are from Venus,* by John Gray; and *Genderflex: Men and Women Speaking Each Other's Language at Work,* by Judith C. Tingley.

All of these authors seem to agree that women are inclined to listen more intently than men do and to give more feedback in the form of responses such as *mhm, uh-uh,* and *yeah.* A man who expects his listener to be quiet could interpret such supportive feedback as an intrusion. Similarly, a woman observing a silent male listener might assume he is not interested or is not taking seriously what she has to say. When men and women communicate through a gender-bias filter, the message can be distorted.

There are also gender differences in topics and focus in communications. Men tend to talk about money, sports, and business, whereas women tend to talk about people, feelings, and relationships. Even when talking about the same topic, men and women may appear to be on different wavelengths because their gender-specific focus is different. For example, if a man and woman are discussing a pending layoff in their organization, the man might approach it from a cost-cutting point of view, while the woman may focus on the feelings of the people involved. Neither view is wrong, but the resulting conversation can frustrate both parties. Judith Tingle indicates that men and women "assume that the other gender is trying to accomplish the same goal as their own gender, but assume the other gender is going about it the wrong way. . . . Both men and women often become critical and angry at the other gender for not using the "correct" means to the desired end."[17] This anger and frustration can interfere with effective communication between the genders.

Most authorities agree that the effects of this communication filter can be reduced as women and men become aware of their different communication styles and begin to adapt their communications accordingly. The adaptation process is similar to learning a foreign language — eventually you "think" in that language rather than thinking first in English and then translating. This same learning curve can take place as men and women learn each other's "genderlect."

Nonverbal Messages

When we attempt to communicate with another person, we use both verbal and nonverbal communication. **Nonverbal messages** have been defined as "messages without words" or "silent messages." These are the messages we communicate through facial expressions, voice tone, gestures, appearance, posture, and other nonverbal means. Research indicates that our nonverbal messages carry five times as much impact as verbal messages.[18] This chapter limits its discussion to the form of nonverbal communication commonly referred to as **body language.**

Many of us could communicate more clearly, more accurately, and more credibly if we became more conscious of our body language. We can learn to strengthen our communications by making sure our words and our body language are consistent. When our verbal and nonverbal messages match, we give the impression that we can be trusted and that what we are saying reflects what we truly believe. But when our body language contradicts our words, we are often unknowingly changing the message we are sending. If a manager says to an employee, "I am very interested in your problem" but then begins to look at his watch and fidget with objects on his desk, the employee will most likely believe the nonverbal, rather than the verbal, message.

Listeners become confused when they observe a lack of consistency between the words they hear and the body language they observe. Given a choice, most people tend to believe an individual's nonverbal messages. Intuitively, they feel that such messages are not easily controlled and reveal more of a person's true thoughts and feelings.[19]

Individuals can improve their communications by monitoring the nonverbal messages they send through their eye contact, facial expressions, and gestures.

Eye Contact Eyes transmit more information than any other part of the body. Because eye contact is so revealing, people generally observe some unwritten rules about looking at others. A direct, prolonged stare between strangers is usually considered impolite, even potentially aggressive or hostile.

The expression on the face of this excited soccer fan communicates a powerful nonverbal message. (David Modell/SABA)

People entering elevators or other crowded areas will glance at others briefly — acknowledging their presence — then look away.

In a business setting, however, people expect more direct eye contact. Salespeople, for example, find that a certain amount of eye contact is necessary to build trust with a prospective customer. Research indicates that tips increase when food service personnel squat down beside the table. Apparently this informal posture promotes eye contact by placing the server on the same level as the customer. When customers perceive the server as friendly and attentive, they tend to give more generous tips.[20]

It is not always fair to base judgments about other people on their ability to make eye contact, however. One interviewer complained that a young man with excellent qualifications would not look him in the eye during the interview. A colleague discovered that the young man was Puerto Rican and explained that Puerto Rican youth are taught to look down as a mark of respect when speaking with adults.

As a general rule, when you are communicating in a business setting, your eyes should meet the other person's about 60 to 70 percent of the time. This timing is an effective alternative to continuous eye contact.

Facial Expressions If you want to identify the inner feelings of another person, watch facial expressions closely. A frown or a smile will communicate a great deal. Janet Elsea, author of *The Four Minute Sell*, states: "After overall appearance, your face is the most visible part of you. Facial expressions are the cue most people rely on in initial interactions; they are the 'teleprompter' by which others read your mood and personality."[21]

Albert Mehrabian, author of *Silent Messages*, indicates that 7 percent of our messages are conveyed through our choice of words, while 55 percent are conveyed by our facial expressions.[22] The people to whom we speak are continually looking for congruency between our words and actions. If our words and our facial expressions are saying different things, we create an enormous credibility problem for ourselves. This may lead to a lack of trust and dramatically damage our relationships with others.

Gestures Did you know that you send a nonverbal message every time you place your hand over your mouth, clench your hands together, cross your legs, or grip your arms? These gestures send messages to people about how you are reacting to them and to the situation in which you find yourself.

R. L. Birdwhistell, one of the researchers who helped develop the science of body language, believes that gestures indicate whether people are open or closed to communication, who is the true leader of a group, and how comfortable people are with physical contact.[23] For example, employees usually "elect" a leader from their own ranks while outwardly acknowledging the supervisor or manager as boss. One researcher has noted that in a company's departmental meetings, whenever the manager proposed a change in work procedures, employees would glance at their own "leader" to watch his reaction. Often they unconsciously imitated his sitting posture or his facial expression as he listened to the manager. This mirroring is a nonverbal means by which people can signal agreement. By imitating another's postures and gestures, a person is saying, "As you can see, I think the same as you."

We must be careful when attempting to interpret gestures, however. No one gesture means the same thing all the time or to all people. To make accurate judgments about behaviors, we must first be aware of their context. For example, some experts in the field of nonverbal communication say that the gesture of crossing one's arms communicates defensiveness. However, in some situations, the crossed-arms gesture may simply mean the person is assuming a position of comfort.

In light of our expanding global marketplace, be aware that some gestures that may be common in the U.S. culture may have dramatically different meanings to people from outside the United States. (See Figure 2.3.) Although nodding your head up and down means "yes" in most countries, it

FIGURE 2.3

The hand-ring finger gesture (hand displayed with the thumb and forefinger tips joined) is a sign of approval in North America. In Belgium, France, and Tunisia this gesture symbolizes the precise opposite — a "big zero." The thumb-up gesture means "O.K." or "something good" in almost every part of the world. In Australia, however, it is considered an obscene gesture.

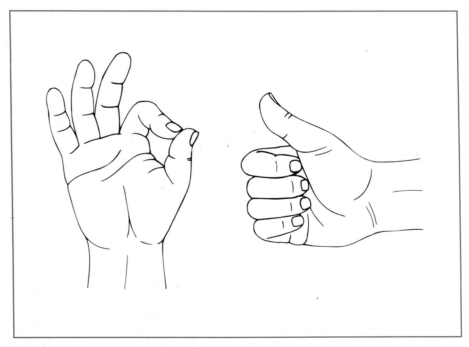

Sources: Hand-ring gesture taken from Desmond Morris, *Bodytalk: The Meaning of Human Gestures,* New York: Crown Trade Paperbacks, 1994, pp. 118–119 and pp. 129–130. Thumb-up gesture: Desmond Morris, *Bodytalk: The Meaning of Human Gestures,* and Rochelle Sharpe, "Work Week," The *Wall Street Journal,* October 31, 1995, p. A-1.

means "no" in Greece and Bulgaria.[24] To use your fingers to call someone forward in a crowd is insulting to most people living in the Middle East or Asia.[25] And that common U.S. gesture of folding your arms in front of you shows disrespect in Fiji.[26]

Thinking / Learning Starters

1. Are you aware of the messages you send through body language? Recall your nonverbal behavior in various situations, including a difficult meeting with a supervisor or a dinner party with friends. Was your behavior consistent with your words? Explain.

2. Acute sensitivity to nonverbal messages is an important skill for people to develop. In general, do you feel that nonverbal messages are more trustworthy than verbal ones? Describe specific nonverbal messages that you have learned to trust in your friends or coworkers.

Who Is Responsible for Effective Communication?

Both the sender and the receiver share equal responsibility for effective communication. The communication loop, as shown in Figure 2.2, is complete when the receiver understands, feels, or behaves according to the message of the sender. If this does not occur, the communication process has broken down.

Individuals can improve their human relations by basing all their communications on a simple premise: The message received *is* the message. If the message the receiver hears differs from the one the sender intended, the communication loop has not been completed. The message the receiver hears is, in effect, the only message that exists. If a serious discrepancy exists between what the sender intended to say and what the receiver heard, disagreements or even fights can occur. When emotions calm down, it does not help for the sender to say, "But that's not what I meant. You misunderstood!" By then, human relations between the sender and receiver have already been damaged.

When the sender accepts complete responsibility for sending a clear, concise message, the communication process begins. But the receiver must accept full responsibility for receiving the message as the sender intended. Receivers must provide senders with enough feedback to ensure that an accurate message has passed through all the filters that might alter it.

HOW TO IMPROVE INTERPERSONAL COMMUNICATION

Now that you have been introduced to the communication process and the various filters that messages must pass through, you can begin to take the necessary steps to improve your own personal communication skills.

Send Clear Messages

Become a responsible sender by always sending clear, concise messages with as little influence from filters as possible. As you formulate your messages, keep in mind how filters creep into all messages from both the sender's and the receiver's vantage points. A general rule of thumb is to give clear instructions and ask clear questions so you won't be misunderstood. A new employee stood before the paper shredder in her new office. An administrative assistant noticed her confused look and asked if she needed some help. "Yes, thank you. How does this thing work?" "It's simple," said the assistant and took the thick report from the new employee and fed it through the shredder. "I see," she said, "but how many copies will it make?" This kind of miscommunication could easily have been avoided if both parties had followed a few simple rules.[27]

Use Words Carefully As noted previously, abstract words, whether spoken or written, often become barriers to effective communication. Edwin Newman, former NBC news commentator and author of *Strictly Speaking,* encourages language that is simple, clear, precise, and, in his terms, "unflossy" — concise words that are not vague or confusing. Avoid buzz words or complex, official language. Tailoring the message to the receiver by using words the listener understands will help ensure that your message is understood.

Keep in mind that busy people do not like to read long memos or letters. According to some estimates, more than two-thirds of the letters, memos, and reports written in industry fail to meet their stated objectives.[28] Some companies are now sponsoring business writing courses for their employees. Bottom line: Keep it short and simple. The opening and closing paragraphs should be limited to approximately three sentences. Condense the remaining information into three to four bullets. The skill of creating memos and letters that convey information clearly and concisely requires practice.[29]

Use Repetition When possible, use parallel channels of communication. For example, by sending a memo and making a phone call, you not only gain the receiver's attention through dialogue but also make sure there is a written record in case specific details need to be recalled. Many studies show that repetition, or redundancy, is an important element in ensuring communication accuracy. Redundant forms help ensure that messages will not be misunderstood.

Use Appropriate Timing   Keep in mind that most employees, particularly at the managerial level, are flooded with messages every day. An important memo or letter may get no attention simply because it is competing with more pressing problems facing the receiver. Some organizations solve the problem by establishing standard times for particular messages to be sent and received. Important financial information, for example, may be sent on the second Thursday of every month. Other organizations send press releases to the media and to employees' computer screens simultaneously at 11:00 A.M. every Monday. Timing the delivery of your message will help ensure that it is accepted and acted on.

Develop Listening Skills

Most of us are born with the ability to hear, but we have to learn how to listen. Tom Peters, in his book *Thriving on Chaos: Handbook for a Management Revolution,* entitles an entire chapter "Become Obsessed with Listening." Psychologist Carl Rogers has said, "Listening is such an incredible and magical thing." Peters, Rogers, and others agree: We need to accept listening as a skill that can be learned.

Research performed at Ohio State University indicates that the amount of time we spend on different parts of the communication process is divided as follows: listening, 45 percent; speaking, 30 percent; reading, 16 percent; writing, 9 percent.[30] Most of us spent first grade learning to write. In second grade, the entire year focused on learning how to read. Every year thereafter provided constant practice in reading and writing. Perhaps we took a speech course in high school or college. Yet schools rarely offer a course in listening. This skill is taught the least, yet it is used the most, according to the Ohio study. This lack of training may help explain why people listen at a 25 percent efficiency rate in typical situations. They miss about 75 percent of the messages spoken by other people.[31]

But there is also a discrepancy between our rate of speaking and our rate of hearing. People speak at approximately 150 words per minute. Our listening capacity is about 450 words per minute. Because the message is usually much slower than our capacity to listen, we have plenty of time to let our minds roam, to think ahead, and to plan what we are going to say next.

All too frequently, most of us hear the message but do not take the time to really listen and blend the message we hear with reason and understanding. Communication expert John T. Samaras of the University of Oklahoma points out five signs of poor listening habits:

1. Thinking about something else while waiting for the speaker's next words or sentence

---

Total Person Insight

"Listening, really listening, is tough and grinding work, often humbling, sometimes distasteful. It's a fairly sure bet that you won't like the lion's share of what you hear."

GERRY MITCHELL

Chairman, Dana Corporation

---

2. Listening primarily for facts rather than ideas
3. Tuning out when the talk seems to be getting too difficult
4. Prejudging from a person's appearance or manner that nothing interesting will be said
5. Paying attention to outside sights and sounds when talking to someone[32]

Active Listening We need to turn these poor listening habits into active listening skills. **Active listening** is the process of feeding back to the speaker what we as listeners think the speaker meant.[33] This feedback takes into consideration the speaker's verbal and nonverbal signals. When the listener shares with the speaker his or her understanding of the content and accompanying feelings of the message, true communication begins.

Active listening takes time, focus, and concentrated energy. Avoid faking your attention. If you do not have time to listen, if your attention is being diverted to other issues, or if you simply do not have the energy to listen, let the speaker know and make arrangements to listen at another time.

When you truly want to create effective communications and enhance your human relations, there are several steps you can follow to become an active listener:

1. *Cultivate a listening attitude.* Regard the person as worthy of respect and attention. Empathize, or "feel with," the speaker, and really try to understand the other person's experience. Drop your expectations of what you are going to hear or what you would like to hear. Be patient, and refrain from formulating your response until the speaker has finished talking.

2. *Focus your full attention.* Establish eye contact. Equalize any difference in height between you and the speaker. Maintain an open body posture and lean forward slightly. This stance communicates your interest and attentiveness. Continually refocus away from distractions, both internal and external.

3. *Take notes.* Note taking is not absolutely essential in every verbal exchange, but it will greatly improve communications in many situations. If your su-

pervisor is giving you detailed instructions, taking notes will ensure greater accuracy and will build the supervisor's confidence in your ability to remember important details.

4. *Ask questions.* This step ensures your own understanding of the speaker's thoughts and feelings and helps you secure additional relevant information. If you want the speaker to expand broadly on a particular point, ask open-ended questions, such as "How do you feel about that?" or "Can you tell us some ways to improve?"[34]

Empathic Listening Many workers today face serious personal problems and feel the need to talk about them with someone. C. Glenn Pearce, a management professor at Virginia Commonwealth University, says that what these workers want is to "put their thoughts about feelings on the table for emotional release. . . . They need an understanding ear to do that."[35] They do not expect specific advice or guidance; they just want to spend some time with an empathic listener. Pearce offers these tips for people who want to practice **empathic listening**.

1. *Avoid being judgmental.* Objectivity is the heart and soul of empathic listening. The person is communicating for emotional release and does not seek a specific response.
2. *Accept what is said.* You do not have to agree with what is being said, but you should let the person know you are able to understand his or her viewpoint.
3. *Be patient.* If you are unable or unwilling to take the time to hear what the person has to say, say so immediately. Signs of impatience send a negative message to the person needing to talk.[36]

FOR BETTER OR FOR WORSE © 1994 Lynn Johnston Prod., Inc. Reprinted with permission of UNIVERSAL PRESS SYNDICATE. All rights reserved.

As a coworker or supervisor, you will likely have many opportunities to engage in empathic listening. Effective empathic listening is one of the highest forms of interpersonal communications.

Thinking / Learning Starters

1. Think of some people you know who are active listeners. How can you tell? Describe an instance when their active listening improved their relations with you or another person.

2. Have you recently been approached by someone who wanted to talk to an empathic listener? Were you able to respond in the manner recommended by Pearce? Explain.

Use Constructive Self-Disclosure

Self-disclosure is the process of letting another person know what you think, feel, or want. It is one of the important ways you let yourself be known by others. The primary goal of self-disclosure is to build strong and healthy interpersonal relationships.

It is important to note the difference between self-disclosure and self-description. **Self-description** involves disclosure of nonthreatening information, such as your age, your favorite food, or where you went to school. This is information that others could acquire in some way other than by your telling them. Self-disclosure, by contrast, usually involves some risk. When you practice self-disclosure, you reveal private, personal information that cannot be acquired from another source. Examples include your feelings about being a member of a minority group, job security, and new policies and procedures.

The importance of self-disclosure, in contrast to self-description, is shown by the following situation. You work in an industrial plant and are extremely conscious of safety. You take every precaution to avoid work-related accidents. But another employee has a much more casual attitude toward safety rules and often "forgets" to observe the proper procedures, endangering you and other workers. You can choose to disclose your feelings to this person or hide your concerns. If you choose to stay silent, it is probably because you are afraid of showing your strong feelings or of failing to get your message across. Either staying silent or speaking out poses a risk.

Benefits of Self-Disclosure There are a number of benefits you gain from openly sharing what you think, feel, or want. As a general rule, relationships grow stronger when people are willing to reveal more about themselves. When two people engage in an open, authentic dialogue, they often develop a high regard for each other's views. Often they discover they share common interests and concerns, and these serve as a foundation for a deeper relationship.

Self-disclosure often results in increased accuracy in communication. It takes the guesswork out of the communication process. No one is a mind reader; if people conceal how they really feel, it is very difficult for others to know how to respond to them appropriately. People who are frustrated by a heavy workload but mask their true feelings may never see the problem resolved.

In many cases, constructive self-disclosure can reduce stress. Sidney Jourard, a noted psychologist who has written extensively about self-disclosure, states that too much emphasis on privacy and concealment of feelings creates stress within an individual.[37] To the extent that persons can share with others their inner thoughts and feelings, they experience less stress. Constructive self-disclosure can be a very important dimension of a stress management program. Too many people keep their feelings bottled up inside, which can result in considerable inner tension.

Guidelines for Appropriate Self-Disclosure In the search for criteria to determine appropriate self-disclosure, many factors must be considered. How much information should be disclosed? How intimate should the information be? Under what conditions should the disclosures be made? The following guidelines will help you develop your self-disclosure skills.

1. *Use self-disclosure to repair damaged relationships.* Many relationships are unnecessarily strained. The strain often exists because people refuse to talk about real or imagined problems. Self-disclosure can be an excellent method of repairing a damaged relationship.
2. *Discuss disturbing situations as they happen.* Your reactions to a work-related problem or issue should be shared as soon after the incident as possible. It is often difficult to recapture a feeling once it has passed, and you may distort the incident if you let too much time go by. Your memory is not infallible. The person who caused the hurt feelings is also likely to forget details about the situation.
3. *Select the right time and place.* Remarks that otherwise might be offered and accepted in a positive way can be rendered ineffective, not because of what we say but because of when and where we say it.[38] When possible, select a time when you feel the other person is not preoccupied and will be able to give you his or her full attention. Also, select a setting free of distractions.
4. *Avoid overwhelming others with your self-disclosure.* Although you should be open, do not go too far too fast. Many strong relationships are built slowly. The abrupt disclosure of highly emotional or intimate information may actually distance you from the other person. Your behavior may be considered threatening.

Thinking / Learning Starter

Mentally review your previous work or volunteer experience. Identify at least one occasion when you felt great frustration over some incident but avoided disclosing your feelings to the person who could have solved the problem. What factors motivated you not to self-disclose? In retrospect, do you now perceive any benefits you might have gained by choosing to self-disclose?

COMMUNICATION CHANNELS IN ORGANIZATIONS

The healthy functioning of any organization, large or small, depends on teamwork. Good communication helps build teamwork by permitting a two-way exchange of information and by unifying group behavior. Poor communication can create an atmosphere of mistrust. Therefore, it is important that workers know the appropriate channels through which communication flows.

Organizations establish formal channels or structures through which communication travels. In most organizations, however, an informal channel, commonly referred to as the grapevine, offers a major communications link. For an organization to function smoothly, everyone needs to know how to use both formal and informal channels of communication.

Formal Channels

The larger an organization is, the "taller" it becomes—that is, the more layers of management it acquires. This complexity makes it difficult to transmit information and to provide channels for feedback to ensure accurate communication. Smaller organizations also have their communication problems, but in many cases misunderstandings can be cleared up fairly quickly. In some instances, the solution may involve a short walk down the hall to the manager's office or a quick phone call to the warehouse.

Communication in an organization generally moves along vertical or horizontal lines. Vertical channels carry messages between the top executive levels and the lowest level in the organization. Horizontal communication occurs between departments, divisions, managers, or employees on the same organizational level.

Vertical Channels Communications moving down through **vertical channels** from top management levels reach a great many people and carry considerable force. In general, if the level of trust between management and employees is fairly high, these messages will usually pass through the organization effectively. Messages will be understood, believed, accepted, and acted on. If the level of trust is low, however, workers will tend to put more faith in word-of-mouth information, even if such information consists mainly of rumors and conflicts with the formal message.

Communication traveling down through vertical channels may be delivered face to face, by phone, or in written form. Many managers find that making brief phone calls to members of their staff is much less expensive and more effective than sending memos; phone calls also allow for immediate feedback. However, sensitive matters are best handled face to face. If someone is denied a promotion, has a personal problem that is affecting his or her work, or needs to be disciplined in some way, the manager should explain the situation in person rather than rely on a memo or letter. Written communications in such cases can be easily misunderstood.

Although communicating down the vertical channel is fairly routine, communicating back up can be more difficult. Top managers sometimes perceive themselves as the senders and their subordinates as the receivers of messages. Upward communication is valuable in any organization. The opportunity for such communication encourages employees to contribute valuable ideas that can lead to substantial savings for the organization. But there are intangible benefits as well. When employees can participate in decisions that directly affect their work, they feel as if they are a part of the organizational community, not just individuals collecting a paycheck.

Horizontal Channels   People on the same level of authority, such as the buyers and store managers, communicate across **horizontal channels**. This communication may take place during structured meetings or informal conversations. Memos dealing with a subject of interest to district managers are sent only to the personnel across that level in an organization. Managers may talk in an informal setting such as over lunch and decide among themselves how directives that have come through the vertical channels are to be carried out. Even though the setting may be informal, the fact that only managers are present confirms that the communication is still proceeding through formal horizontal channels.

In some situations, horizontal channels may intersect with vertical authority lines. Project teams, for example, often bring together people from different departments and with different levels of authority. When project teams are used, the team leader may be giving orders to someone who is officially higher up the organizational ladder. This type of communication can either help break down the rigid barriers of formal reporting lines or put a strain on an otherwise normal relationship between executives and subordinates.

Informal Channels

Top executives are often amazed at how quickly and, in many cases, how accurately information passes along informal channels. Informal channels can work horizontally and vertically. A message, often referred to as gossip, may pass from a vice president's administrative assistant to someone in the mailroom or from a janitor to a department supervisor.

Perhaps the best-known informal communications channel for rumor and gossip (the message) is the organization's **grapevine**. Grapevines exist in all organizations. These informal channels of communication can be positive or negative. The grapevine satisfies employees' social needs and provides a way to clarify orders that come through formal channels, particularly if upward communication is blocked or ineffective. Many officials have come to respect the grapevine's ability to convey even semisecret information quickly.

At times, however, messages that move through the grapevine may be distorted, abbreviated, exaggerated, or completely inaccurate. Many managers have found through personal experience how difficult it is to correct information that has been garbled by the grapevine.

COMMUNICATION IN A GLOBAL ECONOMY

Worldwide telecommunications and international business competition are creating additional communication problems and challenges for modern organizations. U.S. corporations have invested $400 billion abroad and employ more than 60 million overseas workers. More than 100,000 U.S. firms are engaged in global ventures valued at more than $1 trillion.[39] As more and more companies send their employees abroad on temporary or permanent assignments, effective communication becomes more critical. Too often Americans going overseas have little knowledge of the language and culture of the host country. There are many subtle communication traps for the unwary:

Item: In Mexico, you should always inquire about a client's spouse and family. In Saudi Arabia, you should never inquire about a client's family.

Item: In Japan, small gifts are almost obligatory in business situations. In China, gifts to individuals are prohibited in business situations.

Item: In Latin America, people are usually late. In Sweden, you must be prompt to the second.

Item: In the United States, "tabling" something means postponing it until the next meeting. In England, "tabling" means discussing it now.

Item: In a conversation, Japanese prefer to wait and listen; the higher the rank, the more they listen. One Japanese executive explains this tradition: "He who speaks first at a meeting is a dumb ass."[40]

While many companies are sending employees abroad, others are employing more foreign-born workers than ever before. This trend means that supervisors and managers must have the communication skills to manage a multilingual, multicultural work force here at home. Many of these workers speak English only as a second language and may not be fully fluent in either speaking or receiving English messages. In addition to the language barrier, these workers

These Praxair, Inc. employees face special communication problems as the company expands its global markets. At the present time 51 percent of Praxair's sales are generated outside of the United States. (Photo Courtesy of Praxair, Inc.)

may be confused and dismayed by aspects of American culture, such as women occupying positions of authority, top executives performing manual labor, and younger managers openly challenging older managers in meetings.

HIGH-TECH COMMUNICATION

Traditionally, interoffice correspondence, staff meetings, conversations in the break room, and various other face-to-face and telephone conversations throughout the day made up the majority of the communications within an organization. Add to this the phone calls and daily mail deliveries from customers, vendors, and others outside the company, and you have a basic communication system used successfully for generations by most organizations. Today, however, technological advancements are providing many options that speed up and enhance basic communications throughout the office and the global marketplace.

Modems, electronic mail, voice mail, faxes, cellular phones, laptop computers, hand-held pen-based electronic notepads, CD-ROM information storage, videoconferences, and the Internet are making it possible for people scattered all over the country (and world!) to communicate without ever being in the same room. According to one estimate, 100 million people in 135 countries will be using the Internet (the service that links computers on the massive global "superhighway") to retrieve and send messages by 1998.[41]

Many organizations now operate from "virtual offices," which are companies that function like traditional businesses but are actually a network of workers connected with the latest technology.[42] **Telecommuting,** an arrangement that allows employees to work outside the confines of a traditional office, enables people scattered all over the country to work as one office, with no building or room assigned as the headquarters. Often a laptop computer, complete with an internal fax/modem, combines with a cellular phone to function effectively as "an office in a briefcase."

The telecommuting trend is increasing dramatically — according to some estimates, by as much as 20 percent each year.[43] The greatest boost to this trend has been the expansion of electronic mail, often referred to as E-mail. **E-mail** is a message you send or receive through a computer and its modem (the computer's connection to a telephone line). During recent years, most companies have added E-mail capabilities to their in-house computer networks. In such companies, a salesperson calling on a customer can receive up-to-date information on the status of the customer's order by means of a quick E-mail message to the shipping department. An executive could convene an emergency meeting of all department managers by transmitting an E-mail message directly to their computer monitors.

The advantages of using E-mail, both within an organization and globally, are obvious:

- *Time efficiency is unsurpassed:* People can avoid telephone tag by leaving a complete and detailed message on the computer screen, and the concern for crossing time zones virtually disappears.
- *Costs are minimal:* Sending an E-mail message across the country — or the globe — is often less expensive than sending a letter.
- *Accuracy is improved:* Customers can convey their orders exactly as they want them, bypassing customer-service representatives who might enter wrong order data.
- *Customer service is enhanced:* Within minutes, a customer service representative in New York might receive permission from the San Francisco office for a special price consideration on a large order from a Pittsburgh customer, determine inventory availability from the Boston warehouse, and confirm shipping details from Federal Express in Memphis.
- *Some communication filters can be eliminated:* E-mail is often referred to as "the great equalizer" because the sender's gender and skin color are not immediately obvious. Therefore, prejudiced attitudes are less likely to alter the message.

Despite all these advantages, E-mail has some disadvantages you should be aware of if you are going to be using it. Because E-mail is used to speed up the communications process, many people compose and send hastily writ-

With the aid of a well-planned teleconference, employees can maintain communication with coworkers in another part of the country. (Matthew Boroski/Stock, Boston, Inc.)

ten messages, which can be confusing. If you have to send a second message to clarify your first message, E-mail does not save you any time. Think before you write, and carefully edit your message on the screen before sending it. Summarize your main point and indicate the action or response you are seeking. Be sure you provide all the details the receiver needs to take action.

Also, be very careful about the words and the tone of your messages. Since there is no visual contact, senders and receivers are unable to read each other's body language, and as you know, body language often helps to clarify a message. Sara Kiesler, coauthor of *Connections,* says, "E-mail messages are often startlingly blunt because [the senders] feel they must use stronger language to get their message across."[44] Be careful to edit potentially offensive words and phrasing out of your documents.

Another potential hazard in the use of E-mail is lack of privacy. As communication technology advances, individuals and organizations will need to devise guidelines that will maintain every individual's right to privacy.

Summary

Impersonal, one-way communication methods can be effectively used to share basic facts, policies, instructions, and other such information that requires no feedback from the receiver. Interpersonal communication involves a two-way exchange in which the receiver understands the message in the same way the sender intended it.

Communication is often filtered through semantics, emotions, attitudes, gender bias, role expectations, and nonverbal messages. Body language conveys information about a person's thoughts and feelings through eye contact, facial expressions, and gestures.

Individuals can make their messages clearer by using repetition, choosing words carefully, and timing the message so that the receiver can focus on what is being said. They can also learn active and empathic listening skills and use constructive self-disclosure.

Communication in organizations unifies group behavior and helps build teamwork. Formal communication channels follow the structure of the organization and can be vertical or horizontal. Informal channels, such as the grapevine, are both vertical and horizontal. The grapevine often transmits information more rapidly than formal channels but can also have an extremely negative effect on the organization if the rumors are untrue. The dramatic expansion of the global marketplace means that companies must train their employees to be able to communicate in spite of language and cultural differences.

The communication superhighway that connects computers throughout the world has brought with it tremendous opportunities. This technology has also created a major concern about each individual's right to privacy.

Career Corner

Q. The company I work for recently adopted the assessment approach known as 360-degree feedback. Every department head completed a three-day workshop on this feedback strategy. When my boss returned from the workshop she held a staff meeting and said she wants to know what we think of her performance. We have been instructed to schedule a meeting with her and be prepared to "tell it like it is." I think she sincerely wants feedback regarding her strengths and areas needing improvement. Should I share with her the "good" and the "bad"?

A. Although your boss may be seeking assessment feedback, she could be turned off by your complaints or by criticism of the way she manages the department. Most managers respond poorly to direct criticism — even when they seek feedback. Criticism of her leadership may damage your career. Of course it would be a mistake to bottle up a major source of frustration inside you. If you are upset about a particular policy or practice, do find the right time and place to disclose your feelings. Before the meeting, try to think of a good solution to the problem. Most bosses are turned off by employees who complain about something but fail to offer an alternative way of doing things.

Key Terms

impersonal communication
interpersonal communication
feedback
emotions
gender bias
nonverbal messages
body language
active listening

empathic listening
self-disclosure
self-description
vertical channels
horizontal channels
grapevine
telecommuting
E-mail

Review Questions

1. Describe the difference between impersonal and interpersonal communication. Explain the communication process in your own words.
2. Why is feedback essential to good communication?
3. What are the responsibilities of both sender and receiver in the communication process?
4. What are communication filters? How can they be stumbling blocks to effective communication?
5. What techniques can be used to send clear messages? How can you know if you have been successful?
6. What happens when a sender's nonverbal cues do not agree with the verbal message being sent?
7. Why do organizations have formal communication channels? When are they most effective?
8. List and describe four guidelines for appropriate self-disclosure.
9. What types of communication problems exist in an organization that actively participates in the global economy? What steps should organizations take to help eliminate these problems?
10. List the advantages and disadvantages of using E-mail.

Application Exercises

1. Set up an interview with a local businessperson in a small, medium-size, or large organization. Consider your local postmaster, a manager of a grocery store, or a midlevel manager at a large corporation. Ask questions such as, What do you believe is the greatest communication problem in your organization? What methods do you use to try to eliminate or diminish the problem? To what extent do you use electronic technology to communicate? Has there ever been a situation in which a breakdown in communication resulted in a loss of production, a decline in employee morale, or a loss of customer good will?
2. We can all improve our listening efficiency. First, we need to be aware of our listening habits. By completing this form you can become more aware of poor listening habits that might reduce your listening efficiency. The

results will give you an idea of some listening habits you might want to change.

A—Almost never   *B*—Occasionally   *C*—Frequently   *D*—Most of the time

_____ **1.** Do you fail to pay attention? Some listeners allow themselves to be distracted or to think of something else.

_____ **2.** Do you give the appearance of listening when you are not? Some people who are thinking about something else deliberately try to look as though they are listening.

_____ **3.** Do you tune out the person who says something you don't agree with or don't want to hear? Some people are concentrating on what they are going to say next rather than truly listening to the other person's point of view.

_____ **4.** Do you listen only for facts? Some people listen only to facts or details and miss the real meaning of what is being said.

_____ **5.** Do you rehearse what you are going to say? Some people listen until they want to say something, at which point they stop listening and begin planning their response.

_____ **6.** Do you interrupt the speaker? Some people do not wait until the speaker has completely expressed his or her views.

_____ **7.** Do you fail to take notes at a meeting? Some people do not bother to take notes when necessary; consequently, they often forget important details.

3. Observe the nonverbal communications around you for the next day or two. Record the behaviors you notice and the messages those behaviors communicate. Watch facial expressions and gestures made by others. Experiment with your own nonverbal signals and monitor the resulting behavior of others. For example, make a point of maintaining constant eye contact during your next conversation with a teacher, peer, or family member. What was that person's response? Be ready to share with your classmates your discoveries about the power of body language in communications.

Self-Assessment Exercise

The purpose of this application exercise is to help you assess those attitudes and skills that contribute to effective human relations. A similar exercise will appear at the end of each subsequent chapter. Your honest response to each item will help you determine your areas of strength and those areas that need improvement. Completion of this self-assessment will provide you with information needed to develop goals for self-improvement.

   Circle the number from 1 to 5 that best represents your response to each statement: (1) strongly disagree (never do this); (2) disagree (rarely do this); (3) moderately agree (sometimes do this); (4) agree (frequently do this); (5) strongly agree (always do this).

a.	I am an effective communicator who sends clear, concise verbal messages.	1	2	3	4	5
b.	When people talk, I listen attentively and frequently use active listening skills.	1	2	3	4	5
c.	I am conscious of how I express nonverbal messages (facial expression, tone of voice, body language, and so on) when communicating with others.	1	2	3	4	5
d.	I engage in appropriate self-disclosure in order to achieve improved communication and increased self-awareness and to build stronger relationships.	1	2	3	4	5
e.	I am able to share information about myself in appropriate ways, avoiding the extremes of complete concealment and complete openness.	1	2	3	4	5
f.	I understand the positives and negatives surrounding grapevine communications and judge the information accordingly.	1	2	3	4	5

After recording your response to each item, select an appropriate attitude or skill you would like to improve. Write your goal in the space provided. (The instructions for setting and achieving goals are on pages 96–99 in Chapter 4.)

GOAL: _____

_____

_____

Case Problem   ## Mercedes Learns to Speak 'Bama

The German Chamber of Commerce and Industry conducted a survey of 10,000 businesspeople and discovered that 30 percent of them are considering moving their production outside Germany. The reason: German workers earn wages and benefits that, on the average, are worth $25 an hour (the highest in the world), yet in terms of output per hour they are only two-thirds as productive as their American counterparts. In light of this crushing cost of doing business in Germany, Mercedes-Benz AG in Stuttgart formed a new globalization strategy that included building its new $300 million auto plant nearer to its customers. Mercedes was the top-selling import car in Japan in 1993, but the company did not choose that country for its new factory. It could have gone to Mexico and hired low-wage workers, but the company did not make that choice either. Instead, it chose Vance, Alabama (population 350), for the factory that will build the new Mercedes 1997 sport-utility vehicles.

Not only is the Mercedes management team designing a new car and a new factory, but they are also preparing for the cultural upheaval of moving approximately forty German engineers, managers, and their families to Alabama. They are conducting seminars at a retreat in the Black Forest to help their employees adjust to the strange habits of their new home and have flown some native Alabamians to Stuttgart to help with these "cross-cultural encounter groups." The German employees have learned that Americans call strangers by their first names, that they leave their office doors open, and that they rarely use public transportation. They have even learned the meaning of such strange expressions as "y'all" and "Howdy." It appears, however, that mastering the southern drawl may take some time.

Steve Cannon, an American marketing executive for Mercedes involved in the new plant, says, "It's those little things that can cause small cultural rifts. The question is, how can we minimize them?" Roland Folger, who will move from Germany to Alabama, adds, "We don't want a German enclave in Alabama. We want a real cultural mixing."

Questions

1. Both the Americans and the Germans seem committed to making this new multicultural factory operate effectively. What types of training exercises or activities would you use to help these two cultures understand each other better?
2. How might each of the communications filters identified in this chapter affect the messages sent between German-born and American-born workers?
3. What additional communications problems might have been encountered if Mercedes had chosen to build its plant in Japan or Mexico instead of Alabama?

Chapter 3

Attitudes Can Shape Your Life

Chapter Preview

After studying this chapter, you will be able to

1. Understand the impact of employee attitudes on the success of individuals as well as organizations.

2. List and explain the ways people acquire attitudes.

3. Describe attitudes that employers value.

4. Identify ways to change your attitudes.

5. Identify the ways you can help others change their attitudes.

6. Understand what adjustments organizations are making to develop positive employee attitudes.

PRIOR TO OPENING the Grand Hyatt Wailea Beach resort hotel on the island of Maui, the personnel department screened 6,000 applicants to fill 1,200 jobs. When Nordstrom opened its first department store on the East Coast, the company interviewed 3,000 people to fill 400 front-line jobs.[1] Both of these service-driven companies are searching for employees who display a positive attitude toward customer service.

When General Motors opened its Saturn plant, applicants were screened for "compatibility" from a huge pool of people. Hal Rosenbluth, CEO of Rosenbluth International, the nation's fourth-largest travel agency, interviews his potential executives by playing basketball with them. He explains, "I like to see who's passing the ball, who's hogging it, who's taking shots they shouldn't."[2] GM and Rosenbluth are searching for employees who exhibit attitudes that help them work effectively as team members.[3] ■

The qualities that make up the "right attitude" vary from one employment setting to another. Office managers search for employees who display a serious attitude toward accuracy in document preparation. Plant managers focus on employees who are safety conscious. And almost every organization seeks employees who are honest and respectful of company resources. Most employers agree that employees' attitudes are just as important, if not more so, than their technical ability to perform a specific task.

WHAT IS AN ATTITUDE?

A few years ago a group of Scandinavian and American psychologists developed a working definition of the term *attitude*. An attitude, they pronounced, is "a persistent, emotional readiness to think about and behave toward people, institutions, social conditions and so on, in a particular manner."[4] Simply put, an **attitude** is a relatively strong belief or feeling toward a person, object, idea, or event. Throughout life we form attitudes toward political movements, religions, national leaders, various occupations, government programs, laws, and other aspects of our daily lives. Some of our atti-

---

Total Person Insight

"Your attitudes can be the lock on, or the key to, your door of success."

DENIS WAITLEY

Author, *The Psychology of Winning*

These student-owners of Crenshaw High School's Food from the Hood enterprise are learning a new respect for the challenges facing small business owners. Food raised on a former vacant lot in south central Los Angeles generates a modest profit. (Ken Biggs)

tudes are so strong that we encourage others to adopt our views and copy our behaviors. When others hold strong contrasting attitudes, a potential human relations challenge exists.

Attitudes are not quick judgments we make casually. Because we acquire them throughout our lives, they are deeply ingrained in our personalities. We are very much in favor of those things toward which we have a positive attitude. And we are very much against those things toward which we have a negative attitude.

Jerome Kagan, Harvard professor and author, explains, "It is this 'for' or 'against' quality that distinguishes attitudes from more superficial and less influential opinions."[5] The point of view that more women should be entering management-level positions in organizations is an opinion. However, the belief that women should have equal pay and equal access to top-level jobs is an attitude backed by strong emotions.

Some attitudes, such as job satisfaction, are multidimensional. The feelings we have about our work, for example, are made up of attitudes toward the company's compensation plan, opportunities for promotion, coworkers, supervision, the work itself, and other factors.[6] Job satisfaction is usually of major concern to an employer because management knows there is a link between attitudes and behavior. Persons who are dissatisfied with their jobs are more likely to be late or absent from work, to become unproductive, or to quit. Therefore, improved job satisfaction can reduce tardiness, absenteeism, and employee turnover.[7]

The Powerful Influence of Attitudes

Attitudes have a powerful influence on our lives. In fact, our attitudes hold us back more than our aptitudes do.[8] Persons who possess a positive mental attitude and an optimistic view of life are more apt to achieve personal and economic success. Such success does not happen by accident. People with an optimistic view of life are more apt to develop a plan for the future — that is, a series of goals that guide them day after day. Martin Seligman, author of *Learned Optimism,* takes the position that the more control an individual exerts, the more likely the person is to be an optimist. People who have a negative mental attitude simply hope that somehow things will work out for them. They usually have no long-term goals and no definite plan for the future. People with negative attitudes often feel out of control because they have made little attempt to influence the future.

Our attitudes can greatly influence our mental and physical health. Bernie Siegel, author of *Peace, Love and Healing* and *Love, Medicine and Miracles,* sees a strong connection between a patient's mental attitude and his or her ability to heal. Siegel, who is a surgeon, says that when a doctor can instill some measure of hope in the patient's mind, the healing process begins. As part of his treatment plan, Siegel attempts to give patients a sense of control over their destinies. He wants his patients to believe in the future and know that they can influence their own healing.[9] New research findings indicate that people who rate their current health status as good or excellent are significantly more likely to live longer than other people who rate their health as poor. This is true *regardless* of the person's actual physical condition.[10] Could it be that optimism can be a tool for extending life and pessimism can be a killer?

People shape their attitudes about you by what they see and hear. They interpret your attitudes through your behavior. How you feel about something is usually no secret to friends and acquaintances. Office workers who turn out letters filled with typographical errors will no doubt be viewed as people who do not care about their work. Salespeople who always meet or exceed their established quotas will very likely be seen as ambitious and conscientious. They will attract people with the same commitment and attitude toward their work.

Attitudes represent a powerful force in any organization. An attitude of trust, for example, can pave the way for improved communication and greater cooperation between an employee and a supervisor. A sincere effort by management to improve working conditions, when filtered through attitudes of suspicion and cynicism, may have a negative impact on employee-management relations. These same actions by management, filtered through attitudes of trust and hope, may result in improved worker morale. As another example, a caring attitude displayed by an employee can increase customer loyalty and set the stage for repeat business.

HOW ATTITUDES ARE FORMED

Throughout life you are constantly making decisions and judgments that help formulate your attitudes. These attitude decisions are often based on behaviors your childhood authority figures told you were right or wrong, childhood and adult behaviors for which you were rewarded or punished, role models you selected, and the various environmental and corporate cultures you chose to embrace.

Socialization

The process through which people are integrated into a society by exposure to the actions and opinions of others is called **socialization**.[11] As a child, you interacted with your parents, family, teachers, and friends. Children often feel that statements made by these authority figures are the "proper" things to believe. For example, if a parent declares, "People who live in big, expensive houses either are born rich or are crooked," the child is likely to hold this attitude for many years.

Children learn a great deal by watching and listening to family members, teachers, and other authority figures. In some cases, the influence is quite subtle. Children who observe their parents recycling, using public transportation instead of a car to get to work, and turning off the lights to save electricity may develop a strong concern for protection of the environment.

Peer and Reference Groups

As children reach adolescence and begin to break away psychologically from their parents, the **peer group** (persons their own age) can have a powerful influence on attitude formation. In fact, peer-group influence can sometimes be stronger than the influence of parents, teachers, and other adult figures. With the passing of years, reference groups replace peer groups as sources of attitude formation in young adults. A **reference group** consists of several people who share a common interest and tend to influence one another's attitudes and behaviors. The reference group may act as a point of comparison and a source of information for the individual member. For example, a fraternity or sorority may serve as a reference group for a college student. In the business community a chapter of the American Society for Training and Development or of Sales and Marketing Executives International may provide a reference group for its members. As members of a reference group, we often observe other people in the group to establish our own norms. Reference groups often have a positive influence on the professional development of members.

Rewards and Punishment

Attitude formation is often related to rewards and punishment. People in authority generally encourage certain attitudes and discourage others. Naturally, individuals tend to develop attitudes that minimize punishments and maximize rewards. A child who is praised for sharing toys with playmates is likely to develop positive attitudes toward caring about other people's needs. Likewise, a child who receives a weekly allowance in exchange for performing basic housekeeping tasks learns an attitude of responsibility.

As an adult, you will discover that your employers will continue to attempt to shape your attitudes through rewards and punishment at work. Many organizations are rewarding employees who take steps to stay healthy. Dominion Resources, a Virginia-based utility, rewards healthy checkups for both employee and spouse. Some companies offer employees annual health checkups with precise targets for blood pressure, cholesterol levels, and other indicators of good health. Those who achieve the targets get a discount on their health premiums; those who fall short of the goal pay the standard rates.[12]

Role Model Identification

Most young people would like to have more influence, status, and popularity. These goals are often achieved through identification with an authority figure or a role model. A **role model** is that person you most admire or are likely to emulate. Preschoolers are most likely to identify their parents as their role models. At this early stage parents are seen as almost perfect, as real heroes. During early elementary school, children begin to realize that their parents have flaws, and they search for other heroes — perhaps a popular athlete, a rock star, or an actor. During later stages of development, new role models are adopted. As you might expect, role models can exert considerable influence — for better or for worse — on developing attitudes.

The media have a tremendous influence on people's selection of role models. By the time they graduate from high school, most young adults will have spent 50 percent more time in front of a television than in a classroom or in quality experiences with parents, family, or friends.[13] Many television programs are dominated by crime, violence, and stereotyped or deviant characters and life situations. At the other extreme, other programs present positive superheroes with superhuman abilities. With this constant reinforcement from fictional negative and positive role models, young people sometimes have difficulty sorting out which behaviors and attitudes are acceptable in the real world.

Role models at work can have a major influence on employee attitude development. The new salesperson in the menswear department naturally wants help in adjusting to the job. So does the new dental hygienist and the recently hired auto mechanic. These people will pay special attention to the behavior of coworkers and managers. Therefore, if a worker leaves work early and no negative consequences follow, new employees may develop the attitude that staying until quitting time is not as important as they had thought. If a senior employee is rude to customers and suffers no negative consequences, new employees may imitate this attitude and behavior.

In most organizations, supervisory and management personnel have the greatest impact on employee attitudes. The supervisors' attitudes toward safety, cost control, accuracy, dress and grooming, customer relations, and the like become the model for subordinates. Employees pay more attention to what their supervisors *do* than to what they *say*.

If supervisors want to shape employee attitudes, they must demonstrate the kind of behavior they want others to develop. Albert Schweitzer, the French philosopher and Nobel Peace Prize winner, was right on target when he said, "Example is not the main thing in influencing others, it is the only thing." Barbara Meyer points out that a person may not always realize that he or she is serving as a role model to another person: "Most of us do not recognize ourselves as role models, yet we project behavior which people use as a pattern for their own conduct. Everyone who serves as a role model also teaches, since the followers first learn behavior or ideas and then manifest them in their own lives."[14]

E. R. "Buddy" Eanes, president of Warren Trucking Company in Martinsville, Virginia, wanted to restore the "spirit" of his company and build an organization in which employees could grow and prosper. A strike and wage

Reprinted with permission: Tribune Media Services.

rollback had left his drivers and warehouse workers disappointed and angry. As a result, negative attitudes were common. Eanes took one small step toward reestablishing trust by getting physically involved where employees could see him. He and his son began to help load trucks and perform other duties in the warehouse. These efforts, combined with greater involvement of employees in problem solving and decision making, resulted in improved employee morale, positive attitudes, and increased sales.[15]

Cultural Influences

Our attitudes are influenced by the culture that surrounds us. **Culture** is the sum total of knowledge, beliefs, values, and customs that we use to adapt to our environment. It includes tangible items, such as foods, clothing, and furniture, as well as intangible concepts, such as education and laws.[16]

People strive to define themselves in every culture. The definition varies from culture to culture. If you ask an adult living in Japan, "Who are you?" that person is likely to respond, "I'm an employee of Sony Corporation." In Japanese culture, people are more likely to define themselves by the organization for which they work. In the United States, a person's job and employer are somewhat less likely to be the major source of identity. For instance, a young woman who spends hours each week trying to improve the environment may define herself as an environmentalist. That she works as a department supervisor at a local supermarket may be incidental to how she defines herself. Many organizations today are striving to define their own corporate culture in order to influence the attitudes of their workers.

Item: Federal Express Corp., America's first nationwide overnight delivery service, recognizes that a successful service company must do everything possible to keep employees satisfied and highly motivated. After all, it is the employees who make the guaranteed overnight deliveries possible. The Federal Express culture incorporates four basic beliefs that many companies would consider revolutionary: (1) be as concerned about investments in people as investments in machines; (2) use technology to support the efforts of men and women on the front line; (3) make recruitment and training as crucial for salespeople and housekeepers as for managers; and (4) link compensation to performance for employees at the entry level, not just for those at the top.[17] Does all this attention to employees make a difference? The customers say yes. Ninety-five percent of Federal Express customers say they are completely satisfied with services provided.

Item: The management system at the Donnelly Corporation in western Michigan, the major glass products manufacturer for the automobile industry, is based on the assumption that people are intelligent, creative, and motivated when goals are clearly articulated and understood. The philosophy emphasizes participation, fairness, and self-management. Twice the company has won a national award for having the most suggestions per employee of any company in the country. One of their overseas plants in Ireland has operated for twenty-four years with only one day lost because of a labor dispute. Donnelly promises its workers that they will never be displaced by technology. If an employee's job is eliminated, he or she gets a chance to be retrained and integrated into another part of the company. The corporate culture is so strong that Donnelly has approximately 10,000 job applications on file.[18]

Item: Jerry Greenfield, cofounder of Ben & Jerry's Homemade Inc., is a self-proclaimed "minister of joy" and is often quoted as saying, "If it's not fun, why do it?" He created the Joy Gang, a volunteer group of employees whose sole mission is the relentless pursuit of joy in the workplace. Once a month, the Joy Gang sponsors an event for the organization as a whole or for a specific department. For example, one evening they cooked an entire Italian meal for third-shift workers and hired a disc jockey to play songs on request. Competitive wages, outstanding benefits, and a fun-loving atmosphere combine to form a corporate culture that many employees call "employee heaven."[19]

Thinking / Learning Starters

1. Identify at least one matter you feel strongly about. Do you know how you acquired this attitude? Is it shared by any particular group of people? Do you spend time with these people?

2. Think of an attitude that a friend or coworker holds but that you strongly disagree with. What factors do you believe contributed to the formation of this person's attitude?

ATTITUDES VALUED BY EMPLOYERS

Chapter 1 noted that the current labor market is characterized by churning dislocation and uncertainty. The large number of mergers, buyouts, business closings, and downsizing efforts has resulted in the loss of many jobs. Layoffs have come in every segment of the work force. Even managers and professionals have experienced job losses. With a surplus of job applicants, companies are being more selective when hiring. They are looking for candidates who display several important attitudes. The following discussion suggests several of these attitudes.

Be Willing to Assume Self-Leadership

Dawn Overstreet, a lecturer associated with the Americana Leadership College, once said, "People need to be leaders of themselves." In her presentations she emphasizes the importance of self-sufficiency — the ability to handle life despite difficulties.[20] People who display self-leadership are self-directed and, to a large degree, self-motivated. They are inclined to set their own goals and monitor their own progress toward those goals. Self-leadership requires self-observation. For instance, through self-observation, a secretary who sets a goal of producing error-free letters can discover behaviors that enhance and inhibit progress toward that goal. Self-leaders even find ways to administer their own rewards after they achieve their goals.[21]

Learn How to Learn

As the year 2000 approaches, we are seeing rapid and pervasive change. Organizations from hospitals to retail outlets are being forced to train and retrain employees more quickly and more frequently. Established industries are discovering the advantages of adopting new technology, and new industries are developing new processes that offer them a competitive edge in the marketplace. Given this enormous demand for the work force to learn new things faster, people with curiosity and a desire to keep up to date will be in great demand.

Most people are anxious to learn easier and faster ways of performing their work responsibilities, but many do not know *how* to learn. Do you learn best by reading about a new process or by listening to someone describe it? Do you need to watch someone else perform a new procedure, or do you prefer working on it yourself while someone monitors and guides your work? Although there is no right or wrong learning style, it is important to understand the way you learn. Learning how to learn has been described as the most basic of all skills.

> From an employer's perspective, an employee who knows how to learn — who knows how to approach and master any new situation — is more cost effective because time and other resources spent on training can be reduced. More importantly, however, by applying new knowledge efficiently to job duties, employees who have learned how to learn can greatly assist an employer in meeting strategic goals and competitive challenges.[22]

Learning how to learn is closely related to self-leadership. Both attitudes communicate the same message to an employer: "I will assume considerable responsibility for my own progress, my own development." Keeping up in a rapidly changing field may involve joining a professional reference group, listening to audiotapes or watching video training tapes, reading your professional journals, enrolling in continuing technical education classes, and engaging in other learning activities.

Be a Team Player

In sports, the person who is a "team player" receives a great deal of praise and recognition. A team player is someone who is willing to step out of the spotlight, give up a little personal glory, and help the team achieve a victory. Team players are no less important in organizations. Employers are increasingly organizing employees into teams (health teams, sales teams, product development teams) that build products, solve problems, and make decisions. Saturn's automobile manufacturing plant is made up of a network of highly effective teams. Each team functions as a small-business unit responsible for its own product, budget and accounting, and for doing business with the other teams within the organization. Management screens potential employees, but each team has the final say on whether a person will be hired. An employee who is not an effective team member can be thrown off the team.[23]

Be Concerned About Your Own Health and Wellness

The ever-growing cost of health care is one of the most serious problems facing companies today. Like Dominion Resources, many organizations are promoting wellness programs for all employees as a way to keep costs in line. These programs include tips on healthy eating, physical-fitness exercises, stress management practices, and other forms of assistance that contribute to a healthy lifestyle. Employees who actively participate in these programs frequently take fewer sick days, file fewer medical claims, and bring a higher level of energy to work. Some companies even give cash awards to employees who lose weight, quit smoking, or lower their cholesterol levels. Employees who pay a great deal of attention to their health needs can be a real asset. In Chapter 9 we will discuss health and wellness in greater detail.

Value Coworker Diversity

In the future, women and people of color will make up a large majority in the new multicultural, global work force. We will also see increased employment of the over–sixty-five population, and the hiring of more people with physical or mental disabilities. A growing number of progressive organizations see this diversity, or variety, as a strength. Herb Prokscha, owner of La Romagnola, a $5 million pasta maker based in Florida, has built a diverse work force by choice. Two-thirds of his production staff have been referred to him by the

Howard Samuels, an employee of Analog Devices in Wilmington, Massachusetts, is learning sign language on company time and at company expense. Once the company learned he was losing his hearing, steps were taken to organize the class for Samuels and several other workers. (Tom Herde/The Boston Globe)

Catholic Refugee Service in Orlando, and they include Vietnamese, Puerto Ricans, Romanians, and Bulgarians.[24]

To value diversity in a work setting means that an organization intends to make full use of the ideas, talents, experiences, and perspectives of all employees at all levels within that organization. The shift toward valuing diversity is driven by the knowledge that people who differ in terms of race, gender, religious beliefs, age, or physical traits often add richness to the organization. Development and utilization of a talented, diverse work force can be the key to success in a period of fierce global competition.

Many people, however, carry prejudiced attitudes against those who differ from them. Although deeply held prejudices that have developed over a long time are difficult to change, employers are demanding these changes. Chapter 7 contains specific guidance on how to develop positive attitudes toward joining a diverse work force.

Cultivate Enthusiasm for Life and Work

Employers know that the enthusiasm displayed by employees is contagious. An enthusiastic employee can have a positive influence on coworkers, managers, and, most important, the customer. Discontent and pessimism are also contagious. An unhappy or a frustrated employee can exert a negative influence on everyone she or he meets. People with enthusiasm about life and work look for the bright spots. These people have a feeling of optimism about the future and can find the good in almost everything. They try to avoid having too much contact with grumblers and refuse to be drawn into a group of negative thinkers who see only problems, not solutions.

HOW TO CHANGE ATTITUDES

If you begin to notice that successful people will not associate with you, that you have been overlooked for a promotion you thought you should have had, or that you go home from work depressed and a little angry at the world, you can almost always be sure you need an attitude adjustment. Unfortunately, people do not easily adopt new attitudes or discard old ones. It is difficult to break the attachment to emotionally laden beliefs. Yet attitudes can be changed. There may be times when you absolutely hate a job, but you can still develop a positive attitude toward it as a steppingstone to another job you actually do want. There will be times as well when you will need to help colleagues change their attitudes so that you can work with them more effectively. And, of course, when events, such as a recession, are beyond your control, you must strive to maintain a positive attitude. Knowing how to change attitudes in yourself and others can be essential to effective human relations — and your success — in an organization.

Changing Your Own Attitude

You are constantly placed in new situations with people from different backgrounds and cultures. Each time you go to a new school, take a new job, get a promotion, or move to a different neighborhood, you may need to alter your attitudes to cope effectively with the change.

In all these situations, it may help to realize that outside elements, such as the economy, your supervisor, the traffic, and the weather, are out of your control. At the same time, you can control your attitude toward these things and people. If you allow yourself to dwell on negative thoughts or attitudes, you can expect to exhibit negative, self-destructive behaviors. When you screen your thoughts to accentuate the positive, you will find your world a much more pleasant place. When you are happy and feel in control of your life, other people enjoy working with you.

Being able to control your attitudes is a powerful human relations skill that usually involves certain basic changes.

Total Person Insight

"You'll never entirely get rid of the negative voices inside you — but that doesn't mean you have to listen to them. Get into the habit of challenging negative ideas."

PAMELA R. JOHNSON AND CLAUDIA RAWLINS

"Daydreams and Dialogues: Key to Motivation"

1. *Alter your thinking.* Become aware of your negative attitudes toward people and situations. Some people develop a pattern of thinking based on a pessimistic view of life, whereas others maintain an optimistic view of life. You can decide whether to be an optimist or a pessimist.

> The defining characteristic of pessimists is that they tend to believe bad events will last a long time, will undermine everything they do, and are their own fault. The optimists, who are confronted with the same hard knocks of this world, think about misfortune in the opposite way. They tend to believe defeat is just a temporary setback, that its causes are confined to this one case.[25]

A pessimistic pattern of thinking can have unfortunate consequences. Pessimists give up more easily when faced with a challenge, are less likely to take personal control of their life, and are more likely to take personal blame for their misfortune. The good news is that we can change our habits of thinking. An effective way to escape a pessimistic pattern of thinking is to recognize that most of our negative beliefs are distortions. Learn to challenge (dispute) your negative interpretations of events. The chances are good that you will discover that many of your negative beliefs are exaggerated. Once you learn to recognize these distortions and challenge them, you will be on the road to a more optimistic view of life.[26]

2. *Think for yourself.* Determine whether the attitudes that seem to get you in trouble are your own constructions or the result of socialization. If you have been socialized into holding negative attitudes, you need to reexamine them. Authority figures, family ties, and peer pressure are strong influences. But you are an intelligent adult now, and you can control your own thoughts and feelings about people, ideas, and events, rather than being controlled by others' attitudes.

Buckminster Fuller, the respected architect and inventor, stated that learning to think for himself was the turning point in his life. He discovered at age thirty-two that he needed to become a more independent thinker and stop relying on others to influence every aspect of his life. Once he made the decision to think for himself, he became highly motivated to discover what he described as the "operating principles" of his world.[27]

3. *Keep an open mind.* We often make decisions and then refuse to consider any other point of view that might lead us to question our beliefs. Many times our attitudes persist even in the presence of overwhelming evidence to the contrary. A classic example reached headlines around the world when Washington, D.C., Mayor Marion Barry was removed from office following his conviction on drug charges. After serving the prison term, he ran for reelection and won!

For generations, James Allen, the famous Harvard psychologist, has been known for this discovery: By changing the inner attitudes of your mind, you can change the outer aspects of your life.[28] Each generation seems to have to rediscover this truth for itself.

Helping Others Change Their Attitudes

It is true that you are really in control of only your own attitudes. Although you can bend and flex and alter these as often as you find it beneficial,

The Red Hot Mamas, a Connecticut support group, are helping members cope with the physical and emotional turmoil that often accompanies menopause. The group is also attempting to help others develop a more understanding attitude toward this life change. (Andrea Bucci)

sometimes you need to stand firm and maintain your position. At that point, you may want to help other people change their attitudes. Unfortunately, you cannot hand your colleagues "a ready-made box of attitudes." But often you can help produce an atmosphere in which they will want to change their thinking.

If you work in an organization that has adopted a team structure, you will have several opportunities to help others change their attitudes. A healthy work team is characterized by a great deal of discussion about worker-related issues and group objectives. People freely express their thoughts, feelings, and ideas. Some people attempt to beg, plead, intimidate, or even threaten others into adopting new attitudes. This process is similar to attempting to push a piece of yarn across the top of a table. When you *push* the yarn in the direction you want it to go, it gets all bent out of shape. When you gently *pull* the yarn with your fingertips, it follows you wherever you want it to go. Two powerful techniques can help you pull people in the direction you want them to go, often without their even realizing that you are attempting to change their attitudes.

1. Change the *conditions* that precede the behavior.
2. Change the *consequences* that follow when the person exhibits the behavior.

Change the Conditions   If you want people to change their attitudes, identify the behaviors that represent the poor attitudes and alter the conditions that precede the behavior. Consider the following situation.

A new employee in a retail store is having a problem adjusting to her job. From the first day, she has found the job frustrating. Because the store is understaffed and the manager needed her on the sales floor as soon as possible, he rushed through her job training procedures, without taking time to answer her questions. Now she finds there are many customers' questions she cannot answer, and she has trouble operating the computerized cash register. The manager does not seem to care whether she succeeds or fails; he apparently just wanted the job filled. She wants to quit, and her negative attitudes are affecting her job performance and the way she handles her customers.

The manager could easily have prevented this employee's negative attitudes by changing the conditions surrounding her training. He could have been careful to answer all her questions *before* she was placed on the sales floor. Perhaps he could have asked an experienced salesperson to stay with her as she helped her first few customers. Above all, he could have displayed a caring attitude toward her and her success.

Change the Consequences   Another way to help other people change their attitudes is to alter what happens *after* they exhibit the behavior and attitudes you are attempting to change. A simple rule applies: When an experience is followed by positive consequences, the person is likely to repeat the behavior. When an experience is followed by negative consequences, the person will soon learn to stop the behavior. For example, if several of your employees are consistently late for work, you might provide some form of negative consequence each time they are tardy, such as a verbal reprimand or reduced pay. Keep in mind, however, that we tend to focus attention on the people who exhibit disruptive attitudes and to ignore the employees exhibiting the attitudes we want to encourage. Saying: "Thank you for being here on time. I really appreciate your commitment" can be an extremely effective reward for those who arrive at work on time. Attitudes rewarded will be repeated.

One note of caution: It is important to view consequences through the eyes of the person you are trying to influence. What you see as a negative consequence — a one-week leave of absence without pay — might be a positive consequence to someone else — an extra week's vacation. Robert Mager, a nationally known authority in the field of training and development, says:

> It doesn't matter what I might seek out or avoid: It is what is positive or aversive to the person whose behavior I am trying to influence that counts. And this, incidentally, is one reason we don't succeed more often than we do in the area of human interaction. We try to influence others by providing consequences that are positive to us but not to them.[29]

Thinking / Learning Starters

1. Are you holding a grudge against someone? Describe the situation. What are the benefits of holding on to this attitude? What are the benefits of letting go of it and moving on to a more productive relationship?

2. Think of a situation that is upsetting to you at work or home. How can you alter the situation to help change the other person's opinions? If it is absolutely impossible to change the situation, what will result if you change your attitude? Which direction is the best solution to the problem?

Organizations' Efforts Toward Improving Employees' Attitudes

Many companies are realizing that an employee's attitude and output cannot be separated. When employees have negative attitudes about their work, their job performance and productivity suffer. When they have positive attitudes, job performance and productivity improve. For generations, employers and labor unions focused on the salaries and fringe benefits as the rewards that would keep workers producing at top efficiency. But gradually, both labor and management discovered that money was not always the primary ingredient of a satisfying job.

People who are asked what they most want from their job typically cite mutual respect among coworkers, interesting work, recognition for work well done, the chance to develop skills, and so forth. If employers want to maintain or improve the positive attitudes of their workers, and thereby maintain or improve productivity, they need to provide the benefits workers consider important. Of course, workers expect the pay to be competitive, but they want so much more. As author and management consultant Peter Drucker says, "To make a living is not enough. Work also has to make a life."[30] Organizations are having to adjust to this change in worker attitudes.

One attempt to directly influence employee attitudes has been through the improvement of **quality-of-work-life (QWL)** factors. Many popular QWL projects provide opportunities for growth in workers' personal and professional lives. When companies build day-care centers, sponsor drug treatment programs for employees, or pay for employee memberships at local health clubs, they are recognizing the interconnections between work and the other aspects of employees' lives. The QWL movement has even influenced decisions regarding the location of organizations. Many progressive leaders attempt to locate their organizations where their employees will be most happy and therefore most productive. They give attention to quality-of-life criteria such as climate, good schools, cultural opportunities, recreational facilities, and opportunities for two-career couples.[31]

Summary

An attitude is any strong belief toward people and situations. It is a state of mind supported by feelings. People possess hundreds of attitudes about work, family life, friends, coworkers, and the like.

Attitudes represent a powerful force in every organization. If the persons employed by a service firm display a caring attitude toward customers, the business will likely enjoy a high degree of customer loyalty and repeat business. If the employees of a manufacturing firm display a serious attitude toward safety rules and regulations, fewer accidents will likely occur.

People acquire attitudes through early childhood socialization, peer and reference groups, rewards and punishment, role model identification, and cultural influences.

Employers value attitudes that show a willingness to exercise self-leadership, to learn, and to be a team player. Employers also appreciate employees who value coworker diversity, show a concern for health and wellness, and exhibit enthusiasm for life and work.

Although many factors can influence the formation of an attitude, people do not easily adopt new attitudes or discard old ones. You can choose to change your attitude by altering your thinking; thinking for yourself without undue pressure from your peers, family, and others; and keeping an open mind. You can help others change their attitudes by altering the consequences and conditions that surround the situation. Positive consequences and conditions produce positive attitudes. Organizations are also taking steps to improve the quality of work life of their employees to help them be more productive.

Career Corner

Q. I am a twenty-four-year-old recent college graduate. Six months ago I accepted a job as assistant to the office manager of a small manufacturing plant. She is in her late fifties and has been with the company since she graduated from high school. She has made it perfectly clear that she never had the opportunity to go to college. Her attitudes about how work is to be done in our office seem so old-fashioned. I have so many creative ideas to improve our efficiency, but she seems to believe I am too young to know anything. Every time she says "That's the way it has always been done; don't change it," my skin crawls and I feel very bitter for the rest of the day. What can I do to change her attitude toward my potential?

A. Begin by changing your attitude toward her traditional way of performing routine tasks in the office. Remember, she has had to adjust to many changes over the years to keep her organization running smoothly. Respect her past successes and assure her that you are there to help with the changing demands of the future.

Second, begin to alter the conditions in the office so that they are conducive to your creative ideas. Bring your professional journals to work and invite her to read various articles discussing innovative ideas that have been successfully implemented in other offices. Invite her to attend a seminar with you or to enroll in a class on some new software package that makes tedious office tasks easier. If she accepts a new idea, praise her intelligence and openness. When she receives positive feedback from you and others in the organization, she will likely repeat the behavior and seek out additional ways to improve the efficiency of the office. Changing attitudes is not easy, so be patient.

Key Terms

attitude
socialization
peer group
reference group

role model
culture
quality of work life (QWL)

**Review
Questions**

1. It has been said that "attitudes represent a powerful force in any organization." What examples can you give to support this statement?
2. List five ways in which we form our attitudes.
3. Describe how rewards and punishment can shape the attitudes of employees in an organization. Give at least one example of each.
4. How can selecting a positive role model within an organization help an individual reach his or her goals?
5. List and explain three strategies for changing attitudes that might get you in trouble at work.
6. Explain how consequences can influence the shaping of attitudes in an organization.
7. Robert Mager says that the conditions that surround a subject can play an important role in shaping attitudes. Provide at least one example to support Mager's statement.
8. Identify the attitudes employers are seeking in prospective employees.
9. How do QWL factors help companies keep good employees in an age when large numbers of workers change jobs every year?
10. Explain in your own words the meaning of Waitley's Total Person Insight on page 58.

**Application
Exercises**

1. Describe your attitudes concerning
   a. a teamwork environment.
   b. health and wellness.
   c. life and work.
   d. learning new skills.
   How do these attitudes affect you on a daily basis? Do you feel you have a positive attitude in most situations? Can you think of someone you have frequent contact with who displays negative attitudes toward these items? Do you find ways to avoid spending time with this person?
2. Identify an attitude that one of your friends is maintaining and that you would like to see changed. Do any conditions that precede this person's behavior fall under your control? If so, how could you change those conditions so that your friend might change his or her attitude? What positive consequences might you offer when your friend behaves the way you want? What negative consequences might you impose when your friend participates in the behavior you are attempting to stop?

**Self-Assessment
Exercise**

For each of the following statements, circle the number from 1 to 5 that best represents your response: (1) strongly disagree (never do this); (2) disagree (rarely do this); (3) moderately agree (sometimes do this); (4) agree (frequently do this); (5) strongly agree (almost always do this).

a. When forming attitudes about important   1   2   3   4   5
matters, I maintain an open mind, listen
to the views of others, but think for
myself.

b. I make every effort to maintain a positive   1   2   3   4   5
mental attitude toward other people
and the events in my life.

c. I seek feedback and clarification on the   1   2   3   4   5
influence of my attitudes and behaviors
on others.

d. I am willing to change my attitudes and   1   2   3   4   5
behaviors in response to constructive
feedback from others.

Select an appropriate attitude or skill you would like to improve. Write your goal in the space provided.

GOAL: _____

_____

_____

Case Problem

The Prize: A Flounder Fish Light

For the twenty-five years Mary spent with various door-to-door sales organizations, she felt unappreciated. At one company's annual conference, she watched another woman receive an alligator-skin purse for reaching a sales goal. Mary wanted that purse and vowed she would surpass her sales goal the following year and win the coveted prize. Which she did — but that year's prize was a flounder light for night fishing. Years later, Mary told *Savvy* magazine "I made up my mind right then that if I ever ran a company, one thing I would never do was give someone a fish light."

Today Mary Kay Ash, founder of Mary Kay Cosmetics, works hard to provide within her company the conditions that help maintain her employees' positive attitudes toward their work. She also monitors carefully to make sure the rewards her sales consultants earn are meaningful to individual prize winners. She personally sends a birthday card to each employee, a silver bank shaped like a duck to new children of employees, a silver bowl to newlyweds, and, on the Monday before Thanksgiving, a turkey to everyone. Outside her private office at her Dallas headquarters is a sign that reads "Department of Sunshine and Rainbows." She imagines that every person she meets during the day has a sign around his or her neck that says "Make me feel important," and she strives to do just that. Her positive attitude permeates the entire organization, as one employee explained: "It's catching. I was surprised that kind of attitude could be transferred through the whole company."

Many of Mary Kay's 220,000 independent beauty-and-sales consultants attend the three-day seminar held each summer at the Dallas Convention Center. The women are rewarded for their sales achievements and receive queen-for-a-day treatment. Top sellers are crowned with diamond tiaras and wrapped in mink coats or given a set of keys to the Mary Kay trademark — a pink Cadillac.

Questions

1. This chapter states that you can affect other people's attitudes by monitoring conditions in the workplace and influencing the consequences of workers' behavior. How has Mary Kay Ash implemented these principles? Would the conditions and consequences she provides help improve your attitude at work?
2. Employee surveys at Mary Kay show that only 60 percent of the work force feel they are paid fairly. Recently, secretaries at the company were earning $23,000 and production line assemblers $16,800. Christmas bonuses ranged from $25 to $500. Yet, turnover among Mary Kay employees is less than 10 percent. Why do you think these employees are staying in jobs that do not meet their financial goals?

Chapter 4

Building High Self-Esteem

Chapter Preview

After studying this chapter, you will be able to

1. Define self-esteem and discuss how it is developed.

2. Explain how self-esteem influences human relations and success at work.

3. Learn to identify the qualities of people with low and high self-esteem.

4. Discuss the powerful influence of expectations on self-esteem.

5. Explain the roles mentors can play in your professional life.

6. Identify ways to raise your self-esteem.

7. Understand the conditions organizations can create that will help workers raise their self-esteem.

JACKIE JOYNER KERSEE, described by many sports writers as the greatest living female athlete, grew up in humble surroundings. The U.S. Olympics star spent her childhood in East St. Louis, Illinois, a town with more than its share of abandoned public housing projects, burned-out homes, and vacant factory buildings. Although times were tough when she was a child, the young athlete never viewed her family's situation as hopeless. She credits solid hometown roots, close family ties, support from friends, and the guidance of her high school track-and-field coach for helping her achieve many of her goals.

After graduating from high school, Jackie Joyner Kersee attended the University of California at Los Angeles (UCLA) on an athletic scholarship. Although she was a successful college athlete, she was not fully prepared for her first Olympic games. Reflecting on that experience, Kersee says that she was physically ready to compete but she lacked the proper mental conditioning. She did not expect to win, even though sports authorities predicted she would be a gold medal winner for the U.S. team. At the beginning of each event, she fed herself negative thoughts that drained her emotionally. Her defeat that year inspired her to try harder to win at the Olympic games in Seoul. Through the proper mental training, she took control of her thoughts, fed her mind positive self-talk, and came home with two gold medals.[1] ■

The right mental conditioning can be the key to achieving your goals in life. If you expect to fail, you probably will. But if you truly expect to succeed, your mind will take you through your door of success. It all depends on how you feel about yourself.

THE POWER OF SELF-ESTEEM

Nathaniel Branden, author of *The Six Pillars of Self-Esteem,* has spent the past three decades studying the psychology of self-esteem. In countless speeches, articles, and books, he has attempted to describe the connection between self-esteem and many of the human problems common to our society today. The importance of self-esteem is indicated by his statement:

> Apart from disturbances whose roots are biological, I cannot think of a single psychological problem — from anxiety and depression, to underachievement at school or at work, to fear of intimacy, happiness, or success, to alcohol or drug abuse, to spouse battering or child molestation, to co-dependence and sexual disorders, to passivity and chronic aimlessness, to suicide and crimes of violence — that is not traceable, at least in part, to the problem of deficient self-esteem.[2]

The belief that low self-esteem can cause serious problems throughout life prompted the California State Assembly to establish the twenty-five-member Task Force to Promote Self-Esteem and Personal and Social Responsibility.

This action followed testimony that people with low self-esteem are more likely to exhibit violent behavior, discriminate against others, and abuse drugs.[3] The task force's final report defines **self-esteem** as appreciating your own worth and importance, having the character to be accountable for your own behaviors, and acting responsibly toward others.[4]

The importance of self-esteem as a guiding force in our lives cannot be overstated. Alfred Adler, a noted psychiatrist and author, stated, "Everything begins with self-esteem, your concept of yourself."[5]

Self-Esteem = Self-Efficacy + Self-Respect

Nathaniel Branden states that self-esteem has two interrelated components: self-efficacy and self-respect. **Self-efficacy** can be thought of as the confidence you have in your ability to think, understand, and make decisions — to do specific things.[6] When self-efficacy is high, you believe you have the ability to act appropriately. When self-efficacy is low, you worry that you might not be able to do the task, that it is beyond your abilities. Your perception of your self-efficacy can influence which tasks you take on and which ones you avoid. Albert Bandura, a professor at Stanford University and one of the foremost self-efficacy researchers, views this component of self-esteem as a resilient belief in your own abilities. According to Bandura, a major source of self-efficacy is the experience of mastery, in which success in one area builds your confidence to succeed in other areas.[7] For example, an administrative assistant who masters a sophisticated computerized accounting system is more likely to master future complicated computer programs. In contrast, a person who feels computer illiterate may not even try to figure out the new program, regardless of how well he or she *can* do it.

Self-respect, the second component of self-esteem, is what you think and feel about yourself. Self-respect can be described as the deep-down-inside feeling of your own worth. The conviction of your own value is a primary factor in achieving career success. People who respect themselves tend to act in ways that confirm and reinforce this respect. People who lack self-respect may put up with verbal or physical abuse from others because they feel they are unworthy of praise and deserve the abuse.[8] One key to achieving a sense of self-worth is to set realistic standards. People with low self-esteem often set unrealistically high standards for themselves, and then struggle to achieve them. The result may be a persistent need to prove themselves and an inability to enjoy what they have already accomplished.[9] When you respect yourself, you are less likely to feel a constant need to prove yourself to others. You are proud of your accomplishments and goals and are not dependent on the constant approval of others. Branden says the estimate you place on yourself is not a conscious, verbalized judgment but a judgment that exists in the form of a feeling. These feelings can be hard to isolate and identify because you experience them constantly.[10] One of the greatest tragedies in life is that people look for respect from every direction except from within.

Self-esteem includes your feelings about your adequacy in the roles you play in life, such as that of friend, brother or sister, daughter or son, employee or employer, student or teacher, researcher, leader, and so on. Self-esteem also includes the personality traits you believe you have, such as honesty, creativity, assertiveness, flexibility, and many more. Often your self-esteem derives from your physical characteristics and your skills and abilities. Are you tall, slender, short, or heavy? Do you like what you see in the mirror? Are you good at writing, fixing appliances, researching topics, playing the piano, or engaging in some other skill?

Although high self-esteem is the basis for a healthy personality, it does not mean becoming egotistical, that is, thinking and acting with only your own interests in mind. Genuine self-esteem is not expressed by self-glorification at the expense of others or by the attempt to diminish others so as to elevate yourself. Arrogance, boastfulness, and the overestimation of your abilities reflect inadequate self-esteem rather than, as it might appear, too much self-esteem. Someone with an egotistical orientation to the world sees everything and everyone in terms of their usefulness to her or his own aims and goals. This attitude undermines good human relations.

How Self-Esteem Develops

A Sunday school teacher once asked her class of small children, "Who made you?" Instead of giving the expected reply, an insightful child responded, "I'm not finished yet!" You are not born knowing who and what you are. You acquire your image of yourself over time by realizing your natural abilities and by

---

Total Person Insight

"Is it possible to have too much self-esteem? No, it is not; no more than it is possible to have too much physical health. Sometimes self-esteem is confused with boasting or bragging or arrogance. Such traits reflect, not too much self-esteem, but too little; they reflect a lack of self-esteem."

NATHANIEL BRANDEN

Author, *The Six Pillars of Self-Esteem*

constantly receiving messages about yourself from the people closest to you and from your environment.

Childhood   Your self-esteem is a reflection of your image of who you are. This image begins to form the minute you have the first conscious realization that you are a living, functioning being. Your family is the earliest source of information about yourself. An ancient Chinese proverb tells us, "A child's life is like a piece of paper on which every passer-by leaves a mark." Parents do not teach their children self-esteem. But they do shape it with positive and negative messages:

- Bad boy! Bad girl!
- You're so lazy!
- You'll never learn.
- What's wrong with you?
- Why can't you be more like . . . ?
- It's all your fault.

- You're great!
- You can do anything!
- You're a fast learner.
- Next time you'll do better.
- I like you just the way you are.
- I know you did your best.

In most cases, you probably did not stop and analyze these messages; you simply accepted them as true and recorded them in your memory. As a result, your subconscious mind gradually developed a picture of yourself, whether accurate or distorted, that you came to believe as real.

> Everyone was once a child. Our experience today is filtered through the events and feelings of childhood, recorded in detail. We cannot have a feeling today that is "disconnected" from similar feelings recorded in the past, the most intense of which occurred to us in the first five years of life. This does not mean that today's feelings are not real, or that we are to discount them by claiming "they're just an old recording." We are today who we once were.[11]

The type of family discipline you grew up with probably had considerable effect on your self-esteem. Interestingly enough, some psychologists have found that children brought up in a very permissive environment tend to develop lower self-esteem than those raised in a firmer and more demanding home. Parental discipline is one way of telling children that parents care about them and what they do. When someone cares about you, you tend to think more positively about yourself.

The strength of early parental positive feedback can have far-reaching effects in the course of a person's life. Irene Carpenter, the first woman elected a senior vice president in the ninety-year history of Citizens and Southern National Bank in Atlanta, recalls of her childhood, "My parents raised us to believe we could do anything we chose to do. . . . Many women in management do not start out with that concept of themselves. It has enabled me to overcome many of the obstacles I've encountered in the banking industry."[12]

The self-esteem formed in childhood lays the foundation for your attitudes toward work, your future success, your personal abilities, and the roles you play.

Adolescence   Infants love to look at their reflections. They are totally accepting of themselves. As an infant, you looked at pictures of yourself and other children and experienced joy. You probably did not think, "I wish I looked like that baby," or "That baby sure is ugly!" The worth of your own image was not dependent on or measured by the images of others. As you got older, however, and entered your teens, you probably started comparing yourself to other people. Typically you became less happy with who you were. Perhaps you wished you were more like others you perceived as better, and you may even have used put-downs as an equalizer. Teenagers often tear down others to build themselves up, trying to combat their doubts about themselves and their negative self-images. "Friends" add to the level of self-doubt by using "kidding" statements such as "Hi, Klutz!" "You're such a chicken," or "You'll probably be late to your own funeral!" Negative images like these can undermine a person's originally strong self-acceptance. These critical words are often prompted by the speaker's own unmet needs and low self-esteem.

The most critical factor in self-esteem for large numbers of adolescents is physical appearance. The media play a strong part in establishing the standards

Members of this gymnastics team line up to give a hug to a teammate who is a contest winner. This form of positive reinforcement often builds self-esteem. (Spencer Grant/Stock, Boston, Inc.)

by which adolescents judge themselves. In recent years Americans have developed a love affair with thinness. Magazines such as *Glamour, Cosmopolitan,* and *GQ* portray the impossibly thin body as the height of fashion. The common use of fad diets by both men and women can be traced to society's pressure to be thin.[13] It is easy to feel deficient or diminished in comparison to the images projected on television or in our favorite magazines. It is also easy to form a negative self-image when making these comparisons.

The ages of twelve to eighteen are among the most crucial in developing and consolidating your feelings about yourself. During these years, you are moving away from the close bond between parent and child and are attempting to establish ideals of independence and achievement.[14] You must also deal with physical changes; relationships with peer groups; an emerging, often confusing identity; and the loss of childhood and the assumption of some adult responsibilities. Is it any wonder that your self-esteem seemed to change not only day by day but also hour by hour? In fact, many people never move beyond the image they had of themselves while in high school. Outwardly successful, they may still be trying to prove to their old classmates that they can "make it." Adolescent problems should not be underestimated, for it is in the resolution of these problems and conflicts that the self-esteem of the adult is born.

It is unfortunate that many teenagers look for their self-esteem everywhere except within themselves. Strong self-esteem is independent of the opinions of others or of external possessions. It comes mainly from an internal sense of worth. Because many adolescents (and adults) with low self-esteem judge their own value by comparing themselves with others, they have a desperate need for recognition and status. Therefore, they tend to value money and the things money can buy. During a role-playing incident between a teacher instructing a self-esteem unit and a teenage boy, the following exchange occurred:

> The teacher asked, "What's your favorite car? Describe it."
> "A Mustang with black interior," the student replied.
> "Now imagine you just washed that car and drove it to school. I come along in a crane, swing a wrecking ball, your beautiful car shatters. Wham, and the door falls off. Wham, and the body is spread out like scrambled eggs. You are not insured. How would you feel inside?"
> The student looked stricken.
> "If that car is the only image you project," the teacher explains, "I have just destroyed you. I have taken away everything you represent. If you do not work from the inside out, somebody will come along at some point in your life — believe me — and take everything away."[15]

Adulthood   When you reach adulthood, your mind has a time-reinforced picture of who you are, molded by people and events from all your past experiences. You have been bombarded over the years with positive and negative messages from your family, friends, teachers, strangers, and the media. You

may continue to compare yourself to others, as was so common in adolescence, or you may choose to focus on your own inner sense of self-worth. Emmett Miller, a noted authority on self-esteem, says that adults tend to define themselves in terms of their possessions, their work, or their internal value system.[16] Each area can influence feelings of self-worth.

1. *We may define ourselves in terms of the things we possess.* Miller says this is the most primitive source of self-worth. If we define ourselves in terms of what we have, the result may be an effort to accumulate more and more material things to achieve a greater feeling of self-worth. We may be unhappy with an automobile that does not communicate sufficient prestige to others, so we go in debt to buy another model. The house we own may seem small by someone else's standards, so we buy a larger one. People who define themselves in terms of what they have may have difficulty deciding "what is enough" and may spend their life in search of more material possessions.

2. *We may define ourselves in terms of what we do for a living.* Miller points out that too often our self-worth and identity depend on something as arbitrary as a job title. Amy Saltzman, author of *Down-Shifting*, a book on ways to reinvent (or redefine) success, says, "We have allowed our professional identities to define us and control us."[17] She points out that we have looked to outside forces such as the corporation, the university, the media, counselors, or our parents to provide us with a script for leading a satisfying, worthwhile life. People pushed into a rigid career track that offers ample financial rewards but no fulfillment of personal needs may dread going to work in the morning even though others admire the job they hold.

3. *We may define ourselves in terms of an internal value system and emotional make-up.* Miller says this is the healthiest way for people to identify themselves:

> If you don't give yourself credit for excellence in other areas of life, besides your job and material possessions, you've got nothing to keep your identity afloat in emotionally troubled waters. People who are in touch with their real identity weather the storm better because they have a more varied and richer

sense of themselves, owing to the importance they attach to their personal lives and activities.[18]

As an adult, you will constantly be adjusting the level of your self-esteem as you get in touch with your identity. It is important to be aware of how other people have influenced and will continue to influence your beliefs about yourself. You will need to learn how to protect your self-esteem against those who try to diminish or limit your potential and how to listen to those who will encourage and challenge you. Such knowledge can help you distinguish between what is helpful and what is destructive, what is true and what is false. It can also help you expand the range of what you believe you can be and do in the future.

Thinking / Learning Starters

1. Can you recall two or three people from your childhood or adolescence who had a positive effect on your self-esteem? What did these people say or do? Were there any who had a negative effect on you? What did they say or do?

2. Identify at least two people who exhibit the characteristics of people with high self-esteem. What behaviors helped you identify them?

SELF-ESTEEM INFLUENCES YOUR BEHAVIOR

Your self-esteem has a powerful impact on your behavior at work. In general, employees with low self-esteem tend to have more trouble with interpersonal relationships and to be less productive than people with high self-esteem.[19]

Characteristics of People with Low Self-Esteem

1. *They may experience the failure syndrome.* As noted previously in this chapter, you form a mental picture of yourself at a very early age. Your subconscious mind was, and continues to be, "programmed" by other people's negative and positive comments. If your subconscious mind has been saturated with thoughts and fears of failure, these thoughts will continue to undermine your efforts to achieve your goals. If you see yourself as a failure, you will usually find some way to fail. William Glasser, author of *Reality Therapy* and other books on human behavior, calls this the **failure syndrome.** Individuals with a

failure syndrome think, "I always fail....Why try?" They have a fear of taking action because they expect to fail...again.

2. *They tend to maintain an external locus of control.* People with low self-esteem believe their behavior is controlled by someone or something in their environment. When you hear a person say, "It's not my fault. He made me do it," you can be assured that the speaker probably has low self-esteem. Rather than taking responsibility for their own choices, such people blame others for controlling them. Even when they succeed, they tend to attribute their success to luck rather than to their own expertise.

3. *They exhibit poor human relations skills.* Research studies repeatedly show that individuals with low self-esteem are more likely to feel hostile, show a lack of respect for others, and attempt to retaliate against others to save face in difficult situations.[20] Author and psychologist Milton Layden believes that a hostile response to others is a natural outcome of feelings of low self-esteem. It occurs because the emotional system, like other systems of the body, is controlled by a "balancing mechanism." When a person feels a lack of respect toward himself or herself, the mechanism is knocked off balance, and the person starts to feel hostile and anxious. These feelings are then translated into hostile actions.[21]

A person who has low self-esteem and is in a position of power is not likely to treat subordinates or coworkers fairly. Workers with low self-esteem can reduce the efficiency and productivity of a group: They tend to exercise less initiative, hesitate to accept responsibility or make independent decisions, and refuse to ask for help, fearing that others might think them incompetent. Rather than admit an error and handle the consequences, they often lie in an attempt to cover their mistakes.

4. *They tend to participate in self-destructive behaviors.* If you do not like yourself, there is no apparent reason to take care of yourself. Therefore, people with low self-esteem tend to drink too much, smoke too much, and eat too much. Some may develop an eating disorder such as bulimia or anorexia, often with devastating results.

Characteristics of People with High Self-Esteem

1. *People with high self-esteem are future oriented and not overly concerned with past mistakes or failures.* They learn from their errors but are not immobilized by them. Magnifying past failures can lead to depression, anxiety, and feelings of pessimism about the future. Every experience has something to teach—if you are willing to learn. A mistake can show you what does not work, what not to do. One consultant, when asked whether he had obtained any results in trying to solve a difficult problem, replied, "Results? Why, I've had lots of results. I know a hundred things that won't work!" The same principle applies to your own progress. Falling down does not mean failure. Staying down does.

Julia Stasch began to build her future when she accepted a secretarial position with Stein and Company, a Chicago-based construction company, in 1976. Because she had confidence in her own abilities, she took the initiative and began working on projects that gave her added responsibility. Each new project helped her learn more about the construction industry. In 1990, after several promotions, she became president of the company. Today she is one of the top-ranking women builders in the nation. She has worked hard to make sure women get jobs in the male-dominated building industry.[22]

2. *People with high self-esteem are able to cope with life's problems and disappointments.* Successful people have come to realize that problems need not depress them or make them anxious. It is their attitude toward problems that makes all the difference. In his autobiography, Lee Iacocca recalls many disappointments. At the top of his list was the experience of being fired as president of Ford Motor Company after the firm had recorded two years of record profits. After being fired by Henry Ford II, Iacocca moved to Chrysler Corp. and brought the ailing company back from the brink of failure. Years later, he recalled the loss of his job at Ford: "A lot has happened since July 13, 1978. The scars left by Henry Ford, especially on my family, will be lasting, because the wounds were deep. But the events of recent years have had a healing effect. So you move on."[23]

3. *People with high self-esteem are able to feel all dimensions of emotion without letting those emotions affect their behavior in a negative way.* This characteristic is one of the major reasons people with high self-esteem are able to establish and maintain effective human relations with the people around them. They realize emotions cannot be handled either by repressing them or by giving them free rein. Although you may not be able to stop feeling the emotions of anger, envy, and jealousy, you can choose to control your thoughts and actions when you are under the influence of these strong emotions. Without this self-control, you may waste a great deal of energy that could be channeled toward important personal and work-related activities. Robert Conklin, author of *How to Get People to Do Things,* suggests keeping the following statement in mind: "I can't help the way I feel right now, but I can help the way I think and act."[24] Remembering this principle can help you bring an emotionally charged situation under control.

4. *People with high self-esteem are able to help others and accept help.* They are not threatened by helping others to succeed, nor are they afraid to admit weaknesses. If you are not good at dealing with figures, you can bring in an accountant to manage the records. If you see someone whose abilities are not being used to their fullest, you can suggest ways that person might develop his or her talents. An old adage in business goes, "First-rate people hire first-rate people. Second-rate people hire third-rate people." Individuals with secure self-esteem realize that in helping others succeed, they benefit themselves as well.

5. *People with high self-esteem are able to accept other people as unique, talented individuals.* They learn to accept others for who they are and what they can do. As we move toward the year 2000, the changing demographics of the work force will make this attitude even more important. Individuals who cannot tolerate other people who are "different" may find themselves out of a job. People with high self-esteem build mutual trust based on each individual's uniqueness. These trusting relationships do not limit or confine either person because of group attributes such as skin color, religion, gender, lifestyle, or sexual orientation. Accepting others is a good indication that you accept yourself.

6. *People with high self-esteem exhibit a variety of self-confident behaviors.* They accept compliments or gifts by saying "Thank you," without making self-critical excuses and without feeling obligated to return the favor. They can laugh at their situation without self-ridicule. They let others be right or wrong without attempting to correct or ridicule them. They feel free to express opinions even if they differ from those of their peers or parents. They enjoy being by themselves without feeling lonely or isolated. They are able to talk about themselves to others without excessive bragging.

THE POWER OF EXPECTATIONS

Your thoughts about yourself are often expressed in terms of expectations—how far you believe you can go and what you feel you can do. You are also guided by the expectations of other people in your life, especially your authority figures.

Your Own Expectations

Gloria Steinem, author of the book *Revolution from Within—A Book of Self-Esteem,* says "What the future could hold, and what each of us could become, is limited mainly by what we believe."[25] People tend to behave in a way that supports their own ideas of how successful or incompetent they are. This somewhat mysterious power of expectations, often referred to as the **self-fulfilling prophecy,** is at the very heart of self-efficacy.

Earlier in this chapter we indicated that self-efficacy is one of the dual pillars of healthy self-esteem. Individuals with high self-efficacy are confident that they can do whatever is necessary to achieve their goals. Psychologist Albert Bandura states, "When beset with difficulties, people who entertain serious doubts about their capabilities slacken their efforts or give up altogether, whereas those who have a strong sense of efficacy exert great effort to master the challenges."[26] Let's assume that you want to lose one pound a week by following an exercise program and limiting your calorie intake. If you have had success with this weight-loss plan in the past, you will likely be encouraged by this past achievement and believe you can do it again. The encouragement of others can also be a factor. If your doctor says, "If you follow this plan I am sure you will lose weight," your self-efficacy will probably be enhanced. Similarly, if a relative laughs at your weight-loss plan, your self-efficacy will probably diminish.

Your career successes and failures are directly related to your own expectations about your future. In looking over applications for an MBA program, an admissions director noticed that some students had answered questions about their future plans with phrases such as "I am" or "I can." Other students had written "I hope to" or "I might." The words used by the first group represented a statement of belief that they could achieve specific goals. Not surprisingly, their academic records and outside accomplishments showed that these students had set and reached high performance levels. Students in the second group had lower expectations and less confidence in their ability to accomplish their goals. Many managers have witnessed the same phenomenon when talented employees refuse promotions because they do not feel capable of competent performance beyond their current levels. Remember, each person's self-fulfilling prophecy can have a positive or negative effect on his or her future.

The Expectations of Others

Self-fulfilling prophecies reflect a connection between your own expectations for yourself and your resulting behavior. But people can also be greatly influenced by the expectations of others. The **Pygmalion effect** sometimes causes people to become what others expect them to become.

This term was first used by Robert Rosenthal, a professor at Harvard University, and is based on a Greek legend about Pygmalion, the king of Cyprus. In the legend, the king longs for an ideal wife. Because no mortal woman meets his expectations, he fashions a statue of his ideal woman out of ivory and eventually falls in love with his creation. His desire to make the statue his wife is so intense that his belief brings it to life.

Research by Rosenthal and others supports the premise that there is a relationship between a person's level of motivation and the expectation of others. This theory has been applied in such diverse fields as education, sales, medicine, and manufacturing.

Item: In the classic study *Pygmalion in the Classroom,* Rosenthal described the effect of teachers' expectations of student performance. The results of his research were quite astounding. When teachers had high expectations for certain students (those they had been led to believe had excellent intellectual ability and learning capacity), those students learned at a faster rate than other students in the same group — even though the teachers did not consciously treat the former students differently. These teachers unintentionally communicated their high expectations to the students they *thought* possessed strong intellectual abilities.[27]

Item: The medical field has long recognized that a doctor's expectations can have a major influence on a patient's physical health. Healing is more likely to take place if the doctor gives the patient hope that recovery is very likely. Bernie Siegel has written extensively on this phenomenon. In his best-selling book, *Love, Medicine and Miracles,* he says, "When a doctor can instill some measure of hope, the healing process sometimes starts even before treatment begins."[28]

Item: Many manufacturing organizations are beginning to realize the impact of management's expectations on employee productivity. A manager with low expectations for a group of workers may set very low production goals, whereas a manager with high expectations will anticipate peak performance and thus set high production goals. The two types of managers agree, however, that whatever they expect is usually what they get.[29]

The expectations of others can be very powerful. Kimberly Marcus, a native American, hugs her great-aunt after taking first prize in a dance competition. (David Alan Harvey/ Magnum Photos)

Mentors

Mentors are people who have been where you want to go in your career and who are willing to act as your guide and friend. They take you under their wings and show you how to get to the next step in your career. They act as sponsors, teachers, devil's advocates, and coaches.

As sponsors, mentors will create opportunities for you to prove yourself. This might mean they will ask you to help them on a project or analyze a problem. As teachers, mentors will present you with hypothetical situations, ask you, "What would you do?" and then help guide you in the appropriate direction. As devil's advocates, mentors will challenge and confront you to give you practice in asserting your ideas and influencing others. As coaches, mentors will support your dreams by helping you find out what is important to you and what skills you have.

Organizations should nurture mentoring relationships among their employees. Although mentors are not mandatory for success, they certainly help. Indeed, there will always be days when you feel nothing you do is right. Your mentor can help repair damaged self-esteem and encourage you to go on. With the power of another person's positive expectations reinforcing your own native abilities, it is hard to fail.

Thinking / Learning Starters

1. Do you believe you can alter your self-esteem once you have reached adulthood? If so, what actions can you take to raise your current level of self-esteem?

2. Do you agree with the statement "People tend to take you at the value you place on yourself; if you believe in your own potential abilities, so will others"? Explain your answer.

HOW TO BUILD SELF-ESTEEM

"The level of our self-esteem is not set once and for all in childhood," says Nathaniel Branden. It can grow throughout our lives or it can deteriorate.[30] Examining your present self-image is the first step in understanding who you are, what you can do, and where you are going.

The person you will be tomorrow has yet to be created. Most people continue to shape that future person in the image of the past, repeating the old limitations and negative patterns without realizing what they are doing. The development of a new level of self-esteem will not happen overnight, but it can happen. Such a change is the result of a slow evolution that begins with the desire to overcome low self-esteem.

Identify and Accept Your Limitations

The first step toward higher self-esteem is to accept yourself as you are now. Without acceptance, improving your self-esteem is not possible. Accept your limitations and become realistic about who you are and what you can and cannot do. Demanding perfection of yourself is unrealistic—no one is perfect. The past cannot be changed, so stop dwelling on it. Your future, however, can be effectively shaped by how you think and act from this day forward.

> Accepting ourselves begins with an honest look at who we are. We don't need to like everything we find. We can just say, for example, "Oh, yes, I can recognize that I sometimes feel impatient. This is a human feeling, and I don't need to deny it or dislike myself for feeling it."[31]

Some women in business have decided they no longer want to live up to the "superwoman" image, juggling home, family, and career. They realize their time and energy are limited, and they are adjusting their schedules to accommodate those realities. One female executive explains, "I'm concerned about the quality of my existence. I'm willing to work hard; but I don't want to work so hard at everything that nothing gets done well, and I end up feeling like a failure."[32] Many men are rejecting the superachiever image as well.

Acting as an observer and detaching yourself from negative thoughts and actions can help you break the habit of rating yourself according to some scale of perfection and can enable you to substitute more positive and helpful thoughts. A good first step is learning to hate a behavior you may indulge in, rather than condemning yourself. Hating yourself tends to make the behavior worse. If you condemn yourself for being weak, for example, how can you muster the strength to change? But if you become an "observer" and view the activity as separate from yourself, you leave your self-esteem intact, while you work on changing the behavior.

Take Responsibility for Your Decisions

Psychologists have found that children who were encouraged to make their own decisions early in their lives have higher self-esteem than those who were kept dependent on their parents for a longer period of time. Making decisions helps you develop confidence in your own judgment and enables you to explore options. Take every opportunity you can to make decisions both in setting your goals and in devising ways to achieve them.

As you make your decisions, be willing to accept the consequences of your actions, positive or negative. Organizations with supportive management personnel encourage decision making by employees at all levels to help them improve their self-efficacy.

> When Jim Burke became head of a new products division at Johnson & Johnson, one of his first projects was the development of a children's chest rub. The product failed miserably, and Burke expected that he would be fired. When he was called in to see the Chairman of the Board, however, he met a surprising reception. "Are you the one who just cost us all that money?" asked Robert Wood Johnson. "Well, I just want to congratulate you. If you are making mistakes, that means you are taking risks, and we won't grow unless you take risks." Some years later, Burke became the chairman of J&J.[33]

Taking full responsibility for your decisions and actions is an important key to building self-esteem. Most of the factors that generate self-esteem are under your control. You can choose to participate in self-improvement activities that will enhance your career and your personal life. You can choose to build harmonious relationships with your coworkers, supervisors, customers, and family members. Assume full responsibility for the quality of your communications with others. Choose the values by which you want to live your life. Making your own decisions and taking responsibility for the consequences can become a habit that will be a powerful force in your life.

Develop Expertise in Some Area

Developing "expert power" not only builds your self-esteem but also increases the value of your contribution to an organization. Identify and cultivate a skill

---

Total Person Insight

"To feel competent to live and worthy of happiness, I need to experience a sense of control over my existence. This requires that I be willing to take responsibility for my actions and the attainment of my goals. This means that I take responsibility for my life and well-being."

NATHANIEL BRANDEN

Author, *The Six Pillars of Self-Esteem*

or talent you have, whether it is a knack for interviewing people, a facility with math, or good verbal skills. Alice Young, a resident partner in the law firm of Graham & James in New York, developed an expertise in her youth that she did not know would be a major asset in her career. "I speak Japanese, Chinese, French, and English," she says. "I have a knowledge of Asian cultures that I developed before trade with the East opened up." She has been able to capitalize on her expertise to help American and Asian companies do business with each other and to smooth over many cultural differences that would otherwise make negotiations difficult or impossible. She advises others to "use what you know to benefit yourself and your company."[34]

Developing expertise may involve continuing your studies after completing your formal education. Some institutions offer professional courses to enable people to advance in their careers. For example, the Institute of Financial Education conducts courses for persons employed by financial institutions.

Set and Achieve Your Goals

Research points to a direct link between self-esteem and the achievement of personal and professional goals. People who consistently set and achieve their goals are able to maintain high self-esteem. People who fail to set goals wander aimlessly through life with no purpose, and they are more apt to suffer from low self-esteem. Once you set a goal, either personal or professional, you can take three steps to achieve it more easily.

Step One: Visualization The power to visualize is in a very real sense the power to create. We often visualize ourselves succeeding or failing in some enterprise without knowing that such mental pictures can actually affect our behavior. Intentional, successful visualization can slowly lead your self-esteem and your life in the direction you want it to go. Shakti Gawain, author of *Creative Visualization*, states that when we create something, we always create it first in the form of a thought:

> Imagination is the ability to create an idea or mental picture in your mind. In creative visualization you use your imagination to create a clear image of something you wish to manifest. Then you continue to focus on the idea or picture regularly, giving it positive energy until it becomes objective reality . . . in other words, until you actually achieve what you have been visualizing.[35]

Diane Von Furstenberg, noted fashion designer, has used mental imagery to produce positive changes in her life. She started her business using her dining-room table as her office and a small amount of money obtained by pawning her jewelry. Six years later, her business was grossing more than $60 million, and she was on the cover of *Newsweek*—a superstar at twenty-nine. Reflecting on her career, she says, "I believe nothing happens unless you can imagine it. I have to have images of where I want to go next."[36]

Setting and achieving goals is one way to build self-esteem. Visualizing or mentally rehearsing a successful outcome, such as completing a marathon, can help us achieve the goals we've established. (Peter Southwick/ Stock, Boston, Inc.)

Salespeople often visualize closing a sale in advance. Most hosts plan their parties in advance. You can work the same "mental magic" with your own self-esteem by visualizing yourself as the person you want to be.

Step Two: Simulation   Jackie Joyner Kersee mentally rehearsed the perfect running performance repeatedly before she actually ran each race. These rehearsals so firmly planted in her brain the steps toward her goal that they became habit. Most successful Olympic athletes practice this way. Denis Waitley, former chair of psychology for the U.S. Olympic teams, believes it is possible to learn a new self-image through the same process — by vividly imagining yourself being the person you want to become.[37] This mental rehearsal, called **simulation,** can be a powerful step toward improving your self-image. Review the "Characteristics of People with High Self-Esteem" listed earlier in this chapter. If you would like to make them part of your behavior pattern, simulate these behaviors in your mind. Mentally rehearse self-confident behaviors — see yourself walking with your chin up and your shoulders straight and speaking with a strong, confident voice. Picture yourself making appropriate eye contact with other people. As you gain confidence, practice these new skills by actually performing them when you are with your friends, family, and coworkers. You will begin to feel more comfortable with these behaviors every day, and soon they will become habits. This simulation practice will lead you toward a more positive self-image. If it works for the Olympic champions, it can work for you.

Step Three: Monitor Your Self-Talk You silently talk to yourself throughout the day. Through this self-talk, you are constantly in the process of conditioning yourself — negatively or positively, depending on the tone of your thoughts. To be sure you achieve the results you have visualized and simulated, you need to listen very carefully to your self-talk and learn to monitor its tone. Shad Helmstetter, author of *What You Say When You Talk to Yourself,* defines **self-talk** as "a way to override our past negative programming by erasing or replacing it with conscious, positive new directions."[38] It is an extremely effective way to direct your subconscious mind, which will result in a change in your conscious behaviors. As Figure 4.1 indicates, self-talk is part of the cycle of self-esteem, whether that talk is negative or positive. Many people internalize negative self-talk, which produces negative behaviors. When you want to take control of your self-esteem, focus your self-talk on positive thoughts only.

Helmstetter suggests you prepare specific positive self-talk statements and repeat them often to keep yourself on target toward your goals. This intentional, daily repetition of positive self-talk will help reprogram your self-image, just as the repeated comments from others throughout your past have influenced your current feelings about yourself. Learn how to write positive self-talk statements for each of your goals by following these guidelines.

1. Begin each self-talk statement with a first-person pronoun, such as *I* or *my.*
2. Use a present-tense verb, such as *am, have, feel, create, approve, do,* or *choose.* Don't say "My ability to remember the names of other people *will* improve." Instead, focus on the present: "I *have* an excellent memory for the names of other people."
3. Describe the results you want to achieve. Be sure to phrase the statement as though you have already achieved what you want. Say, "I am in control of my habits," as opposed to "I can quit smoking." Table 4.1 offers several general self-talk statements that might help you improve your self-esteem.
4. Use active, vibrant words to describe your new self-image. Pretend you are painting a detailed, verbal portrait of the new you.

Write positive self-talk statements for different facets of your personal and professional life. Put them on three-by-five-inch index cards, and attach them to your bathroom mirror, refrigerator, car dashboard, desk blotter, and so on, and review them often. Barbara Grogan, a successful entrepreneur who founded Western Industrial Contractors, has a placard on the dashboard of her car that reads, "I am powerful, beautiful, creative, and I can handle it!"[39] This positive message helps her through the tough times.

Another technique for internalizing your thoughts is to record your affirming statements on a blank cassette tape while quiet, one-beat-per-second

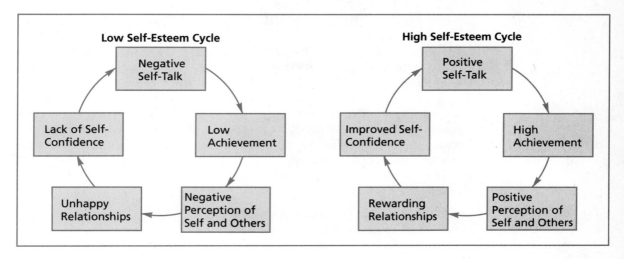

FIGURE 4.1

Self-Esteem Cycles

music (largo) is playing in the background.[40] Play the tape repeatedly, especially when you are in a relaxed state, such as just before you fall asleep at night. Your brain will accept the information without judgment. When these statements become part of your "memory bank," over time your behavior will follow accordingly. Your brain is like a computer. It will put out exactly what you put in. If you put positive self-talk in, positive behavior will result.

TABLE 4.1

Identifying Correct
Self-Talk

Counterproductive Self-Talk	Productive Self-Talk
I can quit smoking.	I am in control of my habits.
I will lose twenty pounds.	I weigh a trim _____ pounds.
I won't worry anymore.	I am confident and optimistic.
Next time I won't be late.	I am prompt and efficient.
I will avoid negative self-talk.	When I talk to myself, I talk with all due respect.
I will not procrastinate.	I do it now.
I'm not going to let people walk all over me anymore.	I care enough to assert myself when necessary.

SEEK A SUPPORTIVE WORK ENVIRONMENT

Even though each of us ultimately is responsible for raising or lowering our own self-esteem, we can make that task easier by seeking employment in a work environment that enhances self-esteem. Many organizations are beginning to realize that low self-esteem affects their workers' ability to learn new skills, to be effective team members, and to be productive. Many of the companies described in *The 100 Best Companies to Work for in America* realize that when employees do not feel good about themselves, the result may be poor job performance. Research has identified five factors that can enhance the self-esteem of employees in any organization.[41] As Figure 4.2 illustrates, workers require the following:

- *Workers need to feel valued.* A major source of worker satisfaction is the feeling that one is valued as a unique person. Self-esteem grows when an organization makes an effort to accommodate individual differences and to recognize individual accomplishments.
- *Workers need to feel competent.* Earlier in this chapter we noted that self-efficacy grows when people feel confident in their ability to perform job-related tasks. One of the best ways organizations can build employee confidence is to involve them in well-designed training programs. Effective

FIGURE 4.2

Factors That Enhance
the Self-Esteem of
Employees

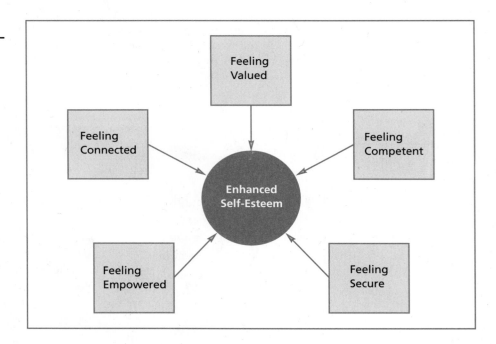

training programs give employees plenty of opportunities to practice newly acquired job skills.

- *Workers need to feel secure.* Employees are more apt to feel secure when they are well informed and know what is expected of them. Managers need to clarify their expectations and provide employees with frequent feedback regarding their performance.
- *Workers need to feel empowered.* Progressive organizations such as Corning Incorporated and Federal Express Corporation are demonstrating to employees that their opinions and views matter and that their ideas are being implemented in significant ways. These companies make sure that each person has a voice in helping the organization achieve its goals.
- *Workers need to feel connected.* People are apt to achieve high self-esteem when they feel their coworkers accept, appreciate, and respect them. Many companies are fostering these feelings by placing greater emphasis on teamwork. Team building efforts help promote acceptance and cooperation.

Summary

Self-esteem is a combination of self-respect and self-efficacy. If you have high self-esteem, you are more likely to feel competent and worthy. If you have low self-esteem, you are more likely to feel incompetent, unworthy, and insecure. Self-esteem includes your feelings of adequacy about the roles you play, your personality traits, your physical appearance, your skills, and your abilities. High self-esteem is the foundation for a successful personal life and professional life.

A person starts acquiring and building self-esteem from birth. Parents, friends, associates, the media, and professional colleagues all influence the development of that person's self-esteem. As an adult, a person often defines herself or himself in terms of possessions, jobs, and/or internal values. People with high self-esteem tend to be future oriented, cope with problems creatively, handle their emotions, and give as well as receive help. They also accept others as unique, talented individuals and exhibit self-confident behaviors.

High self-esteem is essential for success at work. Personal expectations, as well as the expectations of others, have a powerful influence on self-esteem. These expectations can become self-fulfilling prophecies. Managers and mentors can strengthen a person's self-esteem by expressing belief in her or his abilities and talents.

To build high self-esteem, individuals must accept the past and build for the future. They need to accept their limitations and develop expertise in some area. Making decisions and living with the consequences, positive or negative, can also help build self-esteem. Individuals need to set goals by visualizing the person they want to be, simulating specific appropriate behaviors, and monitoring their self-talk.

Many organizations now realize that they need to help build employees' self-esteem and are doing so through training sessions, clear statements of expectations and feedback, giving greater respect to individuals in the workplace, and fostering teamwork.

Career Corner

Q. As a teenager, I was involved in a major car accident in which several bones in my face were broken. I was left with a large scar on my chin. Although I have had several operations to correct the visible damage, I still feel self-conscious whenever I meet new people. It is affecting my career opportunities. What can I do to gain more confidence?

A. In his book *Psycho-Cybernetics,* plastic surgeon Maxwell Maltz demonstrates that what your mind has been conditioned to believe about yourself can override or undermine what you actually see in the mirror. Throughout his twenty-five-year practice, Maltz operated on wounded soldiers, accident victims, and children with birth defects. Many of these individuals saw only their defects and doubted that they could ever be successful. Even after their corrective surgery, these patients' deformities continued to exist in their minds. Their inner self-images had not been changed.

You can learn to use the creative power of your subconscious mind. Even though your external image has been improved, you still need to change the inner self-image you carry within your mind. When you are successful in changing your mental image of yourself, your self-confidence will increase.

Key Terms

self-esteem   Pygmalion effect
self-efficacy   mentors
self-respect   simulation
failure syndrome   self-talk
self-fulfilling prophecy

Review Questions

1. What is self-esteem? Why is the development of high self-esteem important in a person's life?
2. What influences help shape a person's self-esteem?
3. How do the expectations of yourself and others affect your self-esteem? Give examples from your own life.
4. What characteristics do people with high self-esteem exhibit?
5. Describe the behaviors of people with low self-esteem.

6. List the basic guidelines for building high self-esteem. Which two do you feel are the most important? Why?
7. What influence does self-talk have on a person's self-esteem? How can this influence be controlled?
8. In your own words, explain the two cycles portrayed in Figure 4.1.
9. List the four guidelines for constructing positive self-talk statements. Give three examples of such statements.
10. Describe your understanding of the cartoon on page 86.

Application Exercises

1. Describe a situation in which you achieved a goal you had set for yourself. Did any outside positive or negative forces influence your progress toward the goal? If there were negative forces, how did you overcome them? Did you visualize or mentally simulate the completed goal? If so, how did this simulation help?
2. Think about people you know at school, at work, or in your social environment who seem to exhibit low self-esteem. Describe the qualities that give you this impression. Now think about people you know who exhibit high self-esteem. List their qualities. Often these two lists will reflect direct opposites, such as "has a sloppy appearance/keeps a neat appearance," "slumps down the hall/walks tall," or "avoids eye contact during conversations with others/makes eye contact." What steps might the people you identified as having low self-esteem take to enhance their images? How might these steps improve their self-esteem? Could you take any similar steps to improve your own self-esteem? Explain.

Self-Assessment Exercise

For each statement, circle the number from 1 to 5 that best represents your response: (1) strongly disagree (never do this); (2) disagree (rarely do this); (3) moderately agree (sometimes do this); (4) agree (frequently do this); (5) strongly agree (almost always do this).

a. I constantly monitor my self-talk in order to maintain high self-esteem.	1	2	3	4	5
b. I tend to be future oriented and not overly concerned with past mistakes or failures.	1	2	3	4	5
c. I have developed and maintained high expectations for myself.	1	2	3	4	5
d. I accept myself as a changing, growing person capable of improvement.	1	2	3	4	5

  e. My goals are clearly defined, attainable, 1 2 3 4 5
   and supported by positive self-talk.

   Select an appropriate attitude or skill you would like to improve. Write
your goal in the space provided.

GOAL: _____

   _____

   _____

Case Problem   **California Assembly Bill No. 3659**

When the California legislature proposed a major study of the effects of self-esteem on the social ills of society, many critics across the country ridiculed the idea. Some California lawmakers were skeptical of anything dealing with self-esteem and agreed to the study only when the words "and Personal and Social Responsibility" were added to the original title, *The California Task Force to Promote Self-Esteem*. Garry Trudeau satirized the California study in his nationally syndicated comic strip "Doonesbury." Even when the final report was published, the media focused on the seven dissenting committee members who refused to sign the final document rather than on the commission's findings.

Behind the scenes, however, a different story emerged. Even though the work included no salary, more people applied to serve on the task force than on any other legislative body in the state's history. An unprecedented number of people asked to testify before the commission. Positive letters about the task force's work outweighed negative ones by a ratio of ten to one. School districts that addressed self-esteem in light of the study's recommendations met with outstanding success. For example, student discipline problems dropped by 75 percent after self-esteem became part of the curriculum in one mostly Hispanic district that had one of the lowest per capita incomes in the state. In another high school, the number of teenage pregnancies dropped from 147 to 20 over a three-year period following implementation of self-esteem programs. Requests for more information poured in from experts from all fifty states and many foreign countries.

Although California's study focused on ways schools and families could improve self-esteem, one of the key principles listed in the final report was "When possible, we need to form our groups and organizations so that all members participate in establishing decisions, rules, and the consequences of breaking those rules." Since the report was published, companies across the country have begun to implement employee "empowerment" programs to help improve the self-esteem of their workers.

Questions

1. The entire three-year study cost California taxpayers $735,000, less than the cost of maintaining one prisoner facing a life sentence. Do you think the investment was cost effective? Why?
2. Why do you think the task force received so much negative publicity, when the process and results were so dramatically positive?
3. What impact does "empowering" employees to make decisions and rules within an organization have on a worker's self-esteem?

Chapter 5

Developing a Professional Presence

Chapter Preview

After studying this chapter, you will be able to

1. Explain the importance of professional presence.

2. Discuss the factors that contribute to a favorable first impression.

3. Distinguish between assumptions and facts.

4. Define *image* and describe the factors that form the image you project to others.

5. List and discuss factors that influence your choice of clothing for work.

6. Understand how manners contribute to improved interpersonal relations in the workplace.

T HE HERTZ CORPORATION, the U.S. Air Force, Hyatt Hotels Corporation, the City of Dallas, and the Neiman-Marcus Group, Inc., have one thing in common — all have purchased the services of Feedback Plus. Feedback Plus is an agency that dispatches professional shoppers who pose as consumers. These "mystery" shoppers visit the client's business, purchase products or services, and report back to the client on the quality of service they receive. The City of Dallas hired Feedback Plus to see how car-pound employees treat citizens picking up their cars. The Air Force is using professional shoppers to assess customer service at their on-base supply stores. Banks, hospitals, and public utilities are also hiring mystery shoppers. Vickie Henry, chief executive of Feedback Plus, notes that many similar firms compete for clients' business, and service really differentiates one firm from another. Although Henry has a database of 8,800 people who serve as professional shoppers, she sometimes assumes the role of mystery shopper herself. During a recent visit to an upscale women's apparel store, she observed the type of customer service most companies attempt to avoid. None of the many salespeople on the sales floor said hello when she entered the store. When she removed a skirt from a clothing rack, none of the salespeople approached her. Finally, several minutes after entering the store, Henry approached a salesperson and asked to use the dressing room. Needless to say, service at this firm did not receive high marks from Feedback Plus.[1] ■

As organizations experience increased competition for clients, patients, and customers, awareness of the importance of public contact increases.[2] They are giving new attention to the old adage "First impressions are lasting impressions." Research indicates that initial impressions do indeed tend to linger. Therefore, a positive first impression can set the stage for a long-term relationship.

Of course, it is not just those *first* contacts with clients, patients, customers, and others that are important. Positive impressions should be the objective of *every* contact. A major goal of this chapter is to discuss the important factors that help us make positive impressions. Another important goal is to examine the factors that shape the image we project to others.

MAKING A GOOD IMPRESSION

There are many personal and professional benefits to be gained from a study of the concepts in this chapter. You will acquire new insights regarding ways to communicate positive impressions during job interviews, business contacts, and social contacts made away from work. You will also learn how to shape an image that will help you achieve your fullest potential in the career of your choice. Knowledge of how to enhance your professional presence can serve as a foundation for increased self-confidence and positive self-regard. As noted in

Chapter 4, positive self-regard (high self-esteem) is based on your feelings about your adequacy in the multiple roles you play in life.

The material in this chapter will also increase your self-awareness. As we noted in Chapter 1, self-awareness is an important first step toward building more effective relationships with others.

This is not a chapter about ways to make positive impressions with superficial contacts and quick-fix techniques. We do not discuss the "power look" or the "power lunch." The material in this chapter will not help you become a more entertaining conversationalist or win new customers by pretending to be interested in their hobbies or families. Stephen Covey, author of *The Seven Habits of Highly Effective People,* says that the ability to build effective, long-term relationships is based on character strength, not quick-fix techniques. He notes that outward attitude and behavior changes do very little good in the long run unless they are based on solid principles governing human effectiveness. These principles include service (making a contribution), integrity and honesty (which serve as a foundation of trust), human dignity (every person has worth), and fairness.[3]

Few people can fake a sincere greeting or a caring attitude. If you really do not care about the customer's problem, the customer will probably sense your indifference. Your true feelings will be difficult to hide. Ralph Waldo Emerson was right on target when he said, "What you are shouts so loudly in my ears I cannot hear what you say."

Professional Presence

We are indebted to Susan Bixler, president of Professional Image, Inc., and author of *Professional Presence,* for giving us a better understanding of what it means to possess professional presence. **Professional presence** is a dynamic blend of poise, self-confidence, control, and style that empowers us to be able to command respect in any situation.[4] Once acquired, it permits us to be perceived as self-assured and thoroughly competent. We project a confidence that others can quickly perceive the first time they meet us.

Bixler points out that, in most cases, the credentials we present during a job interview or when we are being considered for a promotion are not very different from those of other persons being considered. It is our professional presence that permits us to rise above the crowd. Debra Benton, a career consultant, says, "Any boss with a choice of two people with equal qualifications will choose the one with style as well as substance."[5] Learning to create a professional presence is one of the most valuable skills we can acquire.

The Primacy Effect

The development of professional presence begins with a full appreciation of the power of first impressions. The tendency to form impressions quickly at the time of an initial meeting illustrates what social psychologists call a **pri-**

macy effect in the way people perceive one another. The general principle is that first impressions establish the mental framework within which a person is viewed, and later evidence is either ignored or reinterpreted to coincide with this framework.[6]

Martha Kelly met a middle-aged man at an outdoor cookout. He was wearing cutoff blue jeans and an old pair of worn-out sneakers. He had had several drinks and tended to interrupt people and monopolize any conversation. Throughout the afternoon, people avoided him whenever possible. About two weeks later, Martha stopped at a drugstore to get a prescription filled. To her surprise, the pharmacist was the same man she had met at the cookout, only now he was dressed in a neatly tailored white jacket, blue shirt, and pin-striped tie. Although he projected a very professional image in dealing with his customers, Martha left the store and went to another pharmacy to get her prescription filled. The positive impression communicated in the store was not strong enough to overcome her first, negative impression.

The First Few Minutes

When two people meet, their potential for building a relationship can be affected by many factors. Within a few moments, one person or the other may feel threatened, offended, or bored. Leonard Zunin and Natalie Zunin,

A political candidate must be able to build rapport with a variety of people. A good handshake, eye contact, and a pleasant smile can help you make a good first impression. (Dan Lamont/MATRIX)

coauthors of *Contact — The First Four Minutes*, describe what they call the **four-minute barrier**.[7] In this short period of time, human relationships are established, reconfirmed (in the case of two former acquaintances meeting), or denied. It is during the first few minutes of interaction with others that people's attention spans are at their greatest and powers of retention at their highest.

Why four minutes? According to the Zunins, this is the average time, determined by careful observation, during which two people in a social situation make up their minds to continue the encounter or to separate. During the first few minutes you can benefit from what sociologists call the "halo effect." This means that if you are viewed positively within the first four minutes, the person you made contact with is more likely to assume that everything you say or do is positive.[8]

Thinking / Learning Starters

To test the practical application of the Zunins' theory in a real-life setting, examine it in the context of your past experiences. Review the following questions and then answer each with yes or no.

1. Have you ever gone for a job interview and known instinctively within minutes that you would or would not be hired?

2. Have you ever met a new supervisor who immediately communicated to you the impression that he or she could be trusted and was interested in your welfare?

3. Have you ever entered a restaurant, hotel, or office and experienced an immediate feeling of being welcome after the employee spoke only a few words?

First Impressions in a Work Setting   In a work setting, the four-minute period in which a relationship is established or denied is often reduced to seconds. The U.S. Postal Service is concerned about perceptions created during this brief period of time. In selected regions of the nation, postal workers have completed the Dale Carnegie human relations course.[9] The following examples illustrate the effect that immediate first impressions can have in a variety of work situations:

Item: Paula rushed into a restaurant for a quick lunch — she had to get back to her office for a 1:30 P.M. appointment. The restaurant was not crowded, so she knew she would not have to wait for a table. At the entrance of the main dining area was a sign reading "Please Wait to Be Seated." A few feet away, the hostess was discussing a popular movie with one of the waitresses. The hostess made eye contact with Paula but continued to visit with the waitress. About twenty more seconds passed, and Paula began to feel anxiety build inside her. She tried to get the hostess's attention, but the hostess did not respond. After another ten seconds had passed, Paula walked out of the restaurant.

Item: Sandy and Mike entered the showroom of a Mercedes-Benz dealer. They noticed two salespeople seated at desks near the entrance. One salesperson was wearing a well-tailored blue blazer, gray slacks, and a white shirt with a blue tie highlighted by subtle stripes. The other salesperson was wearing sport slacks (khaki color), a blue knit pullover shirt (short sleeve), and casual shoes. The salesperson wearing the casual clothing walked over to Sandy and Mike and asked, "May I be of assistance?" Mike said, "We're just looking today." The salesperson returned to his desk. As they left the showroom Sandy said, "I can't believe someone selling a $40,000 automobile would wear such casual clothing." "I agree," Mike said.

In each of these examples, the negative first impression was created in less than sixty seconds. The anxiety level of the restaurant customer increased because she was forced to wait while two employees talked about a personal matter. And the potential customers were making judgments about the car salesperson based solely on his appearance. Unfortunately, these employees were probably not fully aware of the impression they communicated to customers.

Assumptions Versus Facts The impression you form of another person during the initial contact is made up of both assumptions and facts. Most people tend to rely more heavily on **assumptions** during an initial meeting. As the Zunins state, people live in an assumptive world:

> When you meet a stranger, and sometimes with friends, much of the information you get is based on assumption. You form positive or negative feelings or impressions but you must realize that only superficial facts can be gathered in four minutes. Depending on assumptions is a one-way ticket to big surprises and perhaps disappointments.[10]

Cultural influences, especially during the early years of your life, lead you to form impressions of some people even before you meet them. People often stereotype entire groups. Here are a few of the common stereotypes that still persist in our society:

- "Older workers are set in their ways."
- "Men have a competition mentality."
- "Executive women are aggressive."

These are just a few of the assumptions that some people perceive as facts. With the passing of time some assumptions tend to lose support as factual information surfaces. The idea that all married couples should have children receives less support today than it did a generation ago. Women are now less likely to be viewed as unacceptable candidates for executive positions. Nevertheless, people rarely reach the point in life where they are completely

---

Total Person Insight

"If people aren't quickly attracted to you or don't like what they see and hear in those first two to four minutes, chances are they won't pay attention to all those words you believe are demonstrating your knowledge and authority. They will find your client guilty, seek another doctor, buy another product, vote for your opponent or hire someone else."

JANET G. ELSEA

President, Communication Skills, Inc.

---

free of assumptions. In fact, the briefer the encounter with a new acquaintance, the greater the chance that misinformation will enter into your perception of the other person.

THE IMAGE YOU PROJECT

Image is a term used to describe how other people feel about you. In every business or social setting, your behaviors communicate a mental picture that others observe and remember. This picture determines how they react to you. Your image depends on more than exterior qualities such as dress and grooming. In the words of James Gray, author of *The Winning Image*, "Image is more than just a veneer."[11] He observes,

> Image is a tool for communicating and for revealing your inherent qualities, your competence, abilities and leadership. It is a reflection of qualities that others associate with you, a reflection that bears long-lasting influence in your bid for success. Image is not a tool for manipulation. Nor is it a false front. It cannot substitute for substance.[12]

In many respects, the image you project at work is very much like a picture puzzle, as illustrated in Figure 5.1. It is formed by a variety of factors, including manners, self-confidence, voice quality, versatility, integrity (see Chapter 6), entrance and carriage, facial expression, surface language, competence, positive attitude, and handshake. Each of these image-shaping components is under your control.

A growing number of organizations have discovered a direct link between profitability and the image projected by employees. Financial institutions, public utilities, airlines, retail stores, restaurants, hospitals, and manufacturers face the problem of not only gaining but also retaining the patronage of clients and

FIGURE 5.1

Major Factors That
Form Your Image

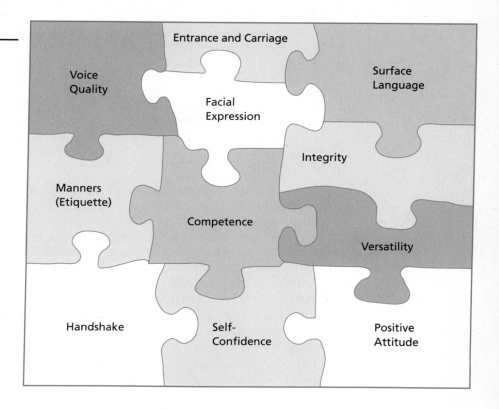

customers. When the Oldsmobile division of General Motors Corp. decided to reshape the image projected by dealers, it developed a $25 million training program. Dealers and employees learned how to improve service to customers and to sell the Aurora, a more luxurious car than Olds dealers have sold in the past.[13]

Surface Language

As noted earlier, we form opinions about other people based on both facts and assumptions. Unfortunately, assumptions often carry a great deal of weight. Many of the assumptions you develop regarding other people are based upon what the Zunins describe as "surface language." **Surface language** is defined as a pattern of immediate impressions conveyed by appearance. The clothing you wear, your hair style, the fragrances you use, and the jewelry you display all combine to make a statement about you to others.

According to many writers familiar with image formation, clothing is particularly important. John Molloy, author of *Dress for Success* and *The Woman's Dress for Success Book,* was one of the first to acknowledge publicly the link between image and wardrobe. According to his research, what you wear influences your credibility and likability.[14] The view that clothing is a very important component of image formation is supported by many other image consultants, including Susan Bixler, William Thourlby, Emily Cho, and Jacqueline Thompson.

Although a more relaxed dress code has evolved in recent years, people judge your appearance long before they judge your talents. It would be a mistake not to take your career wardrobe seriously. Bixler suggests that those making career wardrobe decisions should keep in mind that three things haven't changed:[15]

1. *If you want the job, you have to look the part.* Establish personal dress and grooming standards appropriate for the organization where you wish to work. Before you apply for a job, try to find out what the workers there are wearing. If in doubt, dress conservatively. Some of America's most successful companies still maintain a formal dress code. Roger Penske, best known for his successes in IndyCar racing, owns six auto dealerships in southern California. Men who sell cars at Penske dealerships must follow a strict dress code: No beards, no sunglasses, and proper business attire, with neckties pulled tight.[16]

2. *If you want the promotion, you have to look promotable.* Employees can communicate with their clothing that they are satisfied with their position. A good rule to follow is to dress for the job you want, not the job you have. If you are currently an office clerk and want to become an office manager, identify the successful office managers and emulate their manner of dress. Emily Cho, author of *Looking Terrific,* says that the right wardrobe can transform a person from being part of the corporate scenery to being in the forefront.

3. *If you want respect, you have to dress as well as or better than your industry standards.* One would expect to find conservative dress standards in the fields of banking, insurance, accounting, and law, and more casual dress standards in the fields of advertising, sports entertainment, and agriculture. Spend time researching the dress and grooming standards in the industry where you hope to find a job.

Thinking / Learning Starter

Do you recall a teacher, coworker, or supervisor whose surface language impressed you—either positively or negatively? What specific elements (dress, hairstyle, jewelry, and so on) were evident in this person's surface language? What type of image do you think he or she was trying to project?

Selecting Your Career Apparel

Over 23 million American workers wear a uniform especially designed for a particular job. The judges on the U.S. Supreme Court and the technicians at the local Midas Muffler and Brake shop have one thing in common — both wear a special uniform to work. Today more and more people are donning uniforms to go to work. Companies that have initiated extensive career apparel programs rely on uniforms to project an image of consistent quality, good service, and uniqueness. Uniforms enhance company credibility, which in turn increases customer confidence in the firm.[17] Wearing a uniform can also have a positive effect on employees. Wearing the same uniform seems to create a sort of bond among coworkers. Thus, a uniform can make at least a small contribution to building company spirit at your local McDonald's restaurant or Holiday Inn hotel.

Dress was the focus of a management decision at the GenCorp Automotive plant at Shelbyville, Indiana. The work force there is divided into twenty-five teams of twelve to fifteen production workers. To build company spirit, a decision was made to adopt the same "uniform" for all employees. Everyone, including managers, wears navy blue skirts or trousers and light blue shirts.[18]

Many workers wear special-dress uniforms. Unitog, based in Kansas City, rents and sells uniforms to companies such as Exxon and Anheuser-Busch. Employee uniforms often contribute to a spirit of teamwork. (Eli Reichman)

The uniforms worn by United Parcel Service employees, airline reservation clerks, and the employees at your local restaurant might be classified as special-design **career apparel**. Some work uniforms are designed by top talents in the fashion industry. In addition to special-design uniforms, there is another type of career apparel, somewhat less predictable, worn by large numbers of people in our labor force. Here are some examples:

- A female lawyer representing a prestigious firm would be appropriately dressed in a gray or blue skirted suit. A dress with a suit jacket would also be acceptable. She should avoid clothing in brash colors or casual styles that might reduce her credibility.
- A male bank loan officer would be appropriately dressed in a tailored gray or blue suit, white shirt, and tie. This same person dressed in a colorful blazer, sport shirt, and plaid slacks would be seen as too casual in most bank settings.
- A female receptionist at a prominent accounting firm would be appropriately dressed in a skirt and blouse. This same person would be inappropriately dressed if she showed up for work wearing designer jeans, a sweater, and sneakers.
- A mechanic employed by an auto dealership that sells new cars would be appropriately dressed in matching gray, tan, or blue shirt and pants. The mechanic would be inappropriately dressed in jeans and a T-shirt.

Many organizations seek advice about career apparel from image consultants. One source of image consultants is the Association of Image Consultants International.

Wardrobe Engineering

The term **wardrobe engineering** was first used by John Molloy to describe how clothing and accessories can be used to create a certain image. This concept was later refined by several other noted image consultants in hundreds of books and articles on dress and grooming. Although these authors are not in complete agreement on every aspect of dress, they do agree on a few basic points regarding wardrobe.

The quality of your wardrobe will influence the image you project. A wardrobe should be regarded as an investment, with each item carefully selected to look and fit well. Purchase a few basic items each year and you will soon have everything you need.

The newest dress fad is often inappropriate in a business or professional setting. In most cases, the world of work is more conservative than college, the arts, or the world of sports. If you are a fashion setter, you might be viewed as unstable or insincere. To be taken seriously, avoid clothing that is faddish or too flashy.

FOR BETTER OR FOR WORSE © 1994 Lynn Johnston Prod., Inc. Reprinted with permission of UNIVERSAL PRESS SYNDICATE. All rights reserved.

Women generally have more latitude than men do in selecting appropriate attire, but they should still exercise some caution in choosing their wardrobe. In some cases, women are entering positions formerly dominated by men. They need to be taken seriously, and the wardrobe they select can contribute to this end.

Your wardrobe should be appropriate for your field and for you. Although you should consider the dress and grooming standards of others in your field, don't give in to blind conformity or duplication. As one image consultant noted, "Effective packaging is an individual matter based on the person's circumstances, age, weight, height, coloring, and objectives."[19] In addition to these personal factors, you need to consider what's appropriate for your career. In general, four factors influence your choice of clothing for work:

1. *Products and services offered.*   In some cases the organization's products and services more or less dictate a certain type of dress. For example, a receptionist employed by a well-established law firm would likely wear clothing that is conservative, modest, and in good taste. These same dress standards would apply to a pharmaceutical sales representative who calls on medical doctors.

2. *Type of person served.*   Research indicates that first impressions created by dress and grooming are greatly influenced by unconscious expectations. Throughout life we become acquainted with bank loan officers, nurses, police officers, and others employed in a wide range of occupations. We form mental images of the apparel common to each of these occupations. When we encounter someone whose appearance does not conform to our past experiences, we feel uncomfortable.

3. *Desired image projected by the organization.* Some companies establish dress codes that help shape the image they project to the public. Walt Disney Company, for example, maintains a strict dress and grooming code for all its theme-park employees. They are considered "cast members" and must adhere to dress and grooming standards that complement the image projected by Disney theme parks.

4. *Geographic region.* Dress in the South and Southwest tends to be more casual than in the Northeast. Climate is another factor that influences the clothing people wear at work. In Texas, for example, the warm climate calls for short sleeves and open collars in some work settings.

Thinking / Learning Starter

Assume you are planning to purchase (1) a life insurance policy, (2) a Rolex wristwatch, and (3) eyeglasses. What types of career apparel would you expect persons selling these products to wear? What grooming standards would you recommend?

The Business Casual Look

The terms *business casual* or *corporate casual* have recently been used to describe the movement toward dress standards that emphasize greater comfort and individuality. **Business casual** usually means slacks and sports coats for men, and slacks, casual dresses, or skirts for women.[20] Business casual bridges the gap between the suits, white shirts, and silk blouses traditionally worn in business, and more casual dress, such as jeans, shorts, and T-shirts. Some companies have established "casual Fridays" or "dress-down weeks," while others have shifted from a strict dress code to a relaxed dress code. The casual look in corporate America was triggered, in part, by efforts to improve teamwork and empower employees. Bottom-up initiatives often emphasize getting rid of symbols of top-down authority.[21] The casual trend has also been fueled by the influx of Generation Xers who are entering the work force. These new workers are more relaxed and are looking for ways to express their individuality.

Now that the casual look is gaining acceptance, many companies are struggling to develop casual dress guidelines for their employees. Levi Strauss & Co., maker of jeans, Dockers, and other nonjean clothes, is offering companies an informational kit containing suggestions on how to develop a casual dress code.[22] Image consultants are also offering advice. Most agree that business casual still means dressing for success.

Your Facial Expression

After your overall appearance, your face is the most visible part of you. Facial expressions are the cue most people rely on in initial interactions. They are the "teleprompter" by which others read your mood and personality.[23]

Studies conducted in nonverbal communication show that facial expressions strongly influence people's reactions to each other. The expression on your face can quickly trigger a positive or negative reaction from those you meet. How you rate in the "good-looks" department may not be nearly as important as your ability to communicate positive impressions with a pleasant smile.

If you want to identify the inner feelings of another person, watch the individual's facial expressions closely. A frown may tell you "something is wrong." A smile generally communicates "things are OK." Everyone has encountered a "look of surprise" or a "look that could kill." These facial expressions usually reflect inner emotions more accurately than words.

In many work settings, a cheerful smile is an important key to creating a positive first impression. A deadpan stare (or frown) can communicate a negative first impression to others. If you find it hard to smile, take time to consider the reasons. Are you constantly thinking negative thoughts and simply find nothing to smile about? Are you afraid others may misinterpret your intentions?

Your Entrance and Carriage

The way you enter someone's office or a business meeting can influence the image you project, says Susan Bixler. She notes that "your entrance and the way you carry yourself will set the stage for everything that comes afterward."[24] A nervous or apologetic entrance may ruin your chances of getting a job, closing a sale, or getting the raise you have earned. If you feel apprehensive, try not to let it show in your body language. Hold your head up, avoid slumping forward, and try to project self-assurance. To get off to the right start and make a favorable impression, follow these words of advice from Bixler: "The person who has confidence in himself or herself indicates this by a strong stride, a friendly smile, good posture, and a genuine sense of energy. This is a very effective way to set the stage for a productive meeting. When you ask for respect visually, you get it."[25] Bixler says the key to making a successful entrance is simply believing—and projecting—that you have a reason to be there and have something important to present or discuss.

Your Voice

Several years ago, a Cleveland-based company, North American Systems, Inc., developed and marketed Mr. Coffee, which makes coffee quickly and conveniently. Some credited the quick acceptance of this product to an effective advertising campaign featuring baseball Hall of Famer Joe Di Maggio. He came across to the consumer as an honest, sincere person. When Joe Di Maggio said Mr. Coffee worked and made good coffee, people believed him.

The tone of your voice, the rate of speed at which you speak (tempo), and the volume of your speech contribute greatly to the meaning attached to your verbal messages. In the case of telephone calls, voice quality is critical because the other person cannot see your facial expressions, hand gestures, and other body movements. You cannot trade in your current voice for a new one, but you can make your voice more pleasing to other people and project a positive tone.

Although there is no ideal voice for all business contacts, your voice should reflect at least these four qualities: confidence, enthusiasm, optimism, and sincerity. Above all, try to avoid a speech pattern that is dull and colorless. Joanne Lamm, founder of Professional Speech Associates, says the worst kind of voice has no projection, no color, and no feeling.[26]

Your Handshake

When two people first meet, a handshake is usually the only physical contact between them. The handshake can communicate warmth, genuine concern for the other person, and strength. It can also communicate aloofness, indifference, and weakness. The message you send the other party via your handshake depends on a combination of the following factors.

1. *Degree of firmness.* Generally speaking, a firm handshake communicates a caring attitude, whereas a weak grip communicates indifference.
2. *Degree of dryness of hands.* A moist palm is unpleasant to feel and can communicate the impression that you are nervous. A clammy hand is likely to repel most people.
3. *Duration of grip.* There are no specific guidelines for the ideal duration of a grip. Nevertheless, by extending the handshake, you can often communicate a greater degree of interest in and concern for the other person.
4. *Depth of interlock.* A full, deep grip is more apt to convey friendship and strength to the other person.
5. *Eye contact during handshake.* Visual communication can increase the positive impact of your handshake. Maintaining eye contact throughout the handshaking process is important when two people greet each other.[27]

Most individuals have shaken hands with hundreds of people but have little idea whether they are creating positive or negative impressions. It is a good idea to obtain this information from those coworkers or friends who are willing to provide you with candid feedback. Like all other human relations skills, the handshake can be improved with practice.

Your Manners

The study of manners (sometimes called etiquette) reveals a number of ways to enhance our professional presence. A knowledge of good manners permits us to perform our daily work with poise and confidence. Letitia Baldrige, author of *Letitia Baldrige's New Complete Guide to Executive Manners,* provides us with a basic definition of good *manners:* "It's consideration and kindness and thinking about somebody other than oneself."[28] Another writer says, "Manners are the grace woven into the knotty fabric of our lives. Without them, it's all knots and thorns."[29] Good manners represent an important key to improved interpersonal relations.

Good manners are a universal passport to positive relationships and respect. One of the best ways to develop rapport with another person is to avoid behavior that might be offensive to that individual. Although it is not possible to do a complete review of this topic, some of the rules of etiquette that are particularly important in an organizational setting are covered here.

1. *When you establish new relationships, avoid calling people by their first names too soon.* Jacqueline Thompson, author of *Image Impact,* says assuming that all work-related associates prefer to be addressed informally by their first names is a serious breach of etiquette.[30] Use titles of respect—Ms., Miss, Mrs., Mr., or Dr.—until the relationship is well established. Too much familiarity can breed irritation. When the other party says, "Call me Susan," or "Call me Roy," it is all right to begin using the person's first name. Informality should develop by invitation, not by presumption.

2. *Avoid obscenities and offensive comments or stories.* In recent years, standards for acceptable and unacceptable language have changed considerably. Obscenity is more permissible in everyday conversation than it was in the past. But it is still considered inappropriate to use foul language in front of a customer, a

---

Total Person Insight

"In a society as ridden as ours with expensive status symbols, where every purchase is considered a social statement, there is no easier or cheaper way to distinguish oneself than by the practice of gentle manners."

JUDITH MARTIN

Author, *Miss Manners' Guide for the Turn-of-the-Millennium,* writing in "Low Income Is Not Low-Class"

client, or, in many cases, a coworker. According to Bob Greene, syndicated columnist, an obscenity communicates a negative message to most people.

> What it probably all comes down to is an implied lack of respect for the people who hear you talk. If you use profanity among friends, that is a choice you make. But if you broadcast it to people in general, you're telling them that you don't care what their feelings might be.[31]

Never assume that another person's value system is the same as your own. Foul language and off-color stories can do irreparable damage to interpersonal relations.

3. *Watch your table manners.* Business is frequently conducted at breakfast, lunch, or dinner these days, so be aware of your table manners. When you invite a customer to lunch, do not discuss business before the meal is ordered unless the client initiates the subject. Begin eating only when most of the people around you have their plates. If you have not been served, however, encourage others to go ahead. Assume responsibility for making sure the conversation moves from topic to topic and person to person. No one likes to be left out. Ann Humphries, president of Eticon, Etiquette Consultants for Business, says that knowledge of table manners gives employees the confidence they need to do their jobs well.[32]

4. *Express appreciation at appropriate times.* A simple thank-you can mean a lot. Failure to express appreciation can be a serious human relations blunder. The office worker who works hard to complete a rush job for the boss is likely to feel frustrated and angry if this extra effort is ignored. The customer who makes a purchase deserves a sincere thank-you. You want your customers to know that their business is appreciated.

5. *Be familiar with meeting etiquette.* Business meetings should start and end on time. When you attend a meeting, arrive on time and don't feel obligated to comment on each item on the agenda. Yes, sometimes silence is golden. In most cases, you should not bring up a topic unless it is related to an agenda item. If you are in charge of the meeting, end it by summarizing key points, reviewing the decisions made, and recapping the responsibilities assigned to individuals during the meeting. Always start and end the meeting on a positive note.[33]

6. *Be aware of personal habits that may offend others.* Sometimes an annoying habit can be a barrier to establishing a positive relationship with someone else. Chewing gum is a habit that bothers many people, particularly if you chew gum vigorously or "crack" it. Biting fingernails, cracking knuckles, scratching your head, and combing your hair in public are additional habits to be avoided. If you wear a fragrance (cologne or after-shave lotion), apply it in moderation when going to work. Do not risk causing a client or coworker discomfort with your fragrance.[34]

Letitia Baldrige says that in the field of manners, "Rules are based on kindness and efficiency." She also believes that good manners are those personal qualities that make life at work more livable.[35] In a civilized community, there have to be some restraints.

Assessing Your Professional Presence

To assess your professional presence and determine if small changes are needed, plan to spend ten to fifteen minutes making an informal presentation to someone in front of a video camera. The video footage will let you see what you really look like and how you sound to others. Play the tape several times and pay special attention to your posture, gestures, eye movement, tone of voice, and body movement. After you determine how you come across to others, plan to change the things you don't like. For example, if you notice that you frequently speak in a monotone, make a mental note to work on this problem.[36] Once you complete an assessment of your professional presence and change the things you don't like, you will achieve a new level of confidence in yourself. Increased self-confidence will enhance your self-esteem.

Summary

Professional presence permits us to be perceived as self-assured and competent. These qualities are quickly perceived the first time someone meets us. People tend to form impressions of others quickly at the time they first meet them, and these first impressions tend to be preserved. The four-minute barrier is a term used to describe the average time people spend together before a relationship is either established or denied. In an organizational setting, the time interval is often reduced to seconds. Positive impressions are important because they contribute to repeat business and customer referrals.

The impression you form of another person during the initial contact is made up of assumptions and facts. When meeting someone for the first time, people tend to rely heavily on assumptions. Many of your assumptions can be traced to early cultural influences. Assumptions are also based on perceptions of surface language. Surface language is a pattern of immediate impressions conveyed by appearance. The clothing and jewelry you wear, your hairstyle, and the fragrances you use all combine to make a statement about yourself to others.

Image consultants contend that discrimination on the basis of appearance is still a fact of life. Clothing is an important part of the image you communicate to others. Four factors tend to influence your choice of clothing for work: (1) the products or services offered by the organization, (2) the type of person served, (3) the desired image projected by the organization, and (4) the region where you work.

In addition to clothing, research indicates that facial expressions strongly influence people's reactions to each other. The expression on your face can quickly trigger a positive or negative reaction. Similarly, your entrance and carriage, voice, handshake, and manners also contribute to the image you project when meeting others.

Career Corner

Q. In the near future I will begin my job search, and I want to work for a company that will respect my individuality. Some companies are enforcing strict dress codes and other policies that, in my opinion, infringe on the rights of their employees. How far can an employer go in dictating my lifestyle?

A. This is a good question, but one for which there is no easy answer. For example, most people feel they have a right to wear the fragrance of their choice, but many fragrances contain allergy-producing ingredients. In some parts of California, you will find "non-fragrance" zones. Second-hand smoke is another major issue in the workplace because some research indicates that it can be harmful to the health of workers. Rules regarding weight, hair length, and the type of clothing and jewelry that can be worn to work have also caused controversy. There is no doubt that many companies are trying to find a balance between their interests and the rights of workers. Blockbuster Entertainment Corporation has placed restrictions on the length of an employee's hair and the amount of jewelry that can be worn during work hours. The company believes employee appearance is crucial to the success of the company. The best advice I can give you is to become familiar with the employer's expectations before you accept a job. The company has a responsibility to explain its personnel policies to prospective employees, but sometimes this information is not covered until after a person is hired.

Key Terms

professional presence
primacy effect
four-minute barrier
assumptions
cultural influences

image
surface language
career apparel
wardrobe engineering
business casual

Review Questions

1. Image has been described as "more than exterior qualities such as dress and grooming." What other factors shape the image we project?
2. Define the term *primacy effect*. How would knowledge of the primacy effect help someone who works in patient care or customer service?

3. Why do people tend to rely more heavily on assumptions than on facts during the initial meeting?
4. Why should career-minded people be concerned about the image they project? What factors contribute to the formation of a person's image?
5. What are some of the major decisions people make about others based on career apparel?
6. Susan Bixler suggests that when making wardrobe decisions, you should keep in mind that three things have not changed. List and discuss these three factors.
7. What is meant by the term *unconscious expectations?*
8. Describe the type of speaking voice that increases a person's effectiveness in dealing with others.
9. Provide a basic definition of good manners. Why is the study of manners important?
10. Stephen Covey says that changing outward attitudes and behaviors does very little good in the long run unless we base such changes on solid principles that govern human effectiveness. Do you agree or disagree with his views? Explain your answer.

Application Exercises

1. Harvey Mackay, president of Mackay Envelope Corporation, has designed a 66-question customer profile for his sales staff. Salespeople are encouraged to complete the form for each customer they call on. The profile includes such information as birth date, current position, marital status, professional memberships, and special interests. Mackay takes the position that a salesperson cannot build long-term relationships with customers unless she or he takes a personal interest in them.
   a. Do you support the use of a customer profile to build relationships with customers or clients? Explain.
   b. What type of organization would benefit most from use of a detailed customer profile similar to the one used at Mackay Envelope Corporation?
2. The first step toward improving your voice is to hear yourself as others do. Listen to several recordings of your voice on a dictation machine, tape recorder, or VCR, and then complete the following rating form. Place a checkmark in the appropriate space for each quality.

Quality	Major Strength	Strength	Weakness	Major Weakness
Projects confidence	_____	_____	_____	_____
Projects enthusiasm	_____	_____	_____	_____
Speaking rate is not too fast or too slow	_____	_____	_____	_____
Projects optimism	_____	_____	_____	_____

Voice is not too loud   _____   _____   _____   _____
   or too soft
Projects sincerity   _____   _____   _____   _____

**Self-Assessment
Exercise**

1. For each of the following statements, circle the number from 1 to 5 that
best represents your response: (1) strongly disagree (never do this); (2) disagree (rarely do this); (3) moderately agree (sometimes do this); (4) agree
(frequently do this); (5) strongly agree (always do this).

a. I project to others an image   1   2   3   4   5
   that matches my talents and
   aspirations.
b. The clothes I wear to work and   1   2   3   4   5
   school are appropriate and project
   the image I want to exhibit to
   others.
c. My entrance and carriage project   1   2   3   4   5
   total confidence.
d. When I meet an acquaintance or   1   2   3   4   5
   someone new, I make eye contact
   and shake hands with a firm grip.
e. I believe that good manners is an   1   2   3   4   5
   important key to improved human
   relations.

Select an appropriate attitude or skill you would like to improve. Write
your goal in the space provided.

GOAL: _____

_____

_____

Case Problem   ## What You See Is Not Necessarily What You Get

The clothing we wear at work shapes other people's expectations of us.
Feelings about people's competence, intelligence, attitudes, trustworthiness, and many other aspects of their personalities are conveyed by the colors,
styles, and fit of their attire. Although some organizations such as Levi Strauss
& Co. have adopted business casual dress codes, others encourage more conservative dress. Susan Bixler, well-known image consultant, says traditional

business dress is generally classic and conservative and changes little from year to year. In a conservative business setting, men and women should avoid clothing that is more appropriate for leisure activities.

Some companies, such as the National Car Rental Company and the Century 21 Real Estate Corporation chain, encourage their employees to wear specially designed uniforms, called "career wear," to ensure that the employees will convey the "right" message and instill confidence in their customers.

Just how important is the "right look," and how does what people wear influence our expectations of them? Imagine that you have just checked into a hospital to be operated on the next day. When you get to your room, you are told that the following people will be coming to speak with you within the next several hours:

1. The surgeon who will do the operation
2. A nurse
3. The secretary for the department of surgery
4. A representative of the company that supplies televisions to the hospital rooms
5. A technician who does laboratory tests
6. A hospital business manager
7. The dietitian

You have never met any of these people before and do not know what to expect. The only thing you do know is that they are all women.

About half an hour after your arrival, a woman appears at your door dressed in a straight, red wool skirt, a pink-and-white striped polyester blouse with a bow at the neck, and red medium-high-heel shoes that match the skirt. She is wearing round gold earrings, a gold chain necklace, a gold wedding band, and a white hospital laboratory coat. She is carrying a clipboard.

Questions

1. Of the seven people listed, which of them do you think is standing at your door? Why?
2. If the woman had not been wearing a white hospital laboratory coat, how might your perceptions of her differ? Why?
3. Assume you find out that she is the surgeon who will be operating on you in the morning, and that you had thought she was someone different initially. How confident would you feel in her ability as a surgeon? Why?

Chapter 6

Personal Values Influence Ethical Choices

Chapter Preview

After studying this chapter, you will be able to

1. Explain the advantage of developing a strong sense of character.

2. Understand how personal values are formed and how they influence ethical choices.

3. Understand value conflicts and how these conflicts influence ethical choices.

4. Identify ways to resolve value conflicts.

5. Learn how to make the right ethical decisions based on your personal value system.

6. Understand the danger of corporate crime and the steps being taken to eliminate it.

WHEN DENNIS LEVINE meets with students at New York University, Columbia University, and elsewhere to talk about ethical issues, they pay attention. The students know that Levine was faced with some important ethical decisions on Wall Street and made the wrong choices. At age thirty-three, he was a leading merger specialist and partner at Drexel Burnham Lambert, one of the most powerful investment banks on Wall Street. Several years before achieving this prestigious position, he had started trading on nonpublic information to make some fast money. Eventually he became addicted to the illegal practice of insider trading. After years of breaking the law, he was finally arrested, convicted, and sent to prison. Reflecting on those fast-paced years at Drexel Burnham Lambert, Levine says, "The numbing effect of 60- to 100-hour work weeks helped erode my values and distort my judgment." He admits his ambition was so strong that it went beyond rationality and says, "I gradually lost sight of what constitutes ethical behavior."[1] In his book, *Inside Out,* we learn about the period of "easy morality" that existed on Wall Street. The results of such corruption can be devastating. While Levine and his junk-bond-dealer colleague Michael Milken went to jail, their company, Drexel Burnham Lambert, was forced into bankruptcy. ∎

Why did well-educated, professional people make such poor ethical choices? This is one of the questions we attempt to answer in this chapter.

CHARACTER AND INTEGRITY

"The candidate has the kind of work experience we are looking for, but can he pass the 'character' test?" "I always know exactly where she stands . . . she has character." "When I'm in a conflict with someone, I know I can defeat them if they lack character. If they don't stand for something, they'll fall for anything." Statements like these sprinkle daily conversations in every organization because character is such an important element of effective interpersonal relations. **Character** is composed of your personal standards of behavior, including your honesty, integrity, and moral fiber.[2] Your character is based on your internal values and the resulting judgments you make about what is right and what is wrong.

One dimension of character that is getting a great deal of attention today is integrity. Integrity is a basic ingredient of career success. Robert Ringer, author of *Million Dollar Habits,* defined **integrity** as adherence to your moral values, or practicing what you claim to believe in.[3] When your behavior is in tune with your professed standards and values — when you practice what you believe in — you have integrity.

In a world of uncertainty and rapid change, integrity has become a valuable character trait. People with integrity can be trusted to do what they say they will do. We know what they stand for and what they will fight for. On the other hand, it is difficult to trust people whose behavior contradicts their words.

How can we achieve integrity? One approach, recommended by author Stephen Covey, is to keep your commitments. "As we make and keep commitments, even small commitments, we begin to establish an inner integrity that gives us the awareness of self-control and courage and strength to accept more of the responsibility for our own lives."[4] Covey says that when we make and keep promises to ourselves and others, we are developing an important habit. We cannot expect to maintain our integrity if we consistently fail to keep our commitments.

Your character and integrity strongly influence your relationships with others. But where can you learn these qualities? College catalogs rarely list a course like "Character Building 101." The Josephson Institute of Ethics acknowledged this lack of character training by forming the Character Counts Coalition. The coalition is an alliance of such organizations as the American Federation of Teachers, the American Association of State Boards of Education, and the American Association of Community Colleges. Their mission is to address the issue of character development through educational institutions and organizations throughout the country. Their efforts focus on a variety of grassroots training activities that encourage the development of the following six "pillars of character":

- **Trustworthiness** Be honest and sincere. Don't deceive or mislead, and never betray a trust. Demonstrate your integrity by standing up for your beliefs. Never ask a friend or colleague to do something that is wrong.
- **Respect** Be courteous and polite by being appreciative and accepting of differences. Respect others' rights to make decisions about their own lives. Don't abuse, demean, mistreat, manipulate, exploit, or take advantage of others.

- **Responsibility**   Be accountable for your actions. Think about the consequences of your behavior before you act. Don't make excuses or take credit for others' work.
- **Fairness**   Treat all people fairly, be open-minded, and listen to opposing points of view. Don't take unfair advantage of others' mistakes.
- **Caring**   Show you care about others through kindness, caring, sharing, compassion, and empathy. Be considerate and sensitive to others' feelings.
- **Citizenship**   Play by the rules and obey the laws. Respect authority. Stay informed and vote.[5]

If you want to enhance your character, consider building these "pillars" into your lifestyle.

HOW PERSONAL VALUES ARE FORMED

Throughout life you learn a set of values that determine the nature and strength of your character. This set of values forms your **value system.** You are

Our values can be shaped by religious experiences. This young boy is participating in a ceremony held at an Ethiopian Orthodox church. (Chester Higgins)

not born with the six pillars of character or any other internal set of values. You learn such traits by observing the behaviors of others and watching their results. But psychologists agree that individuals' values are formed early in life.

Values are so deep-seated in our personalities that they are never actually "seen." What we "see" are the ways values manifest themselves through our behaviors and attitudes.[6] For example, an individual may stay overtime to help trace a customer's lost order. We can see this behavior. The attitude displayed is a willingness to help a customer solve a problem. The value, which serves as the foundation for this attitude, may be that of service to others.

Your values are more enduring than your attitudes. Although your attitudes toward various situations or people may change, **values** represent the enduring beliefs and deep preferences that motivate you. What really motivates you can be discovered only through careful examination and clarification of your values. (Use the process described in Table 6.1 to help determine whether or not you truly value something.) Values exist at different levels of awareness, so it is important that you spend the time necessary to truly clarify the values that determine the decisions you make every day.[7]

An understanding of values is important in studying human relations because values strongly influence people's actions. If people of different races, ethnic groups, religions, and backgrounds understand one another's value systems, they may be more appreciative and tolerant of behaviors that differ from their own. Let us look at some of the important factors that shape our values.

Environmental Influences

Aristotle said "If you would understand virtue, observe the conduct of virtuous men." But where are these "virtuous men," the role models we should observe? As a nation, we have witnessed many examples of shabby values. When you look to Wall Street you learn about the transgressions of Dennis Levine and Michael Milken. Turn to religion and you learn about the moral failures and financial excesses of leaders such as Jim Bakker and Jimmy Swaggart. Look at sports and you discover that some of our heroes are motivated by greed and lust. And our political leaders often seem to lack the moral courage to do the right thing.

Many events and individuals have influenced the formation of values in the United States in this century. Some of them are shown in Figure 6.1. In general, the major environmental influences that shape our values are the family, religious groups, schools, the media, and those we admire.

Influence of the Family   Parents influence the values of their children by what they say and do. In many families in contemporary society, one parent must assume full responsibility for shaping children's values. Some single parents — those overwhelmed with responsibility for career, family, and rebuilding their own personal lives — may lack the stability necessary for the

TABLE 6.1

By learning this five-part valuing process, we can clarify and develop our values.

Thinking

We live in a confusing world where making choices about how to live our lives can be difficult. Of major importance is developing critical thinking skills that help distinguish fact from opinion and supported from unsupported arguments. Learn to think for yourself. Question what you are told. Engage in higher-level thinking that involves analysis, synthesis, and evaluation.

Feeling

This dimension of the valuing process involves being open to your "gut-level" feelings. If it doesn't "feel right," it probably isn't. Examine your distressful feelings such as anger, fear, or emotional hurt. Discover what you prize and cherish in life.

Communicating

Values develop not in a vacuum but in an ongoing process of interaction with others. Learn to send clear messages. Be an active listener and hear what others are really saying. Be constantly alert to communication filters such as emotions, body language, and positive and negative attitudes.

Choosing

Your values must be freely selected with no outside pressure. In some situations, telling right from wrong is difficult. Therefore, you need to be well informed about alternatives and the consequences of various courses of action. Each choice you make reflects some aspect of your value system.

Acting

Act repeatedly and consistently on your beliefs. One way to test whether or not something is of value to you is to ask yourself "Do I find that this value is persistent throughout all aspects of my life?"

Source: Sidney B. Simon, Leland W. Howe, and Howard Kirschenbaum, *Values Clarification* (New York: Hart Publishing, 1972).

transmission of traditional values. And in two-parent families, both parents may work outside the home and at the end of the day may lack the time or energy to intentionally direct the development of their children's values. The same may be true for families experiencing financial pressures or the strains associated with caring for elderly parents. Author James Michener, who was an orphan and had no family, offers another perspective: "It is thoughtless

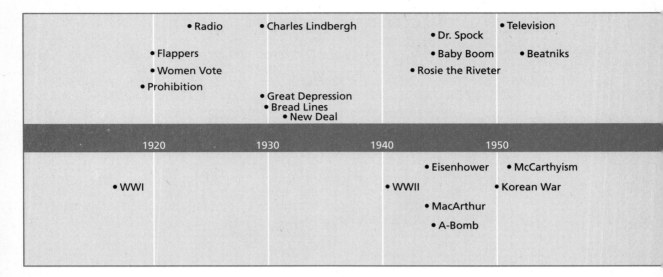

FIGURE 6.1

People and Events That Have Influenced the Formation of Values
in the United States

Source: Reprinted, by permission of publisher, from *AMA Survey Report*, 1982, © 1982
American Management Association, New York. All Rights Reserved. Updated each year
between 1982 and 1996.

beyond imagination for older people to say rigidly, 'The child must learn his or her values at home' when there is no home. Some substitution must be found."[8]

Influence of Religious Groups Many people learn their value priorities through religious training. This may be achieved through the accepted teachings of the church, through religious literature such as the Koran and the Bible, or through individuals in the churches or synagogues who are positive role models. William Wilson, founder of Pioneer/Eclipse Corporation of Sparta, North Carolina, when asked to comment on the impact of religious beliefs on his success, responded:

> I guess my religious beliefs did have one important impact on my approach to business—in terms of the ethics and principles I live by. I've always had the attitude that profits don't come first. They can never come first. People have to come first—customers and employees. The funny thing is, if you treat people right, the profits always follow.[9]

Religious groups that want to define, instill, and perpetuate values may find an eager audience. Stephen Covey and other social observers say that many peo-

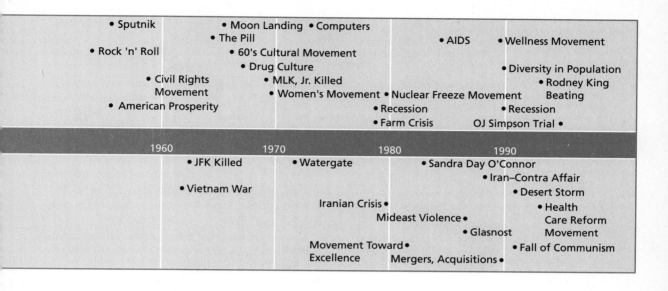

ple are determinedly seeking spiritual and moral anchors in their lives and in their work. People who live in uncertain times seem to attach more importance to spirituality.[10] Healthy spirituality will be discussed in Chapter 9.

Influence of the Schools   Many parents, concerned that their children are not learning enough about moral values and ethical behavior, want character education added to the curriculum.[11] Some have been influenced by William J. Bennett's *The Book of Virtues*. He sees moral education as a fundamental purpose of education. In support of this practice, Thomas Lickona, professor of education at the State University of New York, says children have very little sense of right and wrong, so schools must help out.[12]

In the 1970s, many schools included values clarification in their curriculum. As various factions of society objected, fearing that values would be "imposed" on children, schools eliminated these classes, and teachers learned to be "value neutral." Today, however, there is a nationwide resurgence of the movement to teach moral values and ethics in the classrooms. In Dayton, Ohio, all forty-seven public schools are teaching values education after a dramatic success was achieved in a pilot program at Allen Traditional Academy Elementary School. In Irving, Texas, the school board passed "A Resolution Authorizing the Teaching of Traditional Moral Values" throughout the district's twenty-seven schools. In Maryland, state law requires teachers to promote values found in the Declaration of Independence, the Constitution, and the Bill of Rights — values such as respect, tolerance, protection of others' rights, courage, humility, honesty, and trust. In higher education, we are now seeing the addition of more courses on values and ethics. Over 500 business-ethics courses are currently taught on American campuses.[13] In some cases, entire departments or centers are devoted to this type of education.

Influence of the Media   Some social critics say that if you are searching for signs of civilization gone rotten, you can simply tune into the loud and often amoral voices of mass entertainment on television and radio. Of course, some parts of the media also exert a positive influence. "Mr. Roger's Neighborhood" and "Sesame Street" have a positive influence on children's understanding of right and wrong behaviors. "The Cosby Show" was recognized for its straightforward communication of strong moral values. But gone are the days of Opie and Andy Taylor, John Boy and the Waltons. During that time, viewers were surrounded with moral lessons on a daily basis. Today's Ninja Turtles and Power Rangers solve their problems in distinctly different ways. Bart Simpson's unique family relationships teach children, and adults, a new way of interacting with authority figures. Most mainstream television includes situational comedies, cartoons, soap operas, and dramas that feature a great deal of violence and antisocial behavior. It is estimated that the average preschool child watches more than twenty-seven hours of television per week and that the average teenager spends twenty-one hours watching TV.[14] Is it any wonder that, with this constant bombardment, our children have difficulty determining right from wrong?

Influence of Those We Admire   In addition to being influenced by the media, your values are likely to be influenced by **modeling** — shaping your behavior to resemble that of people you admire and embracing the qualities those people demonstrate. The heroes and heroines you discover in childhood and adolescence help you form a "dominant value direction."[15] But as we grow older, these role models sometimes fall from grace, and we begin to question the values they instilled in us. Pete Rose and O. J. Simpson influenced the values of many young sports enthusiasts until they met major legal problems. Michael Jackson, an outstanding musician and entertainer, struggled with negative publicity that damaged his reputation and strongly affected his fans' opinions and behaviors. Madonna proved to be a strong performer and businesswoman, but some of her extreme public displays turned off a lot of her former admirers. We would all be wise to focus on and emulate the positive qualities of those we admire, but to examine their values and behaviors carefully before accepting them as our own.

Thinking / Learning Starters

1. Identify the events and individuals that have been influential in forming your value system. Are those of your childhood and adolescence still important to you?

2. Based on the media's influence and the concept of modeling, what do you predict the next generation's values will be? The children of today will be your coworkers in the future. Will their attitudes and values be a potential problem for you?

VALUE CONFLICTS

One of the major causes of conflict in organizations is a clash in individuals' values. Don Beck, a leading proponent of value system analysis, points out that when it comes to values, people are different: "These differences pop out in offices, factories . . . anywhere and anytime people get together. . . . They prefer different jobs, work environments, learning systems, social relationships, and other expressions of their uniqueness."[16]

In fact, many observers suggest that organizations look for **value conflicts** when addressing such problems as declining quality, absenteeism, and poor customer service. The trouble may lie not so much in work schedules or production routines as in the mutual distrust and misunderstanding brought about by clashes in workers' and managers' value systems. Here are some examples of value conflicts:

Item: Manny Garcia, a very successful Burger King franchise owner, was upset when the company launched an advertising campaign that included the slogan "Sometimes you gotta break the rules." He felt the slogan sent the wrong message to his teenage customers. To protest the ad campaign, he flipped his Burger King signs upside down.[17]

Item: Daryl Castleberry decided to leave the mortgage banking field to work on an MBA degree at the University of Denver because he was troubled by some of his colleagues' ethical lapses. Castleberry is now studying ethics and social responsibility in many of his classes.[18]

Item: Workers struck the General Motors plant at Flint, Michigan, to protest excessive required overtime. They complained that workweeks that sometimes stretched to sixty-six hours disrupted their personal lives. Management said the overtime was necessary because the cost of health insurance and other benefits for new workers was so high the company couldn't afford to hire more workers.[19]

Internal Value Conflicts

Value conflicts within an individual usually force the person to choose between strongly held values. A common **internal value conflict** surfaces when people cannot find enough time for work and for personal life. The Hilton National survey of time and time values produced some surprising findings regarding the attitudes of Americans toward time spent at work. Nearly two-thirds (65 percent) said they would be willing to take less pay to get more time off.[20] Of course, less work usually means less pay, so for some people the time-off-versus-money dilemma is not easily resolved. This issue will be discussed in more detail in Chapter 9.

You may experience many kinds of internal value conflicts on the job. As a manager, you may be torn between loyalty to workers and loyalty to upper management. As an employee, you may find yourself in conflict between fulfilling family obligations and devoting the time and energy required to succeed at work. Whichever value proves to be the stronger over time is the one that will determine which choice you make. How you resolve these internal value conflicts will greatly affect your attitude toward yourself, your career, and the people close to you.

The purpose of this neighborhood meeting with police is to discuss crime and drug activity in northeast Austin, Texas. Conflicting values can divide people who live in the same community. (Bob Daemmrich/Stock, Boston, Inc.)

Value Conflicts with Others

Some of the most common interpersonal value conflicts arise between workers of different generations, races, cultures, ethnic backgrounds, or religions; between men and women; and between supervisors and workers. Older and younger employees may clash over different interpretations of the work ethic and the priorities of job and personal life.

Value conflicts based on age, race, ethnic background, gender, or religious differences often provoke deep emotional reactions among workers. Unless such conflicts are handled skillfully, confrontation can make the situation worse, not better. The Fiber Industries subsidiary of Hoechst/Celanese Corporation in Charlotte, North Carolina, developed a ten-session training program to teach employees how to deal with such value conflicts.[21] The final session outlined the issues to be resolved, which ranged from interracial distrust to on-the-job discrimination experienced by women. In bringing up concerns, workers were encouraged to talk about the kind of workplace they wanted. This strategy focused their attention on improving the quality of life for everyone, not just for one group. The remaining sessions helped employees discover the common ground they shared and provided methods for solving their differences.

At the end of the workshop, employees felt they had forged a set of values that reflected more clearly their own expectations and needs. For example, managers were surprised to learn how strongly workers valued knowing more about the "whys" of business. All levels of employees were impressed by the commonality of their work values and their standards for personal relationships.

PERSONAL VALUES AND ETHICAL CHOICES

Ethics, as distinguished from values, consists of the rules of conduct that reflect the character of the community. Kickbacks and payoffs may be acceptable practices in one part of the world yet may be viewed as unethical practices elsewhere. Ethics is the link between our values and our actions, helping us translate values into appropriate and effective behaviors in our day-to-day lives.[22]

Ethical and Moral Dilemmas

As competition in the marketplace increases, moral and ethical issues can become cloudy. Although most organizations have adopted the point of view that "good ethics is good business," exceptions do exist. Some organizations encourage, or at least condone, unethical behavior. Thus, you must develop your own personal code of ethics. Every job you hold will present you with new ethical and moral dilemmas. To illustrate, let's look at two different positions in the labor market.

Supervisor   Ethical dilemmas can surface almost daily for people who direct and supervise the work of others. It may be tempting to tell employees to "do whatever is necessary" to get a job done on time, or to look the other way when employees engage in unethical or illegal acts. Simply taking credit for the accomplishments of others or displaying favoritism when establishing the work schedule represents a lapse in ethical conduct. Each of these behaviors is unethical because it can cause some degree of psychological, financial, or even physical harm.[23]

Secretary   One of the major temptations facing a secretary is the misuse of company resources. Is it unethical to make copies of your family Christmas letter on the office photocopy machine? Is it unethical to use the office telephone to make a long-distance call to a friend or relative in another state? The answer to both questions, of course, is yes. Unfortunately, many otherwise law-abiding people steal from their employers. Employee theft of supplies, products, and money has increased sharply in recent years.

How to Make the Right Ethical Choices

In today's turbulent, fast-paced, highly competitive workplace, ethical dilemmas surface frequently, and telling right from wrong has never been more difficult. Here are a few guidelines to help you make the right ethical choices.

Learn to distinguish between right and wrong.   Although selecting the right path can be difficult, a great deal of help is available today. Many current books and articles offer good advice. The book *The Measure of Our Success* by Marian Wright Edelman presents a collection of "lessons for life" that can offer guidance in making ethical choices. A few examples follow:

- There is no free lunch. Don't feel entitled to anything you don't sweat and struggle for.
- Never work just for money or for power. They won't save your soul or build a decent family or help you sleep at night.
- Be honest. Struggle to live what you say and preach.
- Sell the shadow for the substance. Don't confuse style with substance; don't confuse political charm or rhetoric with decency or sound policy.[24]

Help in making the correct ethical choices may be as close as your employer's code of ethics, ethical guidelines published by your professional organization, or advice provided by an experienced and trusted colleague.

Total Person Insight

"Nothing is more powerful for employees than seeing their managers behave according to their expressed values and standards; nothing is more devastating to the development of an ethical environment than a manager who violates the organization's ethical standards."

DAN RICE AND CRAIG DREILINGER

Management Consultants; Authors, "Rights and Wrongs of Ethics Training"

Make certain your values are in harmony with those of your employer. You may find it easier to make the right ethical choices if your values are compatible with those of your employer. Many organizations have adopted a set of beliefs, customs, values, and practices that attract a certain type of employee (see Figure 6.2). Harmony between personal and organizational values usually leads to success for the individual as well as the organization. These **shared values** provide a strong bond among all members of the work force.

Item: The employees at more than 1,100 locations of The Body Shop, a cosmetic chain founded by Anita Roddick, do more than sell shampoo, body lotions, and other toiletries. They are also involved in helping save whales and in stopping the destruction of the Brazilian rain forests. Roddick does not see a fundamental conflict between business and environmental concerns. She sees nothing wrong with pushing a cause along with cosmetics. She encourages her employees to be proactive in the area of environmentalism and human rights.[25]

Item: In a recent Duke University survey of 650 MBA graduates of eleven top schools, 70 percent indicated that they would not work for certain industries because of ethical or political concerns. About 82 percent said they would shun tobacco companies, 36 percent would avoid firms with environmental problems, 26 percent would refuse to work for liquor marketers, and 20 percent would not get involved with defense contractors. Dan Nagy, who conducted the survey for Duke's Fuqua School of Business, says, "Today's students have strong values and limit the compromises they're willing to make for money."[26]

Item: Lotus Development Corp. was awarded the *Personnel Journal*'s coveted Optimas Award, Quality of Life Category, for its continual reevaluation of its values relative to its workers. One of Lotus's operating principles, treating people fairly and valuing diversity, led to the creation of an innovative benefits policy in 1991. Lotus was one of the first large companies to offer medical, dental, vision, and hearing insurance benefits to gay and lesbian partners of

FIGURE 6.2

Lotus Operating
Principles

OPERATING PRINCIPLES

*These Operating Principles are intended to
serve as guidelines for interaction between
all employees. Their purpose is to foster and
preserve the spirit of our enterprise and to
promote the well-being of all concerned.*

Commit to excellence

Insist on integrity

Treat people fairly; Value diversity

Communicate openly, honestly, and directly

Listen with an open mind; Learn from everything

Take responsibility; Lead by example

Respect, trust, and encourage others

Encourage risk-taking and innovation

Establish purpose before action

Work as a team

Have fun

Source: © Lotus Development Corporation. Used with permission.

employees. Russell Campanello, vice president of human resources for Lotus, stated this about the company's prior plan: "Our benefits program was out of synch with our stated values around not discriminating based on sexual orientation. It has to reflect the needs, interests and values [of the workers] because that's what makes [the relationship] mutual."[27]

Don't let your life be driven by the desire for immediate gratification. To many people in America, progress and prosperity have almost identical meanings. Large numbers of people equate progress with the acquisition of material things. Some observers link the deterioration of business ethics to the materialism of the 1980s. One explanation is that young business leaders entering the corporate world at that time were under a great deal of pressure to show the trappings of success. This is the view expressed by John Delaney, who is a professor at the University of Iowa and who has done extensive research on ethics. He says, "You're expected to have the requisite car and summer house to show you're a contributor to society, and many people do whatever it takes to get them."[28]

To achieve instant gratification often means taking shortcuts. It involves pushing hard, cutting corners, and emphasizing short-term gains over the achievement of long-term goals. M. Scott Peck, author of the best-selling book *The Road Less Traveled,* discusses the benefits of delaying gratification: "Delaying gratification is a process of scheduling the pain and pleasure of life in such a way as to enhance the pleasure by meeting and experiencing the pain first and getting it over with. It is the only decent way to live."[29]

If delaying gratification is "the only decent way to live," why do so many people seek immediate gratification? The answer to this question is somewhat complex. Some people feel pressure from friends and family members to climb the ladder of success as quickly as possible. Others are under pressure to display the trappings of success — a new car, a new boat, or some other indicator of prosperity. They fail to realize that the road to peace of mind and happiness is not paved with Rolex watches, Brooks Brothers suits, and a Lexus. In Chapter 9 we will describe a new definition of success and discuss the nonfinancial resources that make the biggest contribution to a happy and fulfilling life.

CORPORATE VALUES AND ETHICAL CHOICES

This chapter began with a look at the dark side of Wall Street. In the securities industry, as in other industries, it is easy to focus on the individuals and organizations that have been motivated by greed and have failed to establish strict standards of business conduct. Nevertheless, some of the most successful companies play by the rules. At Legg Mason, one of the nation's top ten securities and investment management companies, employees are guided by strict standards of business conduct. Chip Mason, chief executive officer at Legg Mason, has told employees that honesty is the *number one* business principle guiding the company. His leadership has been rewarded with steady revenue growth.[30] Similarly, Ben Edwards, chairman of A. G. Edwards and Sons, Inc., the seventh-largest securities firm in the nation, says that following the golden rule is still the best way to achieve success in business. This attitude has had a positive influence on the company's 7,400 employees. He encourages employees who are faced with an ethical conflict to ask the question "Is it right?"[31]

The Problem of Corporate Crime

James O'Toole, author of *Vanguard Management,* says, "No company has ever gotten into financial trouble because they adhered to ethical principles."[32] By the same token, however, many of America's largest corporations have gotten into serious trouble by ignoring ethical principles. In recent years, the media have carried headlines concerning organizations involved in corporate crime.

Item: Eight former Honda Motor Co. executives pleaded guilty to bribery-related charges. The executives admitted that they accepted bribes from dealers in exchange for generous supplies of fast-selling Honda cars.[33]

Item: John Hancock Mutual Life Insurance Co. was found guilty of routinely violating Massachusetts law by treating state lawmakers to sky-box sports tickets, golf at luxury courses, and lavish meals at tropical resorts. On more than 300 occasions, the company exceeded $50 limits on gifts to legislators.[34]

Item: Stew Leonard, founder of the well-known Stew Leonard's Dairy Store, pleaded guilty to conspiring to defraud the federal government of taxes. He installed a computer software program that reduced sales data on an item-by-item basis and skimmed $17 million in cash.[35]

These items represent only a small fraction of the corporate crime that goes on today. Many offenders are not caught or brought to trial. On the positive side, recent surveys indicate that a large majority of America's major corporations are actively trying to build ethics into their organizations. Many say they have difficulty determining the right course of action in difficult "gray-area" situations. And even when the right ethical course of action is clear, competitive pressures sometimes lead well-intentioned managers astray.[36] Tom Chappell, author of *The Soul of a Business* and founder of Tom's of Maine, explains why organizations often have difficulty doing what is morally right and socially responsible: "It's harder to manage for ethical pursuits than it is to simply manage for profits."[37]

Positive Steps Toward Preventing Corporate Crime

Develop Ethics Codes Mark Twain once wrote, "To be good is noble. To tell people how to be good is even nobler, and much less trouble." Many corporate leaders have decided that it is time to put their views on ethics in writing. More than 90 percent of the Fortune 1,000 companies have written codes of ethics.[38] A written code, highly publicized throughout the company and enforced without exception, can be a powerful force in preventing unethical behavior.

A strong statement on corporate values has guided Ukrop's Super Markets, Inc., since 1937. Despite competitive pressures, the company has attained market leadership in the Richmond, Virginia, area by combining traditional business values with innovative merchandising practices and outstanding customer service. At the same time, Ukrop's stores sell no beer or wine, are closed on Sundays, and stay open shorter hours than most competitors. Ukrop's mission preamble to corporate values reflects the company's commitment to the golden rule: "The mission of Ukrop's Super Markets, Inc. is to serve our customers and community more effectively than anyone else by treating our customers, associates, and suppliers as we personally would like to be treated."[39]

Robert D. Haas, chairman and CEO of Levi Strauss & Company, believes that the corporation should be an ethical creature capable of both making profits and making the world a better place to live. He has established high standards regarding work environment, ethics, and social responsibility. He is pictured here in front of Levi Strauss' contribution to the AIDS quilt, a memorial to victims of the disease. (Andy Freeberg)

Hire with Care   Thomas Melohn, president of North American Tool & Die Inc., located in San Leandro, California, says the key to operating a successful company is to first identify a guiding set of values and then "make sure you find people who have those values and can work together."[40] He says the hiring process should be given a very high priority. Melohn never hires any employee without checking references and conducting a lengthy job interview.

Jerry Pardue, vice president of loss and prevention for Super D Drugs, a southeastern drugstore chain, uses integrity tests (also called honesty tests) to screen out dishonest persons and drug users. He is one of a growing number of businesspeople who use some form of psychological testing. (Reid Psychological Systems developed the first honesty test more than forty years ago.) Company officials say that people who get involved in tangible theft (stealing cash or merchandise) are more likely to commit intangible thefts such as coming to work late or using the telephone for personal calls.[41]

As the popularity of integrity tests grows, so does the debate over their use. Many people are questioning the accuracy of the tests and the fairness of using them to hire or turn away applicants. Some states have made it illegal to deny someone a job on the basis of low test scores. Even the testing companies admit that the tests are not foolproof. But the American Psychological Association has studied the accuracy of integrity tests and has stated that some are in fact reliable.[42]

Provide Ethics Training   Many ethical issues are complex and cannot be considered in black-and-white moral terms. It is for this and other reasons that ethics training has become quite common in the business community. About half of the Fortune 1,000 companies report that they provide ethics training for employees.[43] In some cases, the training involves little more than a careful study of the company ethics code and its implications for day-to-day decision making. In other cases, employees participate in in-depth discussions of ethical decisions. At Martin Marietta Corp., ethics training includes the use of a game called Gray Matters, in which a game leader presents minicases to teams of players. Each team also receives a list of potential responses to an ethical dilemma presented in the minicase. After discussing the responses, each team selects what it thinks is the best answer. The team leader then discloses the point value of each answer. Learning takes place as team members debate the pros and cons of each possible response.[44]

Is it possible to instill ethical values in employees through the use of training programs? Some critics say ethics training programs prepare employees to make the right decision only when actions are covered by specific rules. They see more merit in providing guidelines and tools that employees can use to resolve many ethical issues. Almost everyone agrees that ethics education and training must start at the top of the organization. Business leaders must realize that unethical conduct is self-destructive and usually generates no more than short-term gains. The long-term consequences of ethical misconduct can be very costly.

VALUES AND ETHICS IN INTERNATIONAL BUSINESS

If the situation is complex on the domestic scene, values and ethical issues become even more complicated at the international level. The subject is too broad to treat in detail in this chapter, but we can provide an overview of some conflicts that exist in international business.

In some foreign countries, bribery, under-the-table payments, and kickbacks are part of everyday business. Many company managers in these foreign countries are underpaid and look to these additional "revenue" sources to supplement their incomes.

Here are some other examples of situations in which a lack of shared values can create difficult situations:

Item: In China, the highly regulated economy gives government officials many opportunities to seek payments for special favors. If you make the first payment, expect continued demands for money.[45]

Item: As more Americans complete business transactions with the Japanese, value differences become clearer. *Naniwabushi,* the Japanese expression for establishing close personal terms with someone so that she or he will owe you a favor, is a commonly accepted business practice. In this environment, potentially awkward obligations could arise for Americans if they accept gifts from Japanese business acquaintances.

Item: Value differences can also arise in business matters between French and American business representatives. The French tend to be prompt about considering a decision, but they like to examine all the details involved. This means that decisions can be slow in coming. Once made, however, they are expressed candidly — whether the decision is in your favor or not. The French management style tends to be impersonal and standardized, with rigid procedures and centralized hierarchies.

Now that trade relations have been resumed with countries like Vietnam, South Africa, and China, it is important for all parties to recognize value differences and to spend time and effort building mutual respect and understanding.

Summary

A strong sense of character grows out of your personal standards of behavior. When you consistently behave in accordance with your values, you maintain your integrity. Your values are the personal worth or importance you give to an object or idea. People's value systems serve as the foundation for their attitudes, preferences, opinions, and behaviors. Personal values are largely formed early in life and are influenced by family, religious upbringing, schools, the media, and role models.

Internal value conflicts arise when we must choose between strongly held personal values. Value conflicts with others, often based on age, racial, religious, gender, or ethnic differences, require skilled intervention before they can be resolved.

Once you have clarified your personal values, your ethical decisions will be easier. You must learn to distinguish right from wrong, choose an employer whose values you share, and avoid the pursuit of immediate gratification. Shared values unify employees in an organization by providing guidelines for behavior and decisions.

Corporate values and ethics on both the domestic and international levels are receiving increasing attention because of the devastating effect and expense of corporate crime. Many organizations are developing ethics codes to help guide employees' behaviors, hiring only those individuals who share their corporate values, and offering ethics training opportunities to all employees. As multinational organizations increase in number, the individuals involved will need to consciously examine their values and ethical standards to deal effectively with the differing value structures in each country.

Career Corner

Q. While commuting to work on the train, I picked up a newspaper left behind by another passenger. I was shocked to find folded into the paper an envelope that included facts and figures related to a competitive bid one of my competitors was offering on an upcoming construction project. The lowest bid will win the contract. I have already read the information. . . . Should I notify my competitor or keep my mouth shut and use the information to our advantage? My decision will directly affect my employees and stockholders.

A. Call and tell your competitor what happened. Do not change your own bid on the project, but be sure the contracting agency knows what you have done. If you lose the contract because of your ethical behavior, you may lose short-term income and contract-specific jobs. But you will gain the long-term benefits derived from establishing a solid reputation for honesty and integrity.

Key Terms

character
integrity
value system
values
modeling

value conflicts
internal value conflict
ethics
shared values

Review Questions

1. How do values differ from attitudes, opinions, or behavior?
2. How are our values formed? How have the sources of our value systems changed in recent years?
3. Differentiate between internal value conflicts and value conflicts with others.
4. Explain the five dimensions of Simon, Howe, and Kirschenbaum's valuing process.
5. Describe the advantages of employees sharing the same values as their organization.
6. Explain the negative effects of the pursuit of immediate gratification.
7. How do top management values affect the purpose and direction of an organization?
8. List some of the steps corporations are taking to eliminate crime in their organizations.
9. How might an ethics code help organizations be more productive?
10. How do seemingly accepted unethical business practices in foreign countries affect Americans' ability to compete for business contracts in those countries?

Application Exercises

1. Guilt and a loss of self-respect can result when we say or do things that conflict with what we believe. One way to feel better about yourself is to "clean up" your integrity. Make a list of what you are doing that you think is wrong. Once the list is complete, look it over and determine if you can stop these behaviors. Consider making amends for things you have done in the past that you feel guilty about.[46]
2. In groups of four, discuss how you would react if your manager asked you to participate in some sort of corporate crime. For example, the manager could ask you to help launder money from the company, give a customer misleading information, or cover up a budget inaccuracy and keep this information from reaching upper management. You might want to role-play the situation with your group. Follow up with class discussion.

Self-Assessment Exercise

1. For each of the following statements, circle the number from 1 to 5 that best represents your response: (1) strongly disagree (never do this); (2) disagree (rarely do this); (3) moderately agree (sometimes do this); (4) agree (frequently do this); (5) strongly agree (always do this).

   a. I base my personal and professional decisions on clearly defined personal values.

      1   2   3   4   5

   b. I accept the fact that others' values may differ from mine, and I respect their right to maintain a value system that differs from my own.

      1   2   3   4   5

c. I have a clear sense of what is right   1   2   3   4   5
and wrong, and my character reflects
the fundamental strengths of honesty,
fairness, service, humility, and modesty.

d. I maintain my integrity by practicing what   1   2   3   4   5
I believe in and keeping my commitments.

Select an appropriate attitude or skill you would like to improve. Write your
goal in the space provided.

GOAL: _____

        _____

        _____

Case Problem   Tom's of Maine

When Tom Chappell and his wife, Kate, founded Tom's of Maine in 1971, they had no idea that their earth-friendly detergents, toothpaste, and other cosmetics would meet with the success it has. Even though the company's products sell at a premium price, retailers and customers seem to appreciate the social responsibility that permeates the entire organization.

In 1986, Tom began to question his future and wonder what more he could do besides make money. He had gained tremendous financial success but he still felt empty. His next step was to enroll in the Harvard University Divinity School, where he earned a master's degree in theology. Rather than joining the ministry, however, he implemented his new insight in his own world of business and then wrote a book called *The Soul of a Business: Managing for Profit and the Common Good,* in which he outlined the relationship between solid values and business ethics.

Tom Chappell's message is simple: "Beliefs drive strategy. Your ethics can form the foundation of smart analysis and clear thinking." His strong spirituality has led him to select and cultivate employees who bring with them a strong respect for the beauty and goodness of nature and people. Ten percent of the company's pretax dollars goes to education, people in need, or efforts to save the environment. Employees are encouraged to spend 5 percent of their work time — two hours a week or one day a month — working for a cause of their choice. Employees report that they are proud to be a part of Tom's of Maine and are happier with their own lives after helping the less fortunate in their community.

This humanitarian philosophy affects every aspect of the organization, including its marketing plan. Katie Shisler, vice president of marketing, points out that the company's advertising never claims its products are better than those of its competitors. "We're not in the game of 'we're better.' We just recognize nature provides elegant solutions, and we share the same values you do." Tom's products' market share has grown tenfold, and its annual sales should soon top $20 million.

Questions

1. Identify the values that seem to be driving the management decisions at Tom's of Maine. Do you share any of these values?
2. What could other organizations learn from Tom Chappell's philosophy?

Chapter 7

Valuing Work Force Diversity

Chapter Preview

After studying this chapter, you will be able to

1. Define the primary and secondary dimensions of diversity.

2. Discuss how prejudiced attitudes are formed.

3. Develop an awareness of the various forms of discrimination in the workplace.

4. Understand why organizations are striving to develop organizational cultures that value diversity.

5. Discuss the role affirmative action plays in opening employment doors for individuals.

6. Identify ways individuals and organizations can enhance work force diversity.

WHEN FEDERAL AFFIRMATIVE ACTION GUIDELINES were mandated, Digital Equipment Corp. began complying with the regulations by focusing on the numbers of employees it would need to reach multiracial and male-female equity. Later, management decided to move beyond federal mandates to create an environment where every employee could realize his or her potential, where individual differences were not just tolerated but valued . . . even celebrated.

The resulting philosophy, called "valuing differences," has two components. First, the company helps people get in touch with the stereotypes and false assumptions they hold through voluntary groupings of eight to ten people called "core groups." Trained facilitators encourage discussion and self-development as participants struggle to understand their prejudices. Facilitators also run a voluntary two-day training program called "Understanding the Dynamics of Diversity," which has been completed by thousands of Digital employees.

Second, the company has named a number of senior managers to various in-house cultural boards of directors and valuing differences boards of directors. These boards promote openness to individual differences, encourage younger managers to actively value diversity, and sponsor frequent celebrations of racial, gender, and ethnic differences such as Hispanic Heritage Week and Black History Month. Management believes the valuing differences programs will give Digital the competitive advantage of having a more effective work force, higher morale, and the reputation of being a better place to work. As Al Zimmerle, head of the valuing differences program, puts it, "Digital wants to be the employer of choice. We want our pick of the talent that's out there."[1] ∎

A growing number of progressive organizations are realizing the impact a reputation for valuing diversity in the work force can have on a company's success . . . and they are doing something about it!

THE NATURE OF DIVERSITY

"E Pluribus Unum" — "Out of many, one." No other country on earth is as multiracial and multicultural as the United States of America. This **diversity** is a popular topic and common buzz word in newspaper and magazine articles focusing on the future of American organizations.

The strength of many other nations lies in their homogeneity. Japan is mostly made up of persons of Japanese descent, and their economy and business transactions reflect this heritage. The People's Republic of China is populated mostly with persons of Chinese ancestry, and their values and culture are a major part of their global economic strength. But America has always been "the melting pot" of all the world's cultures. This diversity now represents the country's biggest crisis as well as its greatest opportunity.

Total Person Insight

"Getting along with people from many backgrounds and interests is most important if you are going to be involved in society in any way. We are interdependent upon one another."

JACK PLUCKHAN

Vice president, Panasonic Corporation

In the 1980s alone, 8.7 million people immigrated to America. Their numbers match those of the great immigration decade from 1900 to 1910, when masses of Irish, German, French, and Italian immigrants were processed through Ellis Island. The 1990 Immigration Act, which took effect in 1992, allows a 40 percent boost over the previous decade's limits in the number of legal immigrants permitted into this country.[2] All of these people want and need jobs so that they can become happy, healthy, and productive U.S. citizens. How will this country handle this massive increase in population? How can American organizations benefit from these new workers and their diverse skills and talents? And how will we overcome language and cultural barriers?

PacifiCorp, a major utility company serving residents of Washington, is responding to a more diverse customer base. Here Ylia Casper, a Pacific Power employee, answers calls from Spanish-speaking customers as part of PacifiCorp's new "LaLinea" program. (C. Bruce Forster/ Courtesy of PacifiCorp)

In the past, U.S. organizations attempted to assimilate everyone into one "American" way of doing things. The trend now, however, is to identify, respect, and value the individual differences in this new, diverse work force and to encourage every worker to make his or her full contribution. Organizations that foster the full participation of all workers will enjoy the most powerful competitive edge available in our expanding global marketplace.

Dimensions of Diversity

There are primary and secondary dimensions of diversity; that is, characteristics that describe people. The **primary dimensions** are those core elements about each individual that cannot be changed: age, race, gender, physical and mental abilities, and sexual orientation (see Figure 7.1). Together they form an individual's self-image and the filters through which she or he views the rest of the world. These inborn elements are interdependent. In fact, no one dimension stands alone. Each exerts an important influence throughout life. Marilyn Loden and Judy Rosener describe individual primary dimensions in their book *Workforce America!* They say, "Like the interlocking segments of a sphere, they represent the core of our individual identities."[3]

The greater the number of primary differences between people, the more difficult it is to establish trust and mutual respect. Culture clash, the conflicts that occur between groups of people with different core identities, can have a devastating effect on human relations in an organization.[4] Few organizations are immune to the problems that result from the interaction between the genders and among the races and the generations. When we add the secondary dimensions of diversity to the mix, effective human relations becomes even more difficult.

The **secondary dimensions** of diversity are those elements that can be changed or at least modified. They include a person's health habits, religious beliefs, education and training, general appearance, relationship status, ethnic customs, communication style, and income (see Figure 7.1). These factors all add an additional layer of complexity to the way we see ourselves and others, and in some instances they can exert a powerful impact on our core identities. A single mother who loses her job may be severely affected by her loss of income, whereas a married woman with no children may not be as affected by a similar loss. A vocational-technical school graduate may have far different expectations from a four-year-college graduate. An accountant with ten years of work experience might adjust to a new position far differently than would an accountant with much less experience.

Even though situations like these intensify the impact of particular secondary dimensions, they do not diminish the primary impact of core dimensions. Instead, they add depth to the individual. This interaction between primary and secondary dimensions shapes a person's values, priorities, and perceptions throughout life.[5]

FIGURE 7.1

Primary and
Secondary Dimensions
of Diversity

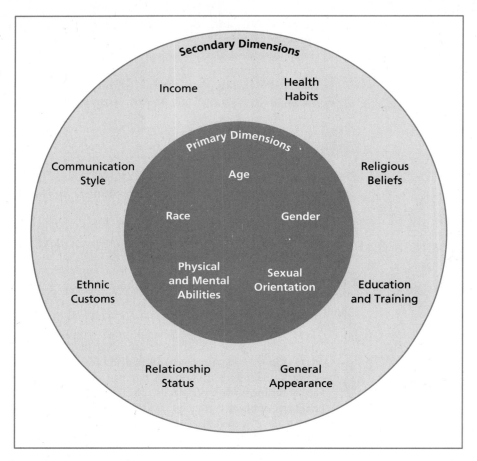

Each of us enters the work force with a unique perspective shaped by these dimensions and our own past experiences. Building effective human relationships is possible only when we learn to accept and value the differences in others. Without this acceptance, both the primary and secondary dimensions of diversity can serve as roadblocks to further cooperation and understanding.

PREJUDICED ATTITUDES

To be prejudiced means to prejudge. Throughout life we prejudge people in light of their primary and secondary dimensions. Attitudes in favor of or against people that are based solely on these traits are **prejudices**. Rather than treat others as unique individuals, prejudiced people tend to think in terms of stereotypes. **Stereotypes** are generalizations made about all members of a particular group. They are focused around widely held beliefs about what various racial groups, socioeconomic classes, men, women, people living in a particular geographic region, and so forth are "really like." When we bring stereotypes to the workplace, we are likely to misinterpret or devalue some primary and secondary differences even after we have been exposed to them.

People holding stereotypes can form prejudiced attitudes toward one group or another person, regardless of other elements that prove the stereotype invalid. For example, suppose two recent graduates of a highly respected building construction program at a local community college apply for one job opening with a building contractor. One applicant is white and has a mediocre grade point average (GPA); the other is African American and has a nearly perfect GPA. If the contractor has stereotyped attitudes in favor of white people, the other applicant may not get the job. The fact that the African American has better credentials may not outweigh the contractor's assumptions based on racial stereotypes.

This **cultural myopia**, the belief that a particular culture is appropriate in all situations, can undermine attempts to establish a cohesive, productive work force.[6] It is often accompanied by negative beliefs about others who do not belong to the preferred group. For example, Jewish women are sometimes stereotyped as materialistic, self-serving, and manipulative, according to Susan Weidman Schneider, editor-in-chief of *Lilith,* a magazine for Jewish women with a feminist orientation.[7] And people without a tendency to gain weight sometimes view an overweight person as someone who lacks the self-discipline and motivation to lose weight. They fail to consider how difficult it is for most overweight people to shed extra pounds. These are negative stereotypes, and they can cause those who are stigmatized to be less productive in their chosen line of work.

If stereotypes can be so harmful, why is it so difficult to rid ourselves of them? The answer is complicated. Stereotypes provide some predictability in our lives, reduce the uncertainty of dealing with other people, and shield us from shock because we see others acting as we expect them to.[8] Stereotypes are often based on one or several real experiences a person has had in dealing with others; yet they are resistant to change because people more readily believe information that confirms their stereotypes than evidence that challenges them.

Most of us object to being stereotyped, yet we forget how often we stereotype others. For instance, you may have learned as a child that certain groups of workers are lazy, not serious about a career, or unable to handle complex decisions. Your experience with one such worker may reinforce your stereotype, and you may discount or not remember many other experiences that prove the stereotype invalid. Perhaps in your organization women are considered too emotional, unable to do quantitative analysis, or less committed to careers than men are. Do you accept this stereotype, or do you examine your own experience to determine whether the stereotype actually conforms to reality? Unchallenged stereotypes can hinder employees' ability to collaborate effectively and to get a job done. Healthy and productive organizations are possible only when human relationships are free from confining stereotypes.

How Prejudicial Attitudes Are Formed

Three major factors contribute to the development of prejudice: childhood experiences, ethnocentrism, and economic conditions.

Childhood Experiences   Today's experiences are filtered through the events and feelings of childhood. Children learn attitudes and beliefs from family, friends, and other authority figures, and they learn how to view and treat different racial, ethnic, religious, and other groups. When the children become adults, they continue to accept these attitudes and beliefs, without testing their validity against their own adult experiences. The result is tension between groups. Hoechst/Celanese Corporation, as noted in the previous chapter, held workshops to help ease racial tensions in the company. Both blacks and whites in the workshops were surprised at the similarity of the messages their parents had given them as children: Each group had taught its children not to trust members of the other race.[9]

Ethnocentrism   The tendency to regard our own culture or nation as better or more "correct" than others is called **ethnocentrism**. The word is derived from *ethnic,* meaning a group united by similar customs, characteristics, race, or other common factors, and *center*. When ethnocentrism is present, the standards and values of our own culture are used as a yardstick to measure the worth of other cultures.

Ethnocentrism is often perpetuated by cultural conditioning. As children, we are conditioned to respond to various situations as we see others in our culture respond to them. Some cultures value emotional control and avoid open conflicts and discussions of such personal topics as money or values. Other cultures encourage a bolder, more open expression of feelings and values and accept greater levels of verbal confrontation. Tension can result when people's cultural expectations clash in the workplace.

In their book *Valuing Diversity,* Lewis Brown Griggs and Lente-Louise Louw compare ethnocentrism in an organization to icebergs floating in an ocean. We can see the tips of icebergs above the water level, just as we can see our diverse coworkers' skin color, gender, mannerisms, and job-related talents. We can hear the words they use and their accents. These are basically "surface" aspects of a person that others can easily learn through observation. These surface aspects of people seldom trigger the emotional responses that come from deep-seated, cultural misunderstandings.

However, just as the enormous breadth of an iceberg's base lies beneath the water's surface, so does the childhood conditioning of people from different cultures. As icebergs increase in number and drift too close together, they are likely to clash at their base even though there is no visible contact at the water's surface.[10] As organizations increase the diversity of their work force, the potential for clashes based on deep-seated cultural conditioning and prejudiced attitudes also increases. These clashes will be emotional, and when they occur effective human relations will become a challenge.

Economic Factors When the economy goes through a recession or depression, and housing, jobs, and other necessities become scarce, people's prejudices against other groups often increase. If enough prejudice is built up against a particular group, members of that group will be barred from competing for jobs. For example, the trade deficit between Japan and the United States indicates that more Japanese-made products are allowed into the American marketplace than American-made products are allowed into the Japanese marketplace. The flood of Japanese goods into the United States has forced some American manufacturers of similar products to cut back production and lay off workers. Resentment has increased, and as a result workers of Japanese descent sometimes find it difficult to obtain jobs in American organizations.

Employment discrimination is not a new event. Each wave of immigrants to the United States has encountered it in one form or another. Prejudice based on economic factors has its roots in people's basic survival needs, and, as a result, it is very hard to eliminate. Until the economy can provide jobs for everyone, competition for work will continue to foster many types of prejudice.

Thinking / Learning Starters

1. Have you ever been the object of prejudice? What were the circumstances? How did this behavior affect your self-esteem?

2. Do you carry any prejudices that are obvious carry-overs from your parents? Explain.

3. Are you doing anything to overcome these prejudices? What would the benefits be if you could overcome them?

DISCRIMINATION

Discrimination is behavior based on prejudiced attitudes. If, as an employer, you believe that overweight people tend to be lazy, that is an attitude. If you refuse to hire someone simply because that person is overweight, you are engaging in discriminatory behavior.

Individuals or groups that are discriminated against are denied equal treatment and opportunities afforded to the dominant group. They may be denied employment, promotion, training, or other job-related privileges on the basis of race, lifestyle, gender, or other characteristics that have little or nothing to do with their qualifications for a job.

Gender

Gender bias (also known as *sexism*) is discrimination on the basis of gender, and it continues to be the focus of much attention. The traditional assumption that women are emotional and weak has hindered their climb into leadership positions. The traditional assumption that men should be aggressive and unemotional is alien to a workplace that rewards sensitivity and teamwork. These traditional roles of men and women have undergone tremendous changes in the past few decades.

Many women now pursue nontraditional jobs or seek management-level positions. When they choose these options, they usually face two challenges: the wage gap and the glass ceiling. The gap between women's and men's earnings has been one of the most compelling statistical benchmarks during the women's movement. Organizations that refuse to adjust unequal pay scales can be sued under the Equal Pay Act of 1963. Yet, in a survey conducted by the Women's Bureau of the U.S. Department of Labor of more than 250,000 persons, respondents clearly indicated that many women, in very different fields, continue to experience wage discrimination.[11]

The **glass ceiling** is a form of discrimination that gives women a view of top management jobs but blocks their ascent in the workplace. Studies indicate that only 1 percent of the Fortune 500 companies' top 2,500 managers are women.[12] Yet women are in the work force in greater numbers than ever before — obviously, something is wrong. A U.S. Department of Labor task force studied nine major U.S. corporations and discovered that the glass ceiling does indeed exist in the workplace.[13] Some companies have found this practice extremely expensive. In a landmark gender-bias lawsuit, Texaco Inc. was ordered to pay $6 million to settle the case brought by Janella Sue Martin, who was twice rejected for management positions that were later assigned to men.[14]

Not long ago, many men felt they had the corporate terrain all to themselves. Some felt discomfort, even resentment, when women became more visible and were promoted to management positions. Today, men generally have more enlightened attitudes toward women who are climbing the career ladder. One reason for this change is that men now in their thirties had a large number of female classmates in professional schools. These men learned during their training not only that they would be competing with such women but also that women are as smart and certainly just as ambitious and talented as they are. Men who would like to see options available for their daughters are particularly helpful to women in business.

One of the most sensitive problems between men and women in organizations is **sexual harassment,** or unwelcome verbal or physical behavior that affects a person's job performance or work environment. Under the law, sexual harassment may take one of two forms. The first is **quid pro quo** (something for something), which occurs when a person in a power position threatens the job security or a potential promotion of a worker who refuses to submit to sexual advances. These kinds of threats are absolutely prohibited, and employers are liable for damages under the Fair Employment Practices section of the Civil Rights Act of 1964.

The second form of sexual harassment involves the existence of a **hostile work environment**. U.S. Supreme Court decisions have held that sexual harassment exists if a "reasonable person" believes that the behavior is sufficiently severe or pervasive to create an abusive working environment, even if the victim is not fired or held back from a promotion. Such an environment exists when coworkers make sexual innuendoes, tell sexually oriented jokes, display sexually explicit photos in the work area, discuss sexual exploits, and so on.

Total Person Insight

"If a mandatory service period here at the [National Association of Female Executives] office could be arranged for all your male associates, it would enlighten them, as it did me. Since that isn't an option, and while men and women still are so different in their approaches and behavior, you still have to talk and talk to us until we all get it. Please give us a hand. It isn't that we don't want to understand. It's just that we have a few centuries of conditioning to overcome. As you do."

GEORGE TUNICK

Publisher, *Executive Female*

Unlike quid pro quo harassment, hostile work environment claims fall in a gray area because what is offensive to one person may not be offensive to another. The bottom line is that most kinds of sexually explicit language, conduct, and behavior are inappropriate in the workplace, regardless of whether such conduct constitutes sexual harassment within the legal meaning of the term.

Age

Discrimination based on age can apply to the older worker—forty to seventy—and the younger worker—eighteen to twenty-five.

Youth can be a disadvantage when potential employers show a reluctance to hire young people because of their lack of practical experience in the workplace. Such employers fail to appreciate that everyone begins his or her career with no experience and needs an opportunity to prove himself or herself. Furthermore, there are advantages to hiring a young person that many employers recognize: (1) they are less expensive to hire than experienced employees, and (2) they tend to be more flexible and willing to learn company procedures. The young worker's chances of employment are increased when he or she acquires a good education and expresses a willingness to learn on the job.

Older workers between the ages of forty and seventy are protected against discrimination by the Age Discrimination in Employment Act. Under an amendment activated on January 1, 1987, employers can no longer require workers to retire at age seventy, as was previously the case.

Even though organizations can no longer require mandatory retirement at a specific age, employees approaching this age are often victims of potent, more subtle forms of discrimination. They may be laid off, have their workload cut back, lose their eligibility for promotion, or be given "make-work" projects that keep them out of the mainstream of the organization.

Americans tend to have a stereotypical notion that older workers are no longer capable of effective work performance. Many employers are reluctant to hire or retrain the older worker. They feel that those educated in the 1950s and 1960s will not understand the technology and methods of the 1990s. Studies indicate, however, that older workers tend to be more dependable, to stay on the job longer, and to learn new technologies in the same amount of time required by younger workers.[15]

The fact remains that the American work force is continuing to mature. By the year 2000, one in three Americans will be over 45 years old.[16] Therefore, it would seem logical for employers to make a commitment to skill upgrading and retraining designed to facilitate acceptance of new techniques and procedures by the older work force. And, indeed, major organizations such as Marriott Corporation, McDonald's Corp., Wal-Mart Stores, Inc., and Red Lobster

Renee Wallace, Executive Director of Vita/Living (a nonprofit organization that creates work and living situations for people with mental retardation and developmental disabilities), is a good example of the changing demographics of the work force. At age seventy she is an energetic, hands-on manager. She is seen here examining a piece of pottery with one of her employees at the ceramic and tile company she started. (Bob Daemmich)

restaurants are recruiting and training older workers across the nation. At the same time, older workers need to bring attitudes of adaptability and flexibility to work. Corning Glass Works hires retirees for short-term projects because it knows these people are highly motivated and eager to do something useful.[17]

Race

Racial discrimination is discrimination based on traits common to a person's national origin or skin color. Because people cannot change their skin color to blend in with the dominant group, this is often the most difficult discrimination to overcome. As DeWayne Wickman, African American and president of Vanita Enterprises, Inc., states it, "The melting pot does not melt blacks."[18] By the year 2050, approximately 50 percent of the U.S. population will be nonwhite.[19] Basically four groups are currently struggling to gain their full place in mainstream U.S. society: African Americans, Hispanics, Asians, and Native Americans.

African Americans currently represent the largest segment of people of color in the country, numbering approximately 30 million, or about 12 percent of the total U.S. population. By the year 2050, projections indicate that percentage will rise to about 16 percent.[20] As a group they have suffered the most from overt discrimination. Even though the Fourteenth Amendment ended slavery, many African Americans continued to be treated as second-class citizens, and a long history of prejudice has created serious inequities in education and employment opportunities for this group.

Hispanics — Mexican-Americans, Puerto Ricans, Cubans, South Americans, Filipinos, and other Spanish-speaking groups — have also suffered from poor education, lack of job skills, and the language barrier. But the picture is changing. A Rand Corporation study of Mexican immigrants in California found that the generation of Hispanics born in this country has high school completion rates as high as those of non-Hispanics. Other studies have found no income gap between male Hispanics who speak fluent English and white males.[21] It is estimated that the Hispanic population is growing at four times the overall U.S. growth rate. By the year 2050, Hispanics will most likely replace African Americans as the largest segment of nonwhites in the United States; their numbers are expected to reach 21 percent of the total population.[22]

Many Asians and Pacific Islanders have immigrated to the United States. This group currently accounts for approximately 4 percent of the total population and is expected to grow to 11 percent by the year 2050.[23] These new citizens are making major strides toward improving their status and stereotyped image. Approximately 35 percent of Asian Americans graduate from college — twice as high as the percentage of whites. At the same time, Asian Americans are rising in corporate America faster than is any other minority group. Gerald Tsai, Jr., a Chinese American, is an example of this success. He became the first Asian American to head a Fortune 500 company when he took over American

Can Company. Robert Nakasone, a Japanese American and graduate of the University of Chicago Business School, was made president of U.S. operations of Toys "R" Us, Inc.[24]

In the nineteenth century and at the turn of the twentieth century, Native Americans were viewed primarily as an obstacle to westward expansion and as racially and culturally inferior to whites. As the country was further settled, many tribes were destroyed, and those that remained were eventually confined to reservations. Nevertheless, Native Americans have made continual efforts to gain control over their political, cultural, and social lives. A militant spirit among the 1980s generation of Native Americans has brought their struggle for equality to public attention. Native American colleges, also, are growing in number and providing curricula intended to strengthen self-identity and self-determination.

Racial tension in the United States is rising as minorities steadily increase in number. Gaps in education and employment between whites and people of color persist. However, because of affirmative action programs, sensitivity training, and the threat of legal action, blatant racism has evolved into a new, more subtle form of discrimination that is difficult to recognize and harder to combat. Strategies to combat this subtle racism should be aimed at all levels within an organization, but they must start at the top.

Disability

Employees whose work assignments are limited by their mental or physical abilities have in the past been referred to as "handicapped" or "disabled." Today, the more politically correct term is *mentally challenged* for those individuals who suffer from mental retardation or a serious emotional disturbance, or *physically challenged* for those individuals who have hearing, speech, visual, or-thopedic, or other health impairments, such as long-term obesity.

Mentally or physically challenged people have found it difficult to enter the job market, even though their right to do so is protected by the Rehabilitation Act of 1973. The Americans with Disabilities Act of 1991 expands the definition of people with disabilities to include people with AIDS, people with tuberculosis, and recovering drug and alcohol abusers, among others. The new law sets forth requirements that businesses with fifteen or more employees must follow in the areas of employment discrimination, public and private transportation, public accommodations, and telecommunications to allow people with disabilities to have equal access to employment, goods, and services.

Discrimination against the mentally and physically challenged takes many forms, but the most common blunders are

- asking a job applicant about his or her impairment,
- requiring a candidate with a disability to have a medical exam,
- reducing health insurance for an employee with a particular infirmity,

- firing a staff member who develops a disability,
- refusing to serve a customer who has a disability.[25]

Mentally or physically challenged people who try to get jobs often encounter such discrimination. Some companies are exceptions, however. Du Pont Corporation, McDonald's, Marriott, and IBM have specific recruiting, training, and retention programs that recognize the skills and abilities of this sector of the work force. Apple Computer, Inc.'s Office of Special Education places physically challenged individuals strategically within the corporation to ensure that Apple designs products with the needs of this population in mind.[26] Red Lobster has been hiring workers with disabilities for over twenty years as a solution to the chronic problem of rapid staff turnover. The restaurant chain's success has proven that mentally and physically challenged people are often the steadiest and hardest working members of the staff.[27]

Sexual Orientation

Discrimination based on a person's sexual orientation is sometimes referred to as *heterosexism,* a bias toward heterosexuality, or *homophobia,* a fear of homosexuals. Not long ago, gays and lesbians went to great lengths to keep their sexuality a secret. But with the women's movement, the gay rights movement, and, more recently, the AIDS crisis, many gays and lesbians have "come out of the closet" to demand their rights as members of society. Indeed, many younger people entering the work force who are used to the relative tolerance of college campuses refuse to hide their orientation once they are in the workplace. Activists want to make people aware that discrimination based on sexual orientation is as serious a problem as discrimination based on race, age, gender, or disability. And some, though not all, states have enacted laws that protect gays and lesbians from discrimination or illegal discharge from their jobs because of their sexual orientation.

An atmosphere in which gays and lesbians are comfortable about being themselves is often more productive than an atmosphere in which they waste their time and energy maintaining alternate, and false, personalities. Brian Mc-Naught, a consultant to AT&T, states, "Homophobia takes a toll on the ability of 10 percent of the work force to produce."[28]

More than thirty major companies throughout the United States — including Xerox, AT&T, Eastman Kodak Company, Digital, and US West, Inc. — have established lesbian and gay employee associations and give them the same access to computer bulletin boards as other groups have.[29] Announcements might include details about an upcoming event or about the legal rights of employees who have tested positive for HIV (human immunodeficiency virus), the virus that causes AIDS. A similar organization at Levi Strauss & Co. prepared a video for the company to use in its diversity training.[30] These groups act as a point of contact for previously invisible employees. Companies have always valued the help of employee groups in dealing with problems of race and gender discrimination. Now gay/lesbian employee associations can be part of the solution to end the discrimination and isolation their members have experienced in the past.

Subtle Forms of Discrimination

Discrimination based on gender, age, race, or disability is prohibited under Title VII of the Civil Rights Act of 1964. This prohibition applies to discrimination in all aspects of employment, including recruitment, hiring, promotion, discharge, classification, training, compensation, and other terms, privileges, and conditions of employment.[31] A person who feels she or he has been the victim of these types of discrimination can take legal action by filing a complaint with the state office of the Equal Employment Opportunity Commission.

But the laws do not specifically protect workers from more subtle discrimination. For example, although some state laws protect gay men and lesbians from discrimination or illegal discharge from their jobs, an atmosphere that allows cruel comments and jokes about their lifestyles can nevertheless occur, adversely affecting their job performance. This lower job performance can be used as a valid reason for dismissing the lesbian or gay person. This more subtle form of discrimination can, of course, be directed against any group and may be based on any of the secondary dimensions of diversity (religious beliefs, personal appearance, marital status). Those who are from another region of the country, speak with an accent, have too much education or too little, or possess some other personal characteristic that marks them as "different" may find themselves victims of subtle discrimination.

Subtle forms of discrimination are extremely hard to prove, in part because employers themselves are often unaware of their prejudices. For instance, many employers subconsciously associate height with assertiveness, self-confidence, and an "executive" image. Studies have shown that as you move up the corporate ladder, individuals get taller and thinner.[32] Some appearance-based job discrimination is quite intentional. When an executive-level position opens, the subtle expectation of hiring a tall, attractive person who fits the "image" of that particular job assignment may not be specifically stated in the job description, but it is clearly understood by all those involved.

What Can You Do?

What can you do if you discover you are the target of these subtle forms of discrimination? If you wish to stay in the organization, you will need to determine whether the "difference" is something you can change—your weight, the way you dress, your manner of speaking. If the difference is something you cannot or choose not to change, you may need to address the situation directly. Assertiveness on your part may help change other people's attitudes, which will in turn alter their discriminatory behaviors. Another powerful method of eliminating subtle discrimination is to compensate for it by excelling in your work. Become an expert on the job, and work to increase your skills and your value to the organization. As your colleagues gain respect for your talents, they will change their attitudes toward you. But if your future appears blocked, investigate other workplaces where management may be more open to diversity. The important point is that you should refuse to allow discrimination to limit your personal and professional success.

Thinking / Learning Starters

1. Describe your primary and secondary dimensions of diversity.

2. Do you hold any prejudices that might create problems for you in your career? In your personal life?

THE ISSUE OF VALUING DIVERSITY

As we look back through the previous decades, we see a pattern of workers continually struggling to be treated alike:

- Labor unions were formed to assure employees that everyone would be treated the same.
- The women's movement fought for equality in the workplace.
- Many organizations implemented strategies to duplicate the Japanese management style, which reinforced teamwork rather than individual accomplishments.

The 1990s, however, have brought a strong shift away from treating everyone the same and toward **valuing diversity.** To value diversity in a work setting means that an organization intends to make full use of the ideas, talents, experiences, and perspectives of all employees at all levels within that organization.

Organizations have traditionally valued assimilation over diversity, with the emphasis placed on changing people to conform to traditional norms and performance expectations. Most American organizations have been shaped primarily by the values and experiences of Western European, white, heterosexual, able-bodied men. Achieving high productivity has frequently been a matter of fitting all workers into the same mold and rewarding those who fit best. The dominant group set and controlled the agenda of the traditional organization, while other groups were expected to follow, conform, or disappear. As people moved up the career ladder, the range of acceptable behavior narrowed and reverted back to the traditional mold of the founding fathers.

However, the changing demographics of the U.S. work force brings with it the realization that organizations must break away from this traditional management approach. By the year 2000, people of color and white women will account for 85 percent of the net growth in the people available for work. To remain competitive, organizations will be forced to recognize and hire the best talent available in the labor pool, regardless of skin color, gender, and cultural background. Once on board, these talented individuals will choose to stay only in an atmosphere where they are appreciated and valued. If their organization does not acknowledge their unique contribution, these diverse employees are likely to move on to an employer that does.

The Economics of Valuing Diversity

Valuing diversity is not only a legal, social and moral issue; it is also an economic issue because an organization's most valuable resource is its people. The price tag for *not* helping employees learn to respect and value each other is enormous in terms of lost time, delayed production, and increased conflict among employees.

- Highly skilled and talented employees will leave an organization that does not value diversity.
- Substantial dollars will be spent on recruiting and retraining because of high employee turnover.
- Discrimination complaints will result from mismanagement of diverse employees.

Total Person Insight

"More and more, organizations can remain competitive only if they can recognize and obtain the best talent; value the diverse perspectives that come with talent born of different cultures, races, and genders; nurture and train that talent; and create an atmosphere that values its work force."

LEWIS BROWN GRIGGS AND LENTE-LOUISE LOUW

Valuing Diversity: New Tools for a New Reality

- A comment, gesture, or joke delivered without malice but received as an insult will create tension between coworkers.
- Deliberate acts of sabotage may be aimed at making coworkers who are different "look bad."
- Absenteeism associated with stress in the workplace will likely occur.
- Time will be wasted because of miscommunication and misunderstanding between diverse employees.[33]

Recognizing the value of diversity and managing it as an asset can help eliminate these negative effects and exert a positive influence on productivity and cooperation within the work force. Companies can succeed only when they have an environment that enables all employees, not just a few, to work to their full potential.

Not only does mismanagement of employee diversity interfere with efficient production, it also poses a significant threat to an organization's ability to provide quality service to its customers. In industries such as retailing, fast food, and banking, a complex set of employee transactions must take place to satisfy a customer's needs. If there is tension, in-fighting, disrespect, and a low level of trust among employees, then there most likely will be human relations problems that stand in the way of quality customer service. Communications break down, leadership is undermined, cooperation among employees is interrupted, service falters, and the customer is lost. Developing a culture where work force diversity is valued is crucial to the profitability of any organization. When discussing the importance of valuing work force diversity, Corning CEO James Houghton states, "It simply makes good business sense."[34]

Thinking / Learning Starters

1. Describe how the student body of your school or your coworkers compare to your community's cultural makeup.

2. Is there a disproportionate number of students of a certain race, gender, or age bracket in your college or workplace? What accounts for this situation? What effect does it have on the environment of your school or workplace?

ENHANCING DIVERSITY

By now you should be aware of the negative effects of prejudice and discrimination as well as the positive effects of valuing diversity. We are no longer asking whether to diversify our work force but rather how well can we manage it. After all, a person's differences don't create human relations problems—other people's responses to those differences do.

What Individuals Can Do

People tend to hang on to their prejudices and stereotypes. If certain white people believe people of color are inferior, they are likely to notice any incident in which a person of color makes a mistake. But when a person of color exhibits competence and sound decision-making abilities, these same white people do not notice anything, or they attribute the positive results to other circumstances. You cannot totally eliminate prejudices that have been deeply held and developed over a long time. But you can learn to do the following:

1. *Monitor and analytically evaluate these prejudices in light of your increased personal involvement with others who are different from you.* The importance of monitoring personal prejudices was underscored in a series of experiments involving hundreds of participants. Researchers found that while all participants were aware of negative racial stereotypes, those who were assessed as "low prejudice" subjects were able to hold their inappropriate behaviors in check and take corrective measures. Those participants deemed "highly prejudiced" were strongly influenced by their attitudes and participated in discriminatory behaviors.[35] Therefore, if you feel you are highly prejudiced against a particular group, try to take that next step toward changing your stereotypical attitudes. This effort will lead you toward a more successful future at work.

2. *Learn to look critically and honestly at the particular myths and preconceived ideas you were conditioned to believe about others.* Psychologists and sociologists have found that contact among people of different races, cultures, and lifestyles can break down prejudice when people join together for a common task. The more contact there is among culturally diverse individuals, the more likely it will be that stereotypes based on myths and inaccurate generalizations will not survive.

3. *Develop a sensitivity to differences.* Do not allow gender-based, racist, or antigay jokes or comments in your presence. If English is not a person's native language, be aware that this person might interpret your messages differently from what you intended. When in doubt as to the appropriate behavior, ask questions. "I would like to open the door for you because you are in a wheelchair, but I'm not sure whether that would offend you. What would you like me to do?" A Hispanic secretary attending a diversity enhancement workshop shared with the instructor that her boss called her into his office by shouting at her from his desk. She said, "In my country, you call dogs, not people." Her boss overheard the discussion and asked if she was talking about him. She said yes. From then on her boss summoned her by using the telephone or by stopping at her desk.[36]

4. *Use appropriate language.* In this way, you show diverse individuals your respect. For instance, the term *minority* is no longer acceptable in reference to people of color because "minority" gives the sense of less power, as in "ma-

TABLE 7.1

Examples of Appropriate Language

When Referring To	Instead Of	Use
Women	Girls, ladies, gals, females	Women
Black people	Negroes, minorities	African Americans, Caribbean Americans, black people, people of color
Asian people	Minorities, Orientals	Asian Americans, Japanese, Koreans, Pakistanis, etc. Differentiate between foreign-born and American-born people of color.
American Indians	Minorities	Native Americans; American Indians; Indians Name of tribe, e.g., Navajo, Iroquois; people of color
People of Hispano–Latin American origin	Minorities	Latinas/Latinos, Chicanas/Chicanos. Use country of national origin, e.g., Puerto Ricans, Chileans; people of color, Hispanics
Gay men and lesbians	Homosexuals	Gay men, lesbians
People with disabilities	Handicapped, crippled, disabled	People who are physically or mentally challenged, people with (the specific disability)
White people	Anglos, WASPs	European Americans. Use country of national origin, e.g., Irish American, Polish American, White people
Older/younger adults	Geriatrics, kids, yuppies	Older adults, elderly, younger people, young adults

Source: Adapted from *Workforce America!* by Marilyn Loden and Judy Rosener, Business One Irwin, 1991, p. 85. Reprinted by permission of Richard D. Irwin, Inc.

jority versus minority." Table 7.1 offers some guidelines for appropriate terminology.

What Organizations Can Do

Organizations must take a critical look at their corporate culture and determine what must change if diversity is to become a constructive, rather than a destructive, force. Managers may have to revamp policies, create new structures, redesign human resource systems, and generally change the way the organization operates. For example, because Procter & Gamble Co. fills its upper-level management positions only from within the company, it formed the Corporate Diversity Strategy Task Force to identify strategies that would help the company value diversity as fully as possible. The task force discovered that the level of diversity was far more complex than imagined. It went far beyond race and gender and included factors such as cultural heritage, personal background, and functional experience.[37]

Enhancing cultural diversity must be an organizationwide endeavor. One or two individual departments or managers will have limited impact if the overall management attitude leans toward preserving the status quo. The following basic steps have been found to be effective:

The Diversity Council at Levi Strauss & Company is seen here working on diversity and communication issues. The council is helping revamp policies, create new structures, and design new human resource systems. Like many other progressive organizations, Levi Strauss views diversity as a constructive force. (Mark Richards/ PhotoEdit)

1. *Make sure top management is committed to the task and vigorously promotes that commitment through the ranks.* Staff members will take their cue from the chief executive. If they see him or her promoting diversity at work yet playing handball at a segregated club, they will question how seriously top management is committed to equality. Unless the policy is carried through at every level, it can be sabotaged somewhere along the line.

AT&T chair Robert E. Allen assigned four of his top executives to lead diverse, cross-functional committees charged with designing a strategic plan to escalate the company's diversity efforts. Their mission was to "create a work environment that sets the world-class standard for valuing diversity."[38] One aspect of the resulting six-page plan recommends that all thirteen top officers should increase their direct interaction with the company's seven caucus groups that represent African Americans, Latinos, Native Americans, Asian Americans, gays and lesbians, women, and people with disabilities. At Hoechst/Celanese, the top twenty-six officers are required to join at least two organizations in which they are a minority. The company believes that managers can break out of their traditional white-male-dominated comfort zone by actually working beside people from diverse backgrounds.[39]

2. *Review standards for recruiting, hiring, and promoting.* Does the organization recruit in places where nonwhite students or workers are likely to be? Some companies form partnerships with schools and colleges that have great diversity in the student body. Merrill Lynch & Co., Inc., for example, helps high schools in multiracial New Jersey prepare students for careers in the financial services area by teaching them to use personal computers and industry-specific software programs. Other companies sponsor professors' research, provide employees as guest lecturers, award scholarships, and hire students for summer jobs. These activities give company recruiters an opportunity to learn more about the specific details of a college's academic programs as well as the qualifications of individual graduates.[40]

3. *Establish a means to monitor nondiscrimination policies, and provide top management with regular reports.* Reports should not be a series of numbers quoting how many Native Americans or Hispanics were hired, for example. Rather, reports should provide an in-depth analysis of the positions that were filled in relation to the available work force and customer base. Hirings, promotions, and dismissals should be monitored carefully to see if a disproportionate number of people from a specific culture are affected. Xerox discovered that white men were underrepresented in entry-level engineering jobs, so it acted quickly to hire more.[41] During downsizing at Dial Corp, reports indicated that the number of African Americans dismissed was two-thirds higher than for other workers.[42] Top managers need quality information about how their policies are being carried out so that they can quickly remedy any situation that might adversely affect their organization's competitive edge in the marketplace.

4. *Celebrate differences.* Celebratory activities bring employees together for ethnic foods and dances and help promote awareness for all cultures within the organization. Digital celebrates Black History Month and Hispanic Heritage Week.[43] In San Jose, California, where thirty-three languages are spoken, the IBM Systems Storage Division began celebrating an annual diversity day in 1993. Employees dress in their various ethnic costumes, perform traditional dances, and prepare authentic dishes for coworkers to taste.[44] Those involved agree that the annual festival successfully defuses multicultural tensions that might otherwise disrupt the productivity of the organization.

Beyond these basic steps for enhancing diversity in the workplace, organizations are beginning to discover additional strategies that help alleviate potential human relations problems in a diverse work force. Approaches include offering training seminars and restructuring benefits to fit individual needs.

Affirmative Action The Civil Rights Act of 1964 established **affirmative action** guidelines to remedy the effect of past discrimination against groups protected under this law. Under these guidelines, employers must identify any discriminatory barriers that limit applicants and employees in their organizations. They are required to eliminate those barriers and establish whatever programs are necessary to facilitate the process of establishing a numerically balanced, diverse work force. Affirmative action programs are mandatory for (1) any organization that contracts with the federal government or receives federal funds, (2) all public employers, and (3) all federal agencies. Xerox chair David T. Kearns believes that a firm and resolute commitment to affirmative action is the first and most important step to work force diversity. "It is a corporate value, a management priority, and a formal business objective."[45]

Affirmative action allowed a tremendous influx of diverse individuals through the front door of thousands of schools and organizations. Many were able to work their way into advanced, top-level positions. At the same time, however, affirmative action reinforced the historical view that the members of protected groups are not qualified for various positions and therefore need assistance just to get a job. Some recipients of affirmative action may be embarrassed to be identified as such. In his book *Reflections of an Affirmative Action Baby,* Steven Carter, an African American and Yale Law School graduate, discusses his search for a teaching position. He found that any school was happy to have a black professor with his credentials, but he wanted to be judged on his merits and was insulted to find himself viewed as "the best black."[46] It is important for organizations to handle affirmative action guidelines with care and integrity — people need to see the program as a positive effort to strengthen the organization.

Preferential policies in schools as well as organizations can backfire on the people who need them the most. When the recipients of affirmative action find they are different from the majority of their coworkers and supervisors, they may experience extreme loneliness and isolation. They may not be able to gain the sense of "belonging" that is essential to self-motivation and eventually may quit their jobs.

The debate concerning affirmative action is far from over. The concept and the means for implementing it are likely to be challenged in court repeatedly over the next decade. As legislators move toward eliminating federally mandated affirmative action programs, human rights activists are pursuing alternative plans that will preserve and maintain the concept of equal opportunity for all.

Training and Education   To develop a culture that values and enhances diversity, organizations will have to move beyond affirmative action and create training programs that develop the full potential of all men and women. Upward mobility should be based on training and competence so that there is no compromise of standards. Many companies have made diversity awareness training programs a prerequisite for promotion. As Judith Katz, a corporate consultant in San Diego, states, "Managers that have not learned to manage diversity by the year 2000 will be incompetent."[47]

Organizations have implemented diversity training with varying degrees of success. Many focus on developing flexible management styles to meet the needs of a diverse work force. Most include techniques for improving communications among workers from different cultural backgrounds. During guided training sessions, managers and employees alike are encouraged to talk openly about their stereotyped attitudes — including those plaguing white men — and to identify how those attitudes might be affecting the work environment.

Unfortunately, diversity training programs themselves can cause backlash. Some white males are tired of being made to feel guilty in every discussion of diversity. Training sessions that cast heterosexual, white American males as the oppressors can create a great deal of resentment. These men point out that being a woman or nonwhite does not guarantee you will be effective working with people from diverse backgrounds. An African-American woman could have just as much difficulty working with a male manager from Saudi Arabia as a white male might have in the same situation. A Japanese engineer working with a Latino supervisor might experience human relations challenges similar to those of a white male in the same position.

Summary

Work force diversity has become an important issue for organizations that want to remain competitive in a global economy. Two dimensions, or sets of characteristics, are the basis of every individual's diversity. Primary dimensions include gender, age, race, physical and mental abilities, and sexual orientation. Secondary dimensions include health habits, religious beliefs, ethnic customs, communication style, parental status, and others.

Prejudice and discrimination are major barriers to effective human relations. Prejudice is an attitude based partly on observation of others' differences and partly on ignorance, fear, and cultural conditioning. Prejudiced people tend to see others as stereotypes rather than as unique individuals. Prejudicial attitudes are formed through the effects of childhood experiences, ethnocentrism, and economic factors. Discrimination is behavior based on prejudicial attitudes. Groups protected by law from discrimination in the workplace include women, older and younger workers, people of color, and those who have disabilities. More subtle forms of discrimination include discrimination arising from sexual orientation, appearance, and lifestyle. These subtle forms of discrimination are often difficult to prove but may be offset through assertiveness, a change in the behavior that causes the discrimination, or a move to a more tolerant organization.

The issue of valuing diversity is an economic one for most organizations. The changing demographics of American society mean that the work force will soon be made up of a minority of white men and a majority of diverse, talented, and well-educated women and people of color. Companies cannot afford to ignore this change in the pool of human resources.

Individuals can enhance diversity by letting go of their stereotypes and learning to monitor their prejudiced attitudes as they work and socialize with people who are different. They will need to develop a sensitivity to differences and use language appropriately.

Finally, organizations must develop a culture that respects and enhances diversity. Affirmative action guidelines will help bring many different individuals into the organization, but training and education will help all men and women reach their potential.

Career Corner

Q. I receive phone calls at work from customers located all over the world. Most of them speak English, but because of their accents, I often have difficulty understanding what they are trying to say to me. How can I handle these calls more effectively?

A. The fact that your customers can speak two languages indicates that they are probably educated and intelligent, so treat them with respect. Statements like "I can't understand you," or "What did you say?" are rude and should be avoided. Instead, take personal responsibility for improving the communications and gently say, "I am having a little difficulty understanding you, but if you will be patient with me I am sure I will be able to help." Ask them to slow down so that you can hear all the information correctly. Listen for key words and repeat them back to the caller. Identify coworkers who are fluent in a particular language and ask them to help when calls come in from customers who share the same culture. Remember, people with foreign accents are not hard of hearing, so don't shout.

Key Terms

diversity	gender bias
primary dimensions	glass ceiling
secondary dimensions	sexual harassment
prejudices	quid pro quo
stereotypes	hostile work environment
cultural myopia	valuing diversity
ethnocentrism	affirmative action
discrimination	

Review Questions

1. Define the *primary* and *secondary dimensions* of diversity, and give examples of each.
2. Why should organizations be concerned about valuing diversity?
3. How do the changing demographics of the American culture affect the human resources pool of the future? Be specific.
4. Define *prejudice* and *discrimination*. What is the difference in meaning between these two terms?
5. What are some of the ways people acquire prejudices?
6. In what ways might valuing diversity impact an organization economically?
7. How can subtle forms of discrimination hurt the victim's chances to succeed in his or her career?
8. What role does affirmative action play in today's organizations? What are some of the positive and negative outcomes of affirmative action?
9. How can organizations enhance work force diversity?
10. What flaws in diversity training programs can cause a negative backlash among participants?

Application Exercises

1. Select a professional journal, the want ads from a local or national paper, or any magazine publication. Examine the ads, articles, and pictures for evidence that the publishers and advertisers are attempting to attract and respect readers from diverse races and cultures. For example, which racial or ethnic groups are pictured in expensive cars, offices, or homes? If your chosen career is traditionally dominated by one gender, do articles in your professional journals include references to one or both genders?
2. For one week, keep a diary that records every instance in which you see actions or hear comments that reflect outmoded, negative stereotypes. For instance, watch a movie and observe whether the villains are all of a particular ethnic group. As you read textbooks from other courses you are taking, notice if the pictures and examples reflect any stereotypes. Listen to your friends' conversations, and notice any time they make unfair judgments about others based on stereotypes.

Share your experiences with class members, and discuss what steps you can take to help rid the environment of negative stereotyping.

Self-Assessment Exercise	1. For each of the following statements, circle the number from 1 to 5 that best represents your response: (1) strongly disagree (never do this); (2) disagree (rarely do this); (3) moderately agree (sometimes do this); (4) agree (frequently do this); (5) strongly agree (always do this).

    a. I refuse to perpetuate negative stereotypes and   1   2   3   4   5
        accept each person as a unique individual worthy
        of my respect.

    b. I make every effort to identify my own preju-   1   2   3   4   5
        diced attitudes and avoid stereotypical attitudes
        toward people of color, older people, persons
        with disabilities, and others who are different
        from me.

    c. I work hard to combat prejudice because it has   1   2   3   4   5
        a negative impact on my self-esteem and the
        self-esteem of the victim.

Select an appropriate attitude or skill you would like to improve. Write your goal in the space provided.

GOAL: _____

_____

_____

Case Problem — Denny's Racial Bias = $54 Million

Denny's, the $1.7 billion restaurant chain, has been fighting racial discrimination charges since the early 1990s. Court documents record a host of charges, including refusing to serve nonwhites, forcing African-American customers to prepay for their meals, temporary closings of restaurants with too many African-American customers, unfair hiring and treatment of nonwhite employees, and blocking nonwhite employees from franchise opportunities and management positions.

One lawsuit was filed when six African-American Secret Service officers, who had allegedly been snubbed by service personnel at a Denny's in Annapolis, Maryland, claimed Denny's "service lapse" had been "racially motivated." Another lawsuit filed in San Jose, California, alleged that thirty-two black customers were ordered to prepay for meals or pay a cover charge while white customers had no such requirement. Denny's parent company, Flagstar, agreed to pay $19.6 million (including $1.9 million in attorneys' fees) to settle the Maryland case. The California case was settled for $34.8 million (including $6.8 million in attorneys' fees).

All this happened while competition for customers was at an all-time high. Innovative new food services were attempting to lure patrons away from full-service, family-type restaurants. To counteract the adverse publicity, which could erode Denny's customer base, Flagstar's chairman and chief executive officer, Jerry Richardson, made an unprecedented sixty-second TV commercial showing a representative sample of Denny's employees endorsing a pledge that all customers would be treated with respect, dignity, and fairness. The commercial ran for two weeks in selected markets across the United States. In other action designed to deal with charges of discrimination, Flagstar (a large corporation whose operations include the Hardee's fast-food chain) launched a $1 billion program that included increasing its minority hiring and its contracting with minority vendors.

Questions

1. Beyond the $54.4 million fines, nationwide television advertising expenses, and the $1 billion diversity program, what other losses might Denny's experience as a result of the charges of discriminatory behaviors?
2. Do you believe that top management officials in the Denny's/Flagstar organization were responsible for creating a climate that encouraged restaurant managers to engage in racially biased activities? Why?
3. How do you think you would respond if you were asked to prepay for your meal while other customers paid after finishing theirs?
4. How would you respond if your manager asked you to blatantly discriminate against someone from another culture?

Chapter 8

Strategies for Resolving Conflict and Achieving Emotional Control

Chapter Preview

After studying this chapter, you will be able to

1. List and describe some of the major causes for conflicts between people in the work setting.

2. Explain the three basic conflict management strategies.

3. Understand the role that assertiveness and cooperation play in personal conflict management.

4. Identify the key elements of the conflict resolution process.

5. Describe how emotions influence our thinking and behavior.

6. Understand the factors that contribute to emotional balance.

7. List and describe the major factors that influence our emotional development.

8. Learn how to deal with your anger and the anger of others.

9. Identify and explain the most common emotional styles.

10. Describe strategies for achieving emotional control.

O RGANIZATIONS TODAY are faced with subtle conflicts among their workers over issues that did not exist fifteen to twenty years ago. For example, most families today depend on two incomes for economic survival. As a result, working parents are demanding and getting new rights and benefits to help balance their personal and professional lives. Flextime, available at some companies, allows working parents to tailor their arrival and departure times at work to fit their child-care arrangements. Many "family friendly" employers allow workers time off to attend special activities that involve their children. Some firms offer parental and maternity leave to both fathers and mothers of newborn babies. These employers are proud of their accomplishments and often recruit new workers more easily because of the benefits they provide for working parents.

But conflicts can arise if workers who have not yet started their families or who have chosen to be child-free feel slighted when benefits and privileges are awarded to workers with children. Child-free workers in some organizations are expected to maintain regular working hours while their coworkers adjust to child-care challenges by arriving late for work or leaving early. They may be denied personal leave time to care for a critically ill spouse while other workers have time off related to a pregnancy. And sometimes — when it comes time to work late into the evening or on weekends — child-free workers are asked or told to put forth extra effort by employers who fear they will be criticized for interfering with the "family time" of working parents. Of course, conflict can also arise if working parents feel employers are exhibiting favoritism when they choose a child-free worker for a special assignment that might eventually lead to a promotion. ■

What are employers to do? Should they change the rules and regulations to avoid conflict? This may not be economically feasible. Should they treat everyone the same? This would be a giant step backward in organizational management, since most employees now want to be treated as unique individuals. As organizations struggle to resolve a wide range of conflicts, managing conflict becomes a necessary human relations skill needed by workers at all levels.

A key element of conflict resolution is emotional balance. This is achieved, in part, by learning to deal with your anger and the anger of others. The factors that contribute to emotional balance will be discussed later in this chapter.

CONFLICT: AN EVERYDAY AFFAIR

Conflict can be defined as individuals striving for their own preferred outcome, which if attained prevents others from achieving their preferred outcome. This process often results in hostility and a breakdown in human relations.[1] Differences, disagreements, and competition generate conflict when the people involved (consciously or unconsciously) try to deny each other the right to satisfy needs. If an organization and its employees have no effective methods of managing conflict, it can undermine employee morale, divert energy from important tasks, decrease productivity by disrupting cooperation, create suspicion and distrust among employees, and overemphasize the differences between individuals.[2]

In many companies, the amount of time spent on conflict management is surprisingly high. Some managers are spending up to half their time attempting to resolve conflicts among workers.[3] These managers have learned that when they address the source of the conflict rather than suppress it, the lines of communication open and people begin talking *to* each other rather than *about* each other. This open communication process helps workers feel that their opinion is valued and that they are a part of the team.

Conflict should not, however, be regarded as a solely negative experience. Sometimes a difference of opinion is the first step in getting rid of outdated rules and regulations. When people work together to resolve conflicts, their solutions are often far more creative than they would be if only one person addressed the problem. Creatively managed conflict can shake people out of their mental ruts and give them new frameworks, new assumptions, and new points of view. The heart of effective human relations lies not in trying to eliminate conflict (an impossible task) but in making constructive use of the energy released by conflict.

Total Person Insight

"The rapid changes of the twentieth century have increased human conflict to the point that our sensibilities toward each other are becoming numb. The human capacity for adaptation may be working against our social relationships as we passively accept conditions that are not conducive to the effective resolution of interpersonal differences. Just as we adapt to bad air, tasteless food, polluted water, congested cities, and loud noise, we are also becoming callous and indifferent to the factors in our environment that are setting us at one another's throats."

GORDON LIPPITT

Consultant, Human Resource Development

Causes of Conflict

Conflicts among workers are caused by a wide range of factors. Some are major and need to be addressed through the legal system or labor union negotiations. Others seem relatively minor, but they can still have a major impact on the productivity of an organization. Here we discuss several causes of conflicts that may help you anticipate, and therefore solve, people problems in your organization.

Poor Communication Skills   The greatest source of personal conflict is the misunderstanding that often results from ineffective communication.[4] In Chapter 2 we discussed the various filters that messages must pass through before effective communication can occur. In the work setting, where many different people work closely together, communication breakdowns are inevitable. Soon workers who should be focusing on the problem are instead placing blame on others for their "failure to communicate." When employees learn to deal with the problem directly, the damage caused by miscommunication can be significantly reduced.

Value Clashes   In Chapter 6 you read that differences in values can cause conflicts between generations, among men and women, and among people with different value priorities. Consider the conflicts that might arise between work-

These Westford, Massachusetts, citizens are sending a message to Wal-Mart stores: "Don't build a store in our community." They fear that a large discount store would be a threat to many of the small businesses serving the community. This clash of values is taking place in several Northeast communities where Wal-Mart plans to open stores. (Rick Freedman/Black Star)

ers who realize the value of vacation time and executives who never take time off. Similarly, conflicts are inevitable between "loyalists," who join their organization for life and make decisions for their own good as well as that of the company, and "job-hoppers," who accept a job in order to position themselves for the next opportunity that might further their personal career advancement. The opportunities for value clashes are almost limitless in today's diverse organizations.

Culture Clashes For generations, culture clashes have occurred between workers not only from other countries but also from different parts of the United States. During the Great Depression, for example, thousands of people left the Texas-Oklahoma-Arkansas dust bowl and migrated to California in search of jobs. The "Okies" and "Arkies," as they were called, dressed, acted, and talked differently from the native Californians, and they encountered prejudice and discrimination. Today's diverse work force, as noted in Chapter 7, reflects a kaleidoscope of cultures, each with its own unique qualities.

Work Policies and Practices Interpersonal conflicts can develop when an organization has arbitrary or confusing rules, regulations, and performance standards. Workers will see little correlation between job performance and salary advancement if they discover that another worker doing the same job is making more money or is being promoted faster than they are. Conflicts over work rules, or the interpretation of work rules, are quite common.

Adversarial Management Under adversarial management, supervisors may view their employees and even other managers with suspicion and distrust, and treat them as "the enemy." Employees usually lack respect for adversarial managers, resenting their authoritarian style and resisting their suggestions for change. This atmosphere makes cooperation and teamwork difficult. Supervisors who display genuine concern for both people and production and are sensitive to employee needs have far fewer conflicts than do adversarial managers. Because of this, most organizations are encouraging a leadership style that fosters openness and mutual respect.

Noncompliance Conflict also surfaces when some workers refuse to comply with the rules and neglect their fair share of the workload. Coworkers get angry if they have to put forth extra effort to get the work done because others are taking two-hour lunch breaks, sleeping on the job, making personal phone calls during office hours, and wasting time. Now that so many organizations are organizing their work forces into teams, noncompliance has the potential for becoming a major source of conflict.

Difficult People The focus of this book is to help you become a valued worker who is easy to get along with and productive regardless of your career path. However, you are likely to encounter coworkers who have not read a human relations text. Some of them will be difficult to get along with, no matter what you do. In their book, *Dealing with People You Can't Stand,* Rick Kirschner and Rick Brinkman identify ten types of difficult personalities (see Figure 8.1). They suggest four options you might consider when you work with difficult people.

1. Suffer in silence.
2. Change your attitude. You may not like the individual, but you can work well together.
3. Change your behavior so that the difficult person has to learn new ways of dealing with you.
4. Look for a new job. Not all situations can be resolved.[5]

Thinking / Learning Starters

1. Have you ever experienced a conflict with a coworker? Explain. How did you handle the situation? Did you confront the other person? What were the results? Could you have handled the situation in a more productive manner? Explain.

2. Identify some of the causes of conflict in an organization in which you worked as an employee or volunteer. What types of conflict seemed to cause the most trouble among people?

STRATEGIES FOR DEALING WITH CONFLICT

In baseball, if two runners try to occupy the same base at the same time, there is conflict. It is an exciting situation, but if a positive solution is not found quickly, both they and their team will be losers. We must accept the fact that any time two or more people are brought together, the stage is set for potential conflict. When conflict does occur, the results may be positive or negative, depending on how those involved choose to approach it.

When a difference of opinion has progressed to open conflict, various conflict management strategies may be needed to resolve the issue. When a conflict management strategy is applied, all opposing parties may or may not be satisfied with the outcome. Generally speaking, if any of the parties involved are dissatisfied, the conflict will probably arise again in the future.

Some of the most common approaches used to resolve conflict include withdrawing from an actual or potential dispute, smoothing it over, compromising, enforcing a solution, and confronting the situation directly. These

Dealing with People You Can't Stand

The Tanks: Pushy and ruthless, loud and forceful, they assume that the end justifies the means.

When under attack, hold your position, make direct eye contact, focus on breathing slowly and deeply. When they finish, say, "When you're ready to speak to me with respect, I'll be ready to discuss this matter."

The Snipers: They identify your weaknesses and use them against you through sabotage behind your back or putdowns in front of the crowd.

Stop in midsentence and focus your full attention on them. Ask them to clarify their grievance. If it is valid, take action; if invalid, express your appreciation and calmly offer new information.

The Know-It-Alls: They will tell you what they know—for hours at a time—but won't take a second to listen to your "clearly inferior" ideas.

Acknowledge their expertise and be prepared with your facts. Use plural pronouns like *we* or *us*. Present your information as probing questions rather than statements so that you are less threatening and appear willing to learn from them.

The Think-They-Know-It-Alls: They don't know much, but they don't let that get in the way. They exaggerate, brag, mislead, and distract.

Acknowledge their input, but question their facts with "I" statements, such as, "From what I've read and experienced . . ."

The Grenades: When they blow their tops, they're unable to stop. When the smoke clears and the dust settles, the cycle begins again.

When the explosion begins, assertively repeat the individual's name to get his or her attention. Then calmly address the person's first few sentences, which usually identify the real problem. Suggest taking time out to cool down, then really listen to the problem.

The Yes Persons: They are quick to agree but slow to deliver, leaving a trail of unkept commitments and broken promises.

When they say yes, ask them to summarize their commitment and write it down. Arrange a weird deadline (9:11 A.M. on Thursday) and describe the negative consequences that will result if they do not follow through.

The Maybe Persons: When faced with a crucial decision, they keep putting it off until it's too late and the decision makes itself.

List advantages and disadvantages of the decision or option. Help them feel comfortable and safe, and stay in touch until the decision is implemented.

The Nothing Persons: No verbal or nonverbal feedback. They tell you nothing and stare past you as if you're not there.

Use open-ended questions that begin with *who, what, where, when* or *how*; use humor; describe negative results of not talking to you.

The No Persons: Doleful and discouraging, they say, "What goes up must come down." And what comes down must never be able to get back up again.

Ask them to critique your idea. This shows you are approaching the problem realistically and with an open mind. Listen to their feedback, fix the problems, then present the plan.

The Whiners: They wallow in their woe, whine incessantly, and carry the weight of the world on their shoulders.

Listen and write down their main points. Interrupt and get specifics; identify and focus on possible solutions. If they remain in "it's hopeless" mode, walk away saying, "Let me know when you want to talk about solving the problem."

FIGURE 8.1

Source: From Rick Brinkman and Rick Kirschner, *Dealing with People You Can't Stand,* Copyright © 1994 by McGraw-Hill, Inc. Reprinted by permission.

and other approaches can be grouped into three basic conflict management strategies:

1. **The win/lose strategy.** This approach eliminates the conflict by having one individual "win" over the other.
2. **The lose/lose strategy.** This approach eliminates the conflict by having both individuals "lose" something.
3. **The win/win strategy.** The conflict is eliminated when all parties accept a mutually satisfying solution arrived at through a step-by-step, problem-solving process.

Win/Lose Strategy

When you rely on the **win/lose strategy,** you achieve your goals at the expense of others.[6] Determining when to use this strategy depends on how severe the problem is and what results are desired from the solution. Although this approach may solve the conflict on a short-term basis, it usually does not address the underlying causes of the problem. When one person wins and the other loses, the loser is likely to resent the solution. In one sense, this approach simply sows the seeds for another conflict.

In a work setting, the strategy can be applied in two principal ways: the manager rules, or the majority rules. In the first way, the manager acts as an autocrat, deciding on the solution and stating that it is final. No feedback or discussion is permitted from those involved in the dispute; a mandate settles the matter. Indeed, the manager can threaten the security of the others if they refuse to accept the solution: "Either do as I say, or find a job somewhere else!" This approach effectively ends the debate. Other participants in the conflict are treated as "nonpersons" who have nothing to say about how the situation is resolved. If they are ignored persistently enough, they will give up, and the manager will have "won." In the second way, a vote can be taken: The majority wins. Unless the vote is unanimous, someone will be on the losing side.

When might the win/lose strategy be used? It can serve in situations where two factions simply cannot agree on any solution or may not even be able to talk to each other. A long-standing feud among workers may also be an instance where a solution may need to be imposed on all parties concerned. In such cases, the concern is not so much to maintain good human relations as it is to ensure that the work gets done.

Lose/Lose Strategy

All parties lose when the **lose/lose strategy** is used. Despite the negative overtones associated with this term, the lose/lose strategy can be called on to eliminate conflicts—again, depending on the results desired. Basically, this strategy can be applied in three ways.

First, both parties can be asked to compromise. Each person involved must "give in" to the other and must judge what degree of compromise is acceptable. When the sacrifices are too great, both parties may feel that too much has been given.

Second, an arbitrator, a neutral third party, can decide how the conflict should be resolved. This process often results in a solution being imposed on the disputing parties. The arbitration process may take from each side as much as it gives in the effort to reach a final settlement.

Third, going by the rules can also resolve a conflict, but it may not take into consideration the particulars of a case. If a worker requests more flexible working hours because he or she must arrange child care, the manager may settle the issue by quoting the company rule that everyone starts at nine and leaves at five, no exceptions. This leaves the worker worrying about child-care concerns, while the manager may lose productivity from the employee.

The lose/lose strategy can be applied when there is little time to find a solution through discussion and mutual problem solving or when the two sides cannot come to an agreement. Union-management disputes, for example, may be submitted to arbitration for a settlement, or citing the company policy manual can cut short a debate that threatens to disrupt a critical work schedule. But the basic problem may persist. Lose/lose strategies seldom address causes.

Win/Win Strategy

The basic purpose of the **win/win strategy** is to fix the problem—not the blame! Those who use this strategy listen to all points of view, define the basic issues, and create an atmosphere of trust among all involved. Everyone must believe that the problem will be settled on the merits of the case rather than through political or personal influence. The leader or mediator of the win/win process should be flexible, sensitive, patient, and calm. It is this person's responsibility to ensure that no one feels threatened or humiliated. The result of the win/win strategy will be a solution to the problem that caused the conflict — one that all parties can accept and that will enhance good human relations and help increase productivity. Table 8.1 cites the assumptions of the win/win strategy.

Almost everyone can improve his or her skills in regard to this basic strategy. Fighting to win has become an extension of the skills we learn to succeed in a world characterized by competition. The winner becomes a powerful victor and the loser a resentful victim. Their interpersonal trust is diminished. When the parties in a conflict put aside their competitive urges and their pride, it is possible to open a sincere dialogue. Mutual trust is built by striving to protect the self-esteem and self-respect of the other person.

TABLE 8.1

Assumptions of the
Win/Win Strategy

> Given these assumptions and the opportunities to act on them, conflicts can be resolved to meet the needs of all involved, if sufficient information is available.
>
> 1. People want to work together.
> 2. People can work together to solve mutual problems.
> 3. People respect each other's right to participate in decisions that affect them.
> 4. People respect each other's integrity.
> 5. People respect each other's capabilities.
> 6. People, working in the same organization, share the common goals of the group.

Source: Adapted, with permission of the publisher, from *Managing Conflict* by Donald H. Weiss. ©1981 AMACOM, a division of the American Management Association. All rights reserved.

CONFLICT MANAGEMENT STYLES

Depending on personality and past experiences in dealing with conflict in the workplace, individuals naturally develop their own conflict management styles. It would be a mistake, of course, to rely on just one style for use in all conflict situations. Robert Maddux has proposed a model of **conflict management styles** that can guide us in resolving a variety of conflicts (see Figure 8.2). The model combines two factors: degree of assertiveness and degree of co-operation. He suggests that there are five different styles resulting from various combinations of assertiveness and cooperation. Maddux takes the position that differing styles may be appropriate in different situations. He says, for example, if you must win at any cost, then the *win/lose style* may be your best option. If your goal is to maximize cooperation, even at the expense of personal goals, then the *accommodating style* would be your best choice. To select the correct style, assess each conflict situation and then decide how much assertiveness behavior and how much cooperation behavior to display. The starting point for effective use of the Maddux model is full understanding of the meaning of assertiveness and cooperation.

Assertiveness

Assertiveness is based on rights. **Assertive behavior** involves standing up for your rights and expressing your thoughts and feelings in a direct, appropriate way that does not violate the rights of others. It is a matter of getting the other person to understand your viewpoint.[7] People who exhibit assertive be-

FIGURE 8.2

Conflict Management
Styles

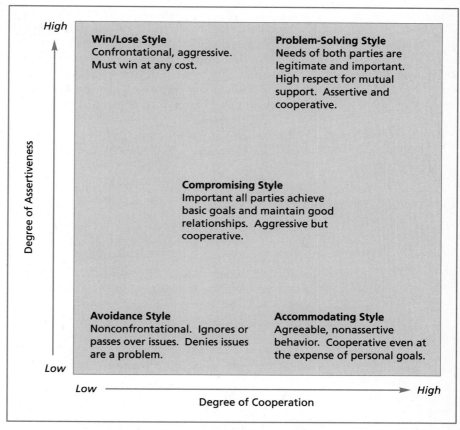

Source: Adapted from Robert B. Maddux, *Team Building: An Exercise in Leadership,* Crisp
Publications, Inc., Los Altos, CA, 1986, p. 53. Reprinted by permission of the publisher.

havior skills are able to handle their conflict situations with ease and assurance
while maintaining good interpersonal relations. Entire books are written de-
scribing assertiveness skills, so it is impossible to explain the various techniques
within the context of this short chapter. Nevertheless, we can offer two practical guidelines that may help you develop assertiveness skills.

1. *Display assertiveness when you sense someone is taking advantage of you, ignoring your needs, or disregarding your point of view.* If a coworker insists
   on playing loud music throughout the workday, which increases your tension level, it is your responsibility to communicate your frustration and try
   to resolve the problem. If you fail to take a firm position when such action
   is appropriate, colleagues may take advantage of you, and management
   may question your ability to lead.[8]

2. *Be aware of the difference between aggressive and assertive behaviors.* **Aggressive behavior** involves expressing your thoughts and feelings and defending your rights in a way that violates the rights of others. Aggressive people believe that others' rights must be subservient to theirs. They will interrupt, talk fast, ignore others, and use sarcasm or other forms of verbal abuse to maintain control. These behaviors, of course, may bring out the worst in those on the receiving end. The receivers are more likely to behave defensively, which just escalates the conflict. It is possible to make a point firmly without upsetting the other person. This can also give the other person the opportunity to change his or her behavior.

Cooperation

Cooperation is an important dimension of the conflict management process. **Cooperation** means working together toward a common end or purpose. To achieve cooperation in a conflict situation, we must draw on our knowledge of factors that contribute to effective person-to-person communication. All parties to the conflict must engage in open communication so the source of conflict is fully understood. Stephen Covey, author of *Seven Habits of Highly Effective People,* said the single most important principle he had learned in the field of interpersonal relations is *"Seek first to understand, then to be understood."*[9] To fully understand the other person's point of view, we need to apply the skills of empathic listening that were discussed in Chapter 2. This approach to listening requires patience and a willingness to avoid being judgmental when the other person is expressing his or her views. Too often people do not listen with the intent to understand; they listen with the intent to reply.[10] Instead of listening to what the other person is really thinking, many listeners are absorbed in their own thoughts about what they will say next. Empathic listening gives us the accurate information we need to resolve conflicts.

Total Person Insight

"Any method of negotiation may be fairly judged by three criteria: It should produce a wise agreement if agreement is possible. It should be efficient. And it should improve or at least not damage the relationship between the parties."

ROGER FISHER AND WILLIAM URY

Authors, *Getting to Yes*

Cooperation also involves letting the other person know what you think, feel, or want. Self-disclosure improves accuracy in person-to-person communication by taking the guesswork out of the communication process. If you describe your thoughts and feelings accurately, the result is likely to be a stronger interpersonal relationship. Keep in mind, of course, that the foundation for constructive self-disclosure is a climate of trust.

Five Conflict Management Styles

Knowledge of how to apply assertiveness and cooperation behaviors prepares us to use any of the five conflict management styles, or variations of these styles, described by Maddux. A brief description of each style follows.

Avoidance Style (Uncooperative/Nonassertive) This style is appropriate when the conflict is too minor or too great to resolve. Any attempt to resolve the conflict might result in damaging a relationship or simply wasting time and energy. Avoiding might take the form of diplomatically side-stepping an issue or postponing your response until a more appropriate time.

Accommodating Style (Cooperative/Nonassertive) This style is appropriate when resolving the conflict is not worth risking damage to the relationship or general disharmony. Individuals who use this approach relinquish their own concerns to satisfy the concerns of someone else. Accommodating might take the form of selfless generosity or blind obedience to another's point of view.

Win/Lose Style (Uncooperative/Aggressive) This style is appropriate when the conflict involves "survival of the fittest," when you must prove your superior position, or when your opinion is the most ethically or professionally correct. This power-oriented position allows you to use whatever means seem appropriate when it is time to stand up for your rights.

Compromising Style (Moderately Aggressive/Moderately Cooperative) This style is appropriate when no one person or idea is perfect, when there is more than one good way to do something, or when you must give to get what you want. Compromise attempts to find mutually acceptable solutions to the conflict that partially satisfy both sides. Never use this style when unethical activities are the cause of the conflict.

Problem-Solving Style (Assertive/Cooperative) This style is appropriate when all parties openly discuss the issues and a mutually beneficial solution can be found without anyone making a major concession. Problem solvers attempt to uncover underlying issues that may be at the root of the problem and then focus the discussion toward achieving the most desirable outcome.

> ## *Thinking / Learning Starters*
>
> 1. Imagine and describe the human relations atmosphere in an organization where win/lose strategies are consistently applied.
>
> 2. Briefly describe the most recent conflict you had with another person. How assertive were you? How assertive was the other person? Who won? Who lost? How might you have changed your conflict management style to better handle the situation?

KEY ELEMENTS OF CONFLICT RESOLUTION

When employees in an organization understand the nature of conflict and know constructive methods to resolve it, they can usually work out disagreements themselves. Let's take a closer look at the three key elements of conflict resolution: attitude adjustment, an effective leader, and a step-by-step plan.

Attitude Adjustment

Conflict triggers the emotional responses of all involved. One of the first steps toward solving a problem is to channel that emotional energy toward constructive ends by adopting the right attitudes.[11] Each person involved in the process should strive to adopt these positive attitudes.

1. Accept anger and conflict as common responses that create the opportunity to share opinions and get things done. Suggested ways to deal with your anger and the anger of others will be discussed later in this chapter.
2. Believe that there is a win/win solution to the problem, and focus on the positive results you expect from the solution.
3. Believe that a difference of opinion is healthy and beneficial, not an attack on an idea or a person.
4. Maintain an attitude of patience. Impatient people get things started. Patient people get things done.

An Effective Leader

According to Gordon L. Lippitt, former professor of behavioral science at George Washington University, leadership in resolving organizational conflict constructively requires empathy and equality but not neutrality.[12] A neutral position recognizes neither side and leaves the problem unresolved. An empathetic leader recognizes the emotions and ideas of both sides without necessarily agreeing completely with either. Equality means that everyone is treated with equal respect and consideration.

A sensitive leader also realizes that there are many reasons people are hesitant to deal with conflict openly. They may feel anxious about confronting others. They may have any one of a number of fears: of losing the acceptance of the group if they talk about their true thoughts and feelings; of taking risks; of solving one problem only to create another, more serious one; or of violating what has been termed *groupthink* — the tendency of people to conform to whatever others in a group think or feel. As a result, the leader has to foster a cooperative, nonthreatening environment in which conflicts may be addressed. Keep in mind that the person most likely to foster such an atmosphere may not be the supervisor or manager. The "leader" may well be a trusted member of the group.

A Formal Conflict Resolution Plan

Most groups have found value in having a plan to follow when dealing with emotional conflicts. A step-by-step plan helps everyone stay focused on solving the problem, saves time, and preserves the self-esteem of all involved. The plan described here has six steps.

Step 1: Define the problem.   The saying "A problem well defined is a problem half solved" is not far from the truth. It is surprising how difficult this step can be. Everyone involved needs to focus on the real cause of the problem, not the symptoms or results.

Step 2: Collect facts and opinions.   Once the parties have defined the basic problem, the next step is to gather the facts and opinions needed to understand the situation. What is the situation? What happened? Who is involved? What policies and procedures are involved?

Step 3: Consider all solutions proposed.   When the problem has been defined and the facts surrounding it have been brought out, the group should brainstorm solutions. It is important to remember that the group is not looking for one final solution but for creative ideas about solving the problem.

Step 4: Define the expected results.   Obviously, not all solutions to a problem are feasible or desirable. How does the group eliminate poor solutions and settle on the most appropriate ones? Part of the process involves focusing on the desired goals: What results should follow from solving this problem? What does the group want to see happen?

Step 5: Select the solution(s).   Which solutions will give the desired results? In light of the goals the group has set, one — or perhaps two or three — of the solutions will stand out as the most appropriate. The group can then systematically select the best solution(s) to achieve the desired goals.

Step 6: Implement the solution(s).   Establish timetables for implementing the solution(s) and provide some way to evaluate the results. On a regular basis, make a point to discuss with others how things are going. Even the best solutions can fail unless all involved make the attempt to follow them through.

ACHIEVING EMOTIONAL CONTROL

To the extent that we can become more aware of our emotions and assess their influence on our daily lives, we have the opportunity to achieve a new level of self-understanding. That greater awareness can help us avoid inappropriate behavior in conflict situations.

An **emotion** can be thought of as a feeling, such as jealousy, fear, love, joy, and grief, that influences our thinking and behavior. It would not be an exaggeration to say that much of the human behavior we observe every day springs from feelings. People are greatly influenced by pride, vanity, bias, anger, and the like.

Throughout each day our feelings are activated by a variety of events (see Figure 8.3). You might feel a sense of joy after learning that a coworker has just given birth to a new baby. You might feel overpowering grief after learning that your supervisor was killed in an auto accident. Angry feelings may surface when you discover that someone borrowed a tool without your permission. Once your feelings have been activated, your mind interprets the event. In some cases, the feelings trigger irrational thinking: "No one who works here can be trusted!" In other cases, you may engage in a rational thinking process: "Perhaps the person who borrowed the tool needed it to help a customer with an emergency repair." The important point to remember is that we can choose how we behave. In the final analysis, each of us is responsible for our own feelings.

Feelings provide us with knowledge of our current emotional condition and the energy to act out our beliefs.[13] For example, after an argument with a coworker you may experience anger over your coworker's comments or regret about your own. Feelings serve as communication links with your anger. If your feelings of anger persist or become more intense, you may be motivated to meet with the coworker and present your views more forcefully. If you feel that some of the comments you made during the argument were inappropriate, you may decide to meet with the person and apologize. Feelings are the internal directives that guide you as you make choices.

FIGURE 8.3

Behavior Is Influenced
by Activating Events

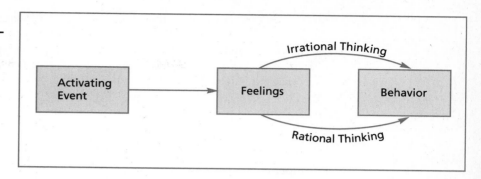

Emotional Balance

We carry inside us a large array of emotions that have been with us since birth and will be with us until death. However, we sometimes suffer from a lack of emotional balance because we learn to inhibit the expression of certain emotions and to overemphasize the expression of others. Some families, for example, discourage the expression of love and affection. Have you ever heard someone say, "In my family, no one ever gives hugs"? Some people are taught from an early age to avoid expressing anger. Others are told that a public display of grief (crying, for example) is a sign of weakness. If as a child you were strongly encouraged to avoid the expression of anger, fear, love, or some other emotion, you may repress or block these feelings as an adult.[14]

Emotional imbalance also develops if we become fixated on a single emotion. The high incidence of violent crime in America has motivated some people to become almost totally fused with the emotion of fear. One writer noted that people who are preoccupied with fear may be intensifying the problem: "We have a habit of keeping ourselves overwhelmed, through the news media, with bad and scary things that have happened all over the world each day; and then the chronic pattern of worrying about which of these bad things might happen to us in the future."[15] To focus on one emotion to the exclusion of others creates a serious imbalance within us. A person obsessed with hatred toward a specific minority group will find it difficult to display compassion toward persons who are not members of that group. The emotion of hatred can overpower and extinguish the emotion of love. The good news is that we can, with practice, take charge of our emotions. We can learn to rely more heavily on the power of rational thinking. Later in this chapter we will discuss ways to achieve greater emotional balance.

FACTORS THAT INFLUENCE OUR EMOTIONS

The starting point in achieving greater emotional balance is to determine the source of emotional difficulties. Why do we sometimes display indifference when the expression of compassion would be more appropriate? Why is it so easy to put down a friend or coworker and so hard to recognize that person's accomplishments? Why do we sometimes worry about events that will never happen? To answer these and other questions it is necessary to study the factors that influence our emotional development.

Temperament

Temperament has been described as the biological shaper of personality. It is a person's natural disposition, the beginning of an individual's identity or personality.[16] Researchers have found that certain temperamental characteristics are apparent in children at birth and remain somewhat stable over time. For example, the traits associated with extroversion and introversion can be observed when a baby is born. Of course, many events take place between infancy and adulthood to alter or shape a person's temperament. Personality at every age reflects the interplay of temperament and of environmental influences, such as parenting.[17]

Subconscious Influences

The **subconscious mind** is a vast storehouse of forgotten memories, desires, ideas, and frustrations, according to William Menninger, founder of the famed Menninger Foundation.[18] He notes that the subconscious mind can have a great influence on behavior. It contains memories of past experiences as well as memories of feelings associated with past experiences. The subconscious is active, continuously influencing conscious decision-making processes.

Although people cannot remember many of the important events of the early years of their lives, these incidents do influence their behavior as adults. Joan Borysenko offers this example:

> Inside me there is a seven-year-old who is still hurting from her humiliation at summer camp. Her anguish is reawakened every time I find myself in the presence of an authority figure who acts in a controlling manner. At those moments, my intellect is prone to desert me, and I am liable to break down and cry with the same desolation and helplessness I felt when I was seven.[19]

This example reminds us that childhood wounds can cause us to experience emotions out of proportion to a current situation. Also, we often relive the experience in a context very different from the one we experienced as a child. A worker who is strongly reprimanded by an angry supervisor may experience the same feelings that surfaced when he was scolded by his mother for breaking an expensive vase.

SALLY FORTH 1/6/95, reprinted with special permission of North America Syndicate.

Cultural Conditioning

A professor at Dartmouth College said, "Culture is what we see and hear so often that we call it reality. Out of culture comes behavior."[20] A number of cultural influences are currently having a dramatic impact on the emotional health of American children and adults. According to the National School Boards Association, U.S. schools are being hit by an epidemic of violence. About one-quarter of all students say they have been victims of violence in or near their public schools.[21] And in a recent Phi Delta Kappa/Gallup poll of public attitudes toward schools, fighting and violence represented the number-one problem area.[22]

The rate of interpersonal violence in the United States is the highest among all industrialized countries. In one category, murder by handgun, the United States stands in stark contrast to other countries: 10,667 U.S. deaths in 1990, compared with sixty-nine in Canada, eighty-seven in Japan, and ten in Australia.[23] The rise of violence and aggression among youth has resulted in a dramatic increase in teen homicide. A report from the American Psychological Commission on Violence and Youth indicates that viewing violence on television promotes an acceptance of violent acts and an increase in aggressive behavior.[24] Critics of television say a steady diet of violence glorifies conflict and desensitizes the viewer.

COPING WITH YOUR ANGER
AND THE ANGER OF OTHERS

In the presence of disagreement or conflict we often experience primary feelings such as frustration, hurt, embarrassment, guilt, or insecurity. These feelings are followed by the secondary feeling of anger. If someone strongly criticizes your work in front of coworkers, you may experience shame, alarm, or insecurity, which are primary feelings. Later, in the privacy of your office or home, you may begin to feel a strong sense of anger. You may say to yourself, "She didn't have to criticize my work in front of everybody!"

Anger is a human emotion that warns us that certain acts or words threaten our well-being and may need attention. Everyone experiences anger from time to time, but few have learned to handle it constructively. Kimes Gustin, author of *Anger, Rage, and Resentment*, says that learning to deal with your anger, and the anger of other people, is one of the most sophisticated and mature skills people are ever required to learn. Intense anger takes control of people and distorts their perceptions, which is why angry people often make poor decisions.[25]

Taking Control of Your Anger

When anger surfaces, we usually have several options. If another driver pulls out in front of your car and almost causes an accident, you will likely feel fear (a primary feeling) followed by anger (a secondary feeling). One option is to suppress the angry feelings. Another is to give way to irrational thinking and act out your angry feelings. You may be tempted to pull alongside the other driver and make a threatening gesture or shout obscenities. The consequences of this action may be quite negative. The other person may respond with further threats, and conflict may evolve to a point where violence takes place. Even if no such response occurs, you may experience feelings of guilt or embarrassment after acting out your anger in a destructive manner. It is important to learn to control angry feelings and to direct your behavior toward defusing the situation before it grows into a damaging event.

Appropriate expressions of anger can reduce your anxiety and help you get rid of unhealthy stress. An expression of anger may also improve communication because the other person learns exactly how you feel. In deciding whether to express your anger, consider these factors:

1. *Try to determine what impact your message will have on the self-esteem of the other person.* Is this person able to hear and understand your feelings without feeling threatened, inferior, or defensive?
2. *Consider the stability of the relationship between yourself and the other person.* Is the relationship strong enough to withstand the impact of your anger? Will your expression of anger evoke defensiveness, resentment, or violence?
3. *Reflect on your need to express anger.* Would it be unhealthy to suppress this anger? Are there less risky outlets for your anger? For example, your anger might dissipate after you discuss the problem with a close friend or colleague who is a good listener.[26]

Effective Ways to Express Your Anger

Buddha said, "You will not be punished for your anger, you will be punished by your anger." Intense anger that is suppressed will linger and become a disruptive force in your life unless you can find a positive way to get rid of it. Expressing feelings of anger can be therapeutic, but many people are unsure about the best way to self-disclose this emotion. To express anger in ways that will improve the chances that the other person will receive and respond to your message, consider these suggestions:

1. *Avoid reacting in a manner that could be seen as emotionally unstable.* If others see you as reacting irrationally, you will lose your ability to influence them.[27] Failure to maintain your emotional control can damage your image.

2. *Do not make accusations or attempt to fix blame.* It would be acceptable to begin the conversation by saying, "I felt humiliated at the staff meeting this morning." It would not be appropriate to say, "Your comments at the morning staff meeting were mean spirited and made me feel humiliated." The latter statement invites a defensive response.[28]

3. *Express your feelings in a timely manner.* The intensity of anger can actually increase with time. Also, important information needed by you or the person who provoked your anger may be forgotten or distorted with the passing of time.

4. *Be specific as you describe the factors that triggered your anger, and be clear about the resolution you are seeking.* The direct approach, in most cases, works best.

In some cases the person who triggers your anger may be someone you cannot confront without placing your job in jeopardy. For example, one of your best customers may constantly complain about the service he receives. You know he receives outstanding service, and you feel anger building inside you each time

---

Total Person Insight

"We all want to live sufficiently free from anger so that it isn't a problem, so that it doesn't prevent us from living successfully and harmoniously with other people and at peace within ourselves. This requires not just a philosophy, or a way of looking at things, it requires some skill-building."

KIMES GUSTIN

Author, *Anger, Rage, and Resentment*

he complains. Yet, any display of anger may result in loss of his business. In this situation you rely on your rational thinking power and say to yourself, "This part of my work is very distasteful, but I can stay calm each time he complains." Similarly, if the person who triggers your anger is your boss, and you cannot confront her without risking the loss of your job, you may have to defuse your anger in some other way. You might practice deep breathing, going for a long walk after work, or taking a few minutes out of your work to meditate.[29]

How to Handle Other People's Anger

Dealing with other people's anger may be the most difficult human relations challenge we face. Most of us are not well prepared to deal with our own anger or the anger of others. The following skills can be learned and applied to any situation where anger threatens to damage a relationship.

1. *Recognize and accept the other person's anger.* The simple recognition of the intense feelings of someone who is angry does a lot to defuse the situation.[30] In a calm voice you might say, "I can see that you are very angry," or "It's obvious that you are angry."

2. *Encourage the angry person to vent his or her feelings.* By asking questions and listening carefully to the response, you can encourage the person to discuss the cause of the anger openly. Try using an open-ended question to encourage self-disclosure: "What have I done to upset you?" or "Can you tell me why you are so angry?" When the other person is talking, never interrupt. You must be perceived as someone who is willing to take the angry person's behavior seriously.

3. *Do not respond to an angry person with your own anger.* To express your own anger or become defensive will only create another barrier to emotional healing. When you respond to the angry person, keep your voice tone soft. Keep in mind the old Biblical injunction, "A soft answer turns away wrath."[31]

4. *Encourage the angry person to discuss the specific details of his or her anger.* You might use closed-ended questions to obtain the facts you need to solve the problem: "Can you tell me why you feel the new compensation plan is unfair?" or "What problems will the transfer create for you and your family?" Getting people to talk about details is not only an effective strategy for reducing anger, it is good therapy for the person who is angry. Talking about your pain can be a liberating experience.[32]

5. *Give the angry person feedback.* After venting feelings and discussing specific details, the angry person will expect a response. You may want to describe how you see the situation. If you are at fault, accept the blame for your actions and express a sincere apology.

Sultan Gangji, an umpire at many major tennis matches, has had to learn not only how to cope with the anger expressed by frustrated tennis players, but how to keep his own anger in check. (Leo Mason/Split Second for TIME)

EMOTIONAL STYLES

A good starting point for achieving emotional control is to examine your emotional style. How do you deal with emotions? Your style started taking shape when you were a child, and it has evolved over a period of many years. As an adult, you are likely to display one of four different emotional styles when confronted with strong emotions.

Suppressing Your Emotions

Many people have learned to suppress their feelings as much as possible. Some have developed intellectual strategies that enable them to avoid dealing directly with emotional reactions to a situation. In response to the loss of a loved one, a person may avoid the experience of grief and mourning by taking on new responsibilities at work. This is not, of course, a healthy way to deal with grief. The inability to express emotions has been linked to a number of mental and physical health problems. Research indicates migraine headaches and back pain can sometimes be traced to suppressed emotions.[33] Some heart attack patients are victims of their inhibited anger. They have blocked the feeling of anger and avoided the expression of this emotion toward the person or situation that provoked the feeling.[34]

Capitulating to Your Emotions

People who display this emotional style see themselves as the helpless victim of feelings over which they have no control.[35] By responding to emotion in this manner, one can assign responsibility for the "problem" to external causes, such as other people or unavoidable events. For example, Paula, a busy office manager, is frustrated because her brother-in-law and his wife frequently show up unannounced on weekends and expect a big meal. Paula has a tight schedule during the week, and she looks forward to quiet weekends with her family. She has never expressed her anger to anyone because the uninvited guests are, after all, "family." People who capitulate to their emotions often experience feelings of helplessness and simply suffer in silence. They also may be overly influenced by other people's attitudes and opinions.

Overexpressing Your Emotions

In a work setting, everyone needs to be seen as a responsible and predictable person. Angry outbursts can damage credibility. One of the quickest ways to lose the respect and confidence of the people you work with is to display a lack of emotional control. Foul and vulgar language in conjunction with an angry outburst can seriously damage a person's image.

One acceptable way to release anger is to sit down with pen and paper and write a letter to the person who triggered your anger. Don't worry about grammar, spelling, or punctuation — just put all your angry thoughts on paper. Write until you have nothing more to say. Then destroy the letter. Once you let go of your angry feelings, you will be ready to deal constructively with whatever caused you to become upset.[36]

Accommodating Your Emotions

At the beginning of this chapter we said an emotion can be thought of as a feeling that influences our thinking and behavior. Accommodation means you are willing to recognize, accept, and experience emotions and attempt to react in ways appropriate to the situation. This style achieves an integration of one's feelings and the thinking process. People who display the accommodation style have adopted the "think before you act" point of view. Let's assume that as you are presenting a new project proposal at a staff meeting, someone interrupts you and strongly criticizes your ideas. The criticism seems to be directed more at you than at your proposal. Anger starts building inside of you, but before responding to the assailant you pause and engage in some rational thinking. During the few seconds of silence, you quickly make a mental review of the merits of your proposal and consider the other person's motives for making a personal attack. You decide the person's comments do not warrant a response at this point. Then you continue with your presentation, without a hint of frustration in your voice. If your proposal has merit, the other members of the group will probably speak on your behalf.

People who display the accommodation style take very few emotional risks. They are more likely to consider the long-term consequences of their behavior.

Do we always rely on just one of these four emotional styles? Of course not. Your response to news that a coworker was killed in an auto accident may be very different from your response to a demeaning comment made by your boss. You may have found appropriate ways to deal with your grief but have not yet learned to avoid lashing out at persons who trigger your anger. Dealing with our emotions is a very complex process. Selecting the most appropriate response can be very challenging.

Thinking / Learning Starters

1. Think about the last time someone expressed their anger to you. Were you able to respond in an appropriate way? Was the relationship between you and the angry person damaged?

2. Try to recall a situation where you either suppressed your feelings or overexpressed your feelings. How did your behavior affect the other person?

STRATEGIES FOR ACHIEVING EMOTIONAL CONTROL

We live our lives in two distinct worlds — one of fact and certainty and one of emotions and ambiguity. The world of certainty is that part of our lives that deals with objects and our rational side; the world of ambiguity deals with people and our feeling, or emotional, side — our human world. Too often we try to handle our human world in the same way that we handle our factual world.[37] Most of us are better prepared to deal with the rational side of our life because most of our previous education (formal and informal) emphasized this area. In this, the final part of the chapter, we share with you some practical suggestions for achieving greater control of the emotions that affect your life. Although emphasis is on the emotion of anger, the information presented here will help you deal with other emotions, such as fear, jealousy, hurt, and grief.

Identifying Your Emotional Patterns

We could often predict or anticipate our response to anger if we would take the time to study our emotional patterns — to take a running inventory of circumstances that touch off our anger. An easy way to do this is to record your anger experiences in a diary or journal, noting such details as when, where, with whom, and to what degree you became angry. How did you respond to the anger? How long did the feelings of anger last? If you expressed your angry feelings to the person who upset you, how did you feel afterwards? These journal entries can provide a path to greater self-awareness and help you determine changes you want to make in your emotional style.

Fine-Tuning Your Emotional Style

Once you have completed the process of self-examination and have identified some emotional patterns you want to change, it is time to consider ways to fine-tune your emotional style. Getting rid of emotional imbalances can help you to live a fuller, more satisfying life. Here are four things you can begin doing today.

- *Take responsibility for your emotions.* How you view your emotional difficulties will have a major influence on how you deal with them. If your anger is triggered by thoughts such as "I can never make my boss happy" or

Total Person Insight

"The problem with emotions is not that we experience them. Experiencing emotions is necessary for personal growth. It is part of being human. The problem comes either when we get stuck in them and can't let go or when we're not even aware that we have them."

JOAN BORYSENKO
Author, *Minding the Body, Mending the Mind*

"Things always go wrong in my life," you may never find an effective way to deal with this emotion. By shifting the blame to others, you only perpetuate the anger.

- *Put your problems into proper perspective.* Why do some people seem to be at peace with themselves most of the time while others seem to be in a perpetual state of anxiety? People who suffer from an emotional imbalance often are unable or unwilling to look at problems realistically and practically, and they view each disappointment as a major catastrophe. Some things are not worth getting upset about. When faced with unpleasant events, pause and ask yourself, "Is this problem worth getting angry about?"

- *Take steps to move beyond anger and resentment.* Some people are upset about things that happened many years ago. Some even nurse grudges against people who have been dead for years. The sad thing is that the anger remains long after we can achieve any positive learning from it.[38] Studies of divorce, for example, indicate that anger and bitterness can linger a long time. Distress seems to peak one year after the divorce, and many people report that it takes at least two years to move past the anger.[39] When anger dominates one's life, whatever the reason, therapy or counseling may provide relief.

- *Give your feelings some exercise.* Several prominent authors in the field of human relations have emphasized the importance of giving our feelings some exercise. Leo Buscaglia, author of *Loving Each Other,* says, "Exercise feelings. Feelings have meaning only as they are expressed in action."[40] Sam Keen, author of *Fire in the Belly,* said, "Make a habit of identifying your feelings and expressing them in some appropriate way."[41] If you have offended someone, how about sending that person a letter of regret? If someone you work with has given extra effort, why not praise that person's work? If you have been nursing a grudge for some time, how about practicing forgiveness?

Every day at work each of us faces some difficult decisions. One option is to take only actions that feel good at the moment. In some cases, this means ignoring the feelings of customers, patients, coworkers, and supervisors. Another option is to behave in a manner that is acceptable to the people around you. If you choose this option, you will have to make some sacrifices. You may have to be warm and generous when the feelings inside you say, "Be cold and selfish." You may have to avoid an argument when your feelings are insisting, "I'm right and the other person is wrong!" To achieve emotional control often requires restructuring our ways of feeling, thinking, and behaving.

Summary

Conflicts among people in organizations happen every day and can arise because of poor communications, value and culture clashes, confusing work policies and practices, or adversarial management. Often, however, conflicts come from coworkers who refuse to carry their fair share of the workload or have a difficult personality. While unresolved conflicts can have a negative effect on an organization's productivity, a difference of opinion sometimes has a positive effect by forcing team members toward creative and innovative solutions to the problem.

There are several approaches for dealing with conflict: win/lose, lose/lose, and win/win. Using the win/win strategy can not only resolve a conflict but also preserve effective human relations. Regardless of the strategy implemented, your ability to display assertiveness and cooperation behaviors are key factors in the effective resolution of conflicts with others. The three key elements of conflict resolution are the needs for attitude adjustment, strong, sensitive leadership, and a clear outline of the steps that need to be taken to resolve the conflict.

We carry inside us a vast array of emotions that come into play when we encounter a conflict situation. An emotion can be thought of as a feeling that influences our thinking and behavior. We sometimes experience emotional imbalance because we learn to inhibit the expression of certain emotions and overemphasize the expression of others.

Our emotional development is influenced by temperament (the biological shaper of personality), our subconscious mind, and cultural conditioning. Throughout the long process of emotional development we learn different ways to express our anger. Appropriate expressions of anger contribute to improved interpersonal relations, help us reduce anxiety, and give us an outlet for unhealthy stress. We must also learn how to handle other people's anger. It takes a great deal of effort to learn how to deal with our own anger and the anger of others.

To achieve emotional balance we need to start with an examination of our current emotional style. When confronted by strong feelings we are apt to display one of four different emotional styles: suppressing emotions, capitulating to them, overexpressing them, or accommodating them.

Emotional control is an important dimension of emotional style. The starting point in developing emotional control is to identify your current emotional patterns. One way to do this is to record your anger experiences in a diary or journal. Once you have completed the process of self-examination, you should consider appropriate ways to fine-tune your emotional style.

Career Corner

Q. I am in my mid-forties, have spent twenty-two years working my way up to supervisor of my department in a major department store, and love my job. The new thirty-one-year-old store manager has started to exclude me from memos and weekly management meetings, saying, "There's no reason for you to attend." Many of my coworkers are much younger than I, dress in jeans instead of professional suits, and seem to lack the traditional work ethic. Those of us over forty are finding it difficult to keep our mouths shut. Any suggestions?

A. It is obvious your conflict stems from a values clash that sometimes develops between older and younger workers. There also seems to be a breakdown in communication. Your younger coworkers and the store manager may be consciously or unconsciously building an "us versus them" scenario in relation to the more experienced members of the team. You need to establish communication with your store manager. Openly discuss your concerns and assertively seek an explanation for the changes that have taken place. When you allow others to ignore your needs and disregard your point of view, you display passive behaviors that will get you nowhere.

Key Terms

conflict
win/lose strategy
lose/lose strategy
win/win strategy
conflict management styles
assertive behavior

aggressive behavior
cooperation
emotion
temperament
subconscious mind
anger

Review Questions

1. What are some of the major causes of conflicts between people in organizations?
2. Discuss the positive aspects of conflict in an organization.
3. What results might you expect when you implement the win/lose strategy? The lose/lose strategy? The win/win strategy?
4. What types of attitudes can you embrace to help avoid conflicts with other people?
5. How does assertive behavior differ from aggressive behavior?
6. What is the relationship between feelings and emotion? What role do feelings play in our life?
7. What is meant by the term *emotional balance*? What factors create an emotional imbalance?
8. What four steps can improve the chances that another person will receive and respond to your feelings of anger?
9. List five skills that can be used effectively to handle anger in other people.
10. List and briefly describe four ways to fine-tune your emotional style.

Application Exercises

1. Describe a conflict that is disrupting human relations at school, home, or work. It might involve academic requirements at school, distribution of responsibilities at home, or hurt feelings at work. Identify all the people involved in the conflict, and decide who should be involved in the conflict

resolution process. Design a conflict resolution plan by following the steps given in this chapter. Implement your plan and report the results of this conflict management process to other class members.

2. To learn more about the way you handle anger, record your anger responses in a journal for a period of five days. When anger surfaces, record as many details as possible. What triggered your anger? How intense was the anger? How long did your angry feelings last? Did you express them to anyone? At the end of the five days, study your entries and try to determine whether any patterns exist. If you find this activity helpful, consider keeping a journal for a longer period of time.

Self-Assessment Exercise

For each of the following statements, circle the number from 1 to 5 that best represents your response: (1) strongly disagree (never do this); (2) disagree (rarely do this); (3) moderately agree (sometimes do this); (4) agree (frequently do this); (5) strongly agree (almost always do this).

a. When I experience conflict with others   1   2   3   4   5
   I strive to determine how much assertive
   behavior and how much cooperative
   behavior to display.

b. In my attempts to resolve conflict   1   2   3   4   5
   I strive for a solution that all
   parties can accept.

c. I am able to solve problems and make decisions 1 2   3   4   5
   in a logical manner without allowing my emo-
   tions to interfere.

d. My relationships with people at home, school, 1   2   3   4   5
   and work do not suffer because of my expres-
   sions of anger or impatience.

e. I have developed effective ways to cope with 1   2   3   4   5
   my own anger and the anger of others.

f. I am familiar with, and can apply, several   1   2   3   4   5
   strategies for achieving emotional control.

Case Problem

Protesting Obligatory Overtime

In 1994 New York City corrections officers were forced to work sixteen-hour shifts for three or four consecutive days until they demanded that the mayor cut back on obligatory overtime. A USAir, Inc., flight attendant, whose six-year-old was in bed with chickenpox, took her case to court when she was fired after arguing with the scheduler who ordered her to work overtime. Laborers at an Allegheny Ludlum Corporation steel plant called a strike against the company after some workers were required to work as much as 174 hours in two weeks.

Over the past decade, many of the nation's largest companies have eliminated 4.7 million jobs, or about one-quarter of their work force. With an improved economy and an increasing demand for consumer products and services, many organizations are now asking their downsized work force to pick up the slack. In 1994, for example, General Motors (GM), which had painstakingly eliminated 52,000 jobs over a three-year period, faced a surge in the demand for its cars. Rather than hire more workers and pay their benefits, the company decided to increase the overtime benefits of its current work force. A bonus, right? Many workers who faced twelve-hour days and six-day weeks didn't think so. Their paychecks were healthy, but their families were not. One assembly-line worker, a single mother, protested her mandatory overtime after revealing that her eighteen-year-old unmarried daughter was pregnant and her son was in counseling. She joined 11,500 other union workers in a successful strike against GM that illustrates a trend in the workplace: resistance to forced overtime.

Overtime demands are not limited to blue-collar jobs. In the white-collar world the *average* workweek is 46.5 hours; male executives average 48.2 hours. Juliet Schor, author of *The Overworked American,* reports that U.S. workers are shifting away from the desire for big paychecks that result from increased overtime and are demanding more free time. She says, "In every poll we see a larger fraction of people saying they want more time off the job." The results of a recent Gallup Poll reveal that one-third of the work force said they would take a pay cut in exchange for shorter hours.

Questions

1. Which do you value more — overtime pay opportunities or a regular forty-hour workweek that allows time for family and recreational activities? Why?
2. Would you participate in a strike or a work slowdown if your organization demanded that you work sixty hours or more each week?
3. What happens when some workers want or need the overtime pay while others do not? Is there any way to resolve this conflict with a win/win solution? How?

Chapter 9

A Life Plan for Effective Human Relations

Chapter Preview

After studying this chapter, you will be able to

1. Define success by standards that are compatible with your needs and values.

2. Learn how to better cope with life's uncertainties and disappointments.

3. Understand the forces that are influencing work schedules and leisure time.

4. Discuss the meaning of *right livelihood*.

5. Describe the four nonfinancial resources that can enrich your life.

6. Provide a rationale for adopting a healthy lifestyle.

7. List six guidelines for a healthy diet.

8. Explain the importance of physical fitness.

9. Develop a plan for making needed changes in your life.

I N THE MID-1980S, Douglas Peterson experienced the exhilaration and personal satisfaction often associated with starting a new business enterprise. With his younger brother as partner, he established Pete's Lights Incorporated, a maker of stage lighting. The business was an initial success and expanded to the point where annual income reached $1.5 million. Although the company was doing well, the relationship between Douglas Peterson and his brother began to deteriorate in the late 1980s. After a series of arguments, his brother, who was well known in the industry, left the company. Concerned about customer reaction to his brother's departure, Peterson began lowering prices. As profit margins dropped, the future of Pete's Lights was in jeopardy. Just when things were looking bad, a new client, the singing group New Kids on the Block, became a customer. This new account would add $250,000 to the company's annual sales. Unfortunately, Douglas Peterson lacked the motivation to work closely with the new client. At that point, he was tired of his work and wanted some time off. His staff had problems providing service to the new account, and finally the lighting director for New Kids on the Block terminated the relationship.[1] A valuable client was lost.

People who would give their right arm to be in Douglas Peterson's shoes have difficulty understanding his behavior. As owner of the company, why did he not do everything possible to keep the new client happy? Why did he not take a more active role in supervising the work done by his employees? Peterson's response to these questions was "I just felt bummed out about the business. I wanted to be left alone." Eventually, he was able to regain his enthusiasm for business by spending more time with employees. He found that teaching employees about various aspects of the business, and learning from employees who possessed unique technical skills, was very rewarding.[2] ■

No amount of training or education can fully prepare us for some of the experiences we will face in our careers. There will usually be some unexpected rewards and a few major disappointments. Consider the experience of Rolf Reinalda, who quit a comfortable position to take a potentially lucrative job with a struggling new firm. One year later he was out of work. With no job and no income, where do you look for self-fulfillment? Reinalda suggests you turn to family, friends, and community. After losing his job, Reinalda discovered his friends were overwhelmingly sympathetic. It took him more than three months to find a new job, but the period of unemployment was filled with worthwhile experiences. Today dinners out for Reinalda consist of potluck gatherings at friends' houses, and he is trying to be a more active citizen in the community. He recently won a seat on the local school board in Fair Haven, New Jersey. Reinalda says, "It was time to give something back."[3]

The experiences of Douglas Peterson and Rolf Reinalda remind us that our personal life and our work life are very much intertwined. The problems we experience at home (conflict with other family members, rebellion by a teenager, divorce) often have an influence on our performance at work. And a negative experience at work may influence how we feel and act away from the job.

Working for a tyrannical boss may result in stress-filled days and sleepless nights. In this chapter we help you construct a life plan that will enhance your relationships with people in your personal life and in your professional life. This plan will also help you better manage the relationship you have with yourself. We discuss the meaning of success and suggest ways to cope with major disappointments such as losing your job or being passed over for a promotion. You will learn how to avoid being trapped by a lifestyle that offers financial rewards but little else. This chapter also helps you define your relationship with money and describes the four nonfinancial resources that give meaning to life. Finally, you will learn how to develop the mental and physical fitness needed to keep up in today's frantic, fast-paced world.

TOWARD A NEW DEFINITION OF SUCCESS

Most of us have been conditioned to define success in narrow terms. Too frequently we judge our own success, and the success of others, by what is accomplished at work. Successful people are described as those who have a "good job" or have "reached the top" in their field. We sometimes describe the person who has held the same job for many years as successful. We do not stop to consider that such a person may find work boring and completely devoid of challenge.

We also measure success by movement on the career ladder. Amy Saltzman, author of *Downshifting*, notes that many people have had a tendency to set goals and measure success along a vertical career path that is often described as the "career ladder" or the "fast track." Saltzman says, "One is not successful, according to this school of thought, unless one is consistently moving up the ladder in some clearly quantifiable way."[4] Too often the person who is striving to achieve an immediate career goal (one more rung on the career ladder, for

---

Total Person Insight

"When it comes to defining a successful life in American Society, today's career professionals seem stuck between two ultimately dissatisfying extremes: dropping out completely and creating their own vision of a better world, or working within the system and speeding up their pace on the success treadmill."

AMY SALTZMAN

Author, *Downshifting: Reinventing Success on a Slower Track*

example) is forced to give up everything else that gives purpose and meaning to life. This may mean spending less time with family members and friends, spending less time keeping physically fit, abandoning vacation plans, and spending weekends at the office. Achieving the next promotion may also require numerous relocations to places dictated by company officials.

Of course, the fast track is no longer an option for many employees. According to some estimates, nearly 25 percent of all middle-management positions in corporate America were eliminated during the 1980s as companies downsized by reducing the number of layers of management.[5] The flattening of hierarchies has continued in the 1990s.

For those persons who have defined success in terms of larger paychecks earned by working overtime, the picture seems to be changing. Giving up time with friends and family, or giving up that part in the local community theater production, in return for more money seems to be less appealing to workers today. Juliet Schor, Harvard economist and author of *The Overworked American,* believes that during the next decade workers will give up income in exchange for more leisure time. She says, "People are very interested in issues like personal development, family, home and those kinds of things, so they are starting to want more from a job than just a paycheck; they're wanting flexibil-

The search for a new definition of success often requires that we spend more time on self-examination. Wisconsin Energy CEO Richard Abdoo spends some eight hours a week in reflection. (Suzanne Opton)

ity, and that usually involves time."[6] She points out that many of the people who are continually required to work overtime feel trapped.

The Need for a New Model of Success

In recent years, we have seen a growing number of people who are angry, disillusioned, and frustrated because they had to abruptly change their career plans. They gave their best efforts to an employer for ten, fifteen, or twenty years, and then the company eliminated their jobs. For years the firm said, "Take care of business and we'll take care of you," but then the situation changed. Under pressure from new global competition, hostile takeovers, and the need to restructure, companies started getting rid of loyal workers. The unwritten and unspoken contract between the company and the employee was broken. Many of those who lost their jobs suffered a crippling loss of self-esteem.[7] Amanda Bennett, in discussing the plight of middle managers who lost their jobs, says:

> It would be hard to overestimate the bitterness and anger that so many of the discarded managers feel. One manager looks back on a whole career of lunches at his desk, 12-hour days and missed evenings with his family, and says that if he had known it would end this way he would never have thought of signing on to begin with.[8]

Many of the people who lost their jobs during the past decade were once told that if they had ambition and worked tirelessly to achieve their career goals, success would be their reward. But the "reward" for many people has been loss of a job, loss of self-esteem, and anxiety about the future.

We should certainly feel sympathy for persons who have lost their jobs and watched their dreams dissolve. But there is another group of people who also merit our concern. These are the persons who put in long hours, climbed the ladder of success, and still have a job but have discovered that something is missing from their lives. These people have a good job, a regular paycheck, and in some cases an impressive title, but they do not *feel* successful. How should we feel about the person who has invested ten, fifteen, or twenty years in a job, given up all or most of his or her leisure time, given up quality time with friends and family, reached the top rung on the career ladder, and then discovered that life was empty and unfulfilling?

The traditional success model is slowly breaking down. This model defined success almost exclusively in terms of work life. The model emphasized working long hours, accomplishing work-related goals, and meeting standards often set by others. Lynn Lannon, president of the Lannon Group, a San Francisco–based consulting firm, says the old model results in "judging one's success by the standards of others, never feeling quite good enough and often feeling dissatisfied."[9]

The old model of success required us to be "one-dimensional" people. In the life of a one-dimensional person (where work is the single dimension),

everything that has meaning seems to be connected to the job. When a person defines himself or herself by a job and then loses that job, what does that person have left? This is the question raised by Robert McCarthy, an outplacement counselor who works with people who have lost their jobs. He takes the position that people who are fired may be the fortunate ones if they come to the realization that they have meaning beyond their jobs. People who are able to broaden their perspectives, develop interests beyond their jobs, and put balance in their lives will usually not only achieve more self-fulfillment but also be more valuable as employees. McCarthy says, "The more balance we add to our lives — the more interests we pursue — the more we've expanded our spheres of information, influence, and competencies."[10] The result is that we may become more appealing to prospective employers.

Total Person Insight

If I had only...
Forgotten future greatness
and looked at the green things and the buildings
and reached out to those around me
and smelled the air
and ignored the forms and the self-styled obligations
and heard the rain on the roof
and put my arms around my wife
... and it's not too late

HUGH PRATHER

Poet; Author, *Notes to Myself: My Struggle to Become a Person*

Loss of Leisure Time

The hard-working Japanese have long understood the costs associated with too much work and too little leisure time. They use the word *karoshi* to describe death from overwork. Many Americans are beginning to understand that "all work and no play" is not good for their long-term mental and physical health. Ironically, it is the competitive pressures from the hard-working Japanese, in part, that have forced American employers to demand more of their employees. The pressure to work longer, to work harder, and, in some cases, to work faster has been linked to a wide range of health problems, from coronary heart disease to fatigue caused by anxiety about work-related goals.

Since the early 1970s, we have seen a steady increase in the number of hours people work per week and a steady decline in leisure time. Some of the pressure to work long hours comes from employers who would rather pay overtime than hire more workers. This approach means the employer spends less on training and less on fringe benefits for new employees. Overtime was intended to make it more costly to employ workers for more than forty hours, but overtime is still viewed by most employers as more cost efficient. The result of this practice is that some workers are working more than they really want, while others are without work.[11]

U.S. workers spend less time on vacation than do workers in most other industrialized countries. A recent report by Hewitt Associates, an employee compensation firm, says a typical American worker with one year of service receives only ten days of paid vacation. By comparison, the same worker in Sweden,

Denmark, Brazil, and Austria would receive thirty paid days off. Companies in Germany, Britain, France, and Spain are required to give eighteen or more days of vacation to almost all employees.[12]

Developing Your Own Life Plan

The goal of this chapter is to help you develop a life plan for effective relationships with yourself and others. The information presented thus far has, we hope, stimulated your thinking about the need for a life plan. We have noted that personal life can seldom be separated from work life. The two are very much intertwined. We have also suggested that it is important for you to develop your own definition of success. Too frequently people allow others (parents, teachers, counselors, a spouse) to define success for them. Judging your success by the standards established by someone else may lead to a life of frustration.

Many people today are discovering that true success is a combination of achievements. Becoming too focused on one narrow goal may not provide the self-satisfaction you are seeking. One author makes this observation: "Everyone wants to be successful. But one person must have a personal definition of what success will feel like, and understand that true success rarely means having just one goal."[13] A narrow definition of success may actually prove to be counterproductive if it means giving up everything else that adds meaning to life.

Because work is such an important part of life, we will now move to a discussion of items that will help you in your career planning. We discuss the concept of "right livelihood."

TOWARD RIGHT LIVELIHOOD

People who watched Lee Iacocca advance rapidly through the ranks of Ford Motor Co. and then become CEO of Chrysler Corp. probably think he studied business in preparation for his executive career. In fact, he earned a bachelor's degree and a master's degree in engineering before joining Ford Motor Co. as an engineer trainee. It did not take him long to discover that he really did not want to pursue a career in engineering. In his best-selling book *Iacocca*, he explains what happened:

> I was nine months into the program (engineer trainee) with another nine to go. But engineering no longer interested me. The day I'd arrived, they had me designing a clutch spring. It had taken me an entire day to make a detailed drawing of it, and I said to myself: "What on earth am I doing? Is this how I want to be spending the rest of my life?"[14]

Right livelihood recognizes that work is a vehicle for self-expression. Geoffrey Macon used a buyout package from his former employer to pursue a deferred dream: to become his own boss. His new company, Ethnicware, is a manufacturer and distributor of Afrocentric stoneware plates, cups, and saucers. (George Selman)

Soon after that experience, he discovered that sales and marketing were his real niche in the corporate world. He loved the work and achieved success at every level as he moved up to president.

Lee Iacocca provides an example of someone who appears to have achieved "right livelihood." The original concept of right livelihood apparently came from the teachings of the Buddha. In recent years, the concept has been described by Michael Phillips in his book *The Seven Laws of Money* and by Marsha Sinetar in her book *Do What You Love . . . The Money Will Follow.* **Right livelihood** is work consciously chosen, done with full awareness and care, and leading to enlightenment. When Jason Wilson gave up a challenging business career to become a carpenter, he embraced the concept of right livelihood. He later started his own home construction business.[15] Bill Donahue felt stifled after eight years as a computer programmer at Merrill Lynch & Co., Inc. After several career-counseling sessions at New York University, he discovered he would be happier working with people than with machines. Today he is working in telecommunications.[16] There are three characteristics to right livelihood.

Right Livelihood Is Based on Conscious Choice

Marsha Sinetar says, "When the powerful quality of conscious choice is present in our work, we can be enormously productive."[17] She points out that many people have learned to act on what others say, value, and expect and thus find conscious choice very difficult:

> It takes courage to act on what we value and to willingly accept the consequences of our choices. Being able to choose means not allowing fear to inhibit or control us, even though our choices may require us to act against our fears or against the wishes of those we love and admire.[18]

Right Livelihood Places Money in a Secondary Position

People who embrace this concept accept that money and security are not the only rewards in life. Michael Phillips explains that "right livelihood has within itself its own rewards; it deepens the person who practices it."[19] Internal motivation is often the result of doing work that is personally rewarding. For example, people who work in the social services usually do not earn large amounts of money, but many receive a great deal of personal satisfaction from their work.

Many people who once viewed success in terms of wealth, material possessions, and status are finding that something is missing from their lives. They do not *feel* successful. They once felt pressured to "have it all" but now feel disappointed that their achievements have not brought them real happiness.

Right Livelihood Recognizes That Work Is a Vehicle for Self-Expression

Most of us spend from forty to fifty hours each week at work. Ideally, we should not have to squelch our real abilities, ignore our personal goals, and forget our need for stimulation and personal growth during the time we spend at work.[20] John Naisbitt and Patricia Aburdene, authors of *Re-Inventing the Corporation,* state that "in their hearts, people know that work should be fun and that it should be related to the other parts of their lives."[21] Most employees know intuitively that work should fulfill their need for self-expression, but this message has not been taken seriously by many leaders. Too few organizations truly empower workers and give them a sense of purpose. When employees feel that the company's success is their own success, they will be more enthusiastic about their work.

Marsha Sinetar says that although their jobs may differ, bicycle repair people, furniture makers, physicians, salespersons, and artists can use work as a means of self-expression and gain the satisfaction of growth and self-understanding.[22] In recent years, many people have abandoned secure, well-paying corporate jobs to start their own businesses. These entrepreneurs often report that their new businesses are a vehicle for self-expression.

What do people who choose right livelihood have in common? They are more apt to have high self-esteem and thus find it easier to make choices. They are more likely to know what they want. By contrast, persons with low self-esteem often do not know what they want out of life.[23] People who choose right livelihood are self-disciplined and have established meaningful goals. They know where they are going and feel a sense of personal happiness as they move toward the realization of their goals.[24] Persons who choose right livelihood have another characteristic in common—they have defined their relationship with money.

Thinking / Learning Starters

1. Do you agree that many people define success in terms that are too narrow? Reflect on your personal knowledge of friends and family members before answering this question.

2. In your opinion, does the concept of right livelihood seem realistic? Is right livelihood an option for everyone, or only a select few? Explain.

Defining Your Relationship with Money

Money has become a compelling force in the lives of many people. It often influences selection of a career and the amount of time and energy invested in that career. Some people are pursuing money with the misguided belief that it is the key to happiness. Melvyn Kinder, author of *Going Nowhere Fast,* says many people are on a money treadmill: "The money treadmill is built on a misconception about what money is, what it does, and what it means. We have been brainwashed into thinking money itself, once we amass it sufficiently, will bring us happiness and an end to insecurity."[25]

The money treadmill can be a trap, especially when you do not know what amount of money is enough. If you think that having *more* money is going to produce happiness or peace of mind, will you ever earn enough? Joe Dominguez, author of a popular course on the role of money in our lives, says the answer is no. He says that when you get to the level of income you have defined as "more," you will be motivated to seek a higher level of income. The danger here is that "more" does not have an endpoint.[26]

Many Americans are locked into a "work-and-spend" cycle. People go into debt to buy products they really do not need and then find it necessary to work longer hours to pay for these items.[27] As debts increase, people must give up leisure time to make more money. As the treadmill continues to roll, some people become too tired to enjoy active leisure activities such as hiking, swimming, or playing a round of golf. The alternative is involvement in less satisfying activities such as sitting passively in front of the television set. The work-and-spend cycle frequently results in a decline in the quality of life.

During the 1980s, the common view was that there would always be more money to pay off debts, and so many people reduced or stopped saving and spent more. (The personal savings rate of Americans is among the lowest in the industrialized world.) Today, we are less certain that income will rise in the years ahead. Most projections suggest only a modest gain in real income for the average worker.[28] We know that many people will likely experience a decline in their standard of living during the years ahead. For these and other reasons, everyone should define her or his relationship with that scarce resource called "money."

If you want to get more from your current income, then learn to manage your financial resources with as much efficiency as possible. The starting point is a good understanding of how much you earn and where your income is going. With a simple recordkeeping system, you can determine how much you spend each month on clothing, food, housing, transportation, and other expenses. These records will help you identify your spending patterns. Good money management also requires setting goals. If one of your goals is to retire at age fifty-five with a monthly income of $3,000, you can develop a plan to meet this goal. Goals give direction and purpose to your money management activities. Goals also motivate and encourage you as you work toward doing what is important to you.[29] When you are feeling anxious about past-due bills, and concerned about future financial obligations, your ability to maintain effective interpersonal relationships with others is hampered.

Nonfinancial Resources

If you become totally focused on your financial resources, if you have adopted the work-and-spend cycle, then chances are you have ignored your **nonfinancial**

Total Person Insight

"Most people most of the time make decisions with little awareness of what they are doing. They take action with little understanding of their motives and without beginning to know the ramifications of their choices."

M. SCOTT PECK

Psychiatrist and author, *The Road Less Traveled*

resources. And it is often the nonfinancial resources that make the biggest contribution to a happy and fulfilling life. A strong argument can be made that the real wealth in life comes in the form of good health, peace of mind, time spent with family and friends, learning (which develops the mind), and healthy spirituality. Paul Hwoschinsky, author of *True Wealth,* makes this observation about nonfinancial resources: "If you are clear about who you are, and clear about what you want to do, and bring your financial and non-financial resources together, it's extraordinary what can happen. I encourage people to really honor their total resources, and magical things happen. New options occur."[30] If you focus most or all of your attention on work, and you suffer a major work-related disappointment, then the result will likely be feelings of depression and despair. Thoughts such as "Now I have lost everything" will likely surface when you fail to get a promotion, find out that you were not selected to be a member of a special project team, or learn that your job has been eliminated. If you fully understand the power of your nonfinancial resources, then work-related disappointments are easier to cope with. The starting point is to realize that *most* of your resources are nonfinancial. During periods of great uncertainty, it is especially important that you think about your nonfinancial assets and consider ways to enhance them. We briefly discuss four nonfinancial resources that can enrich your life: physical and mental health, education and training (intellectual growth), leisure time (time for family, socializing, recreation), and healthy spirituality (see Figure 9.1).

Physical and Mental Health   Is the statement "Health means wealth" just a worn-out cliché, or is this slogan a message of inspiration for people who want to get more out of life? If good health is such an important nonfinancial asset, then why are so many people flirting with self-destruction by eating the wrong

FIGURE 9.1

Put Balance In
Your Life

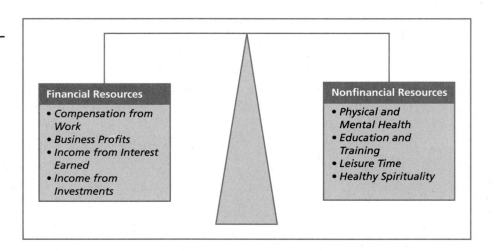

foods, drinking too much, exercising too little, and generally choosing un-healthy lifestyles? The answer to the second question may be lack of awareness of the benefits of physical fitness. Susan Smith Jones, a fitness instructor at UCLA and author of *Choose to Be Healthy,* offers these benefits of good health:

- There is an interrelationship between health and outlook on life. For exam-ple, when the physical body is fit, toned, and strong, this condition has a positive effect on the mind. We are more likely to experience higher levels of self-esteem, feel a greater sense of self-confidence, and have a more posi-tive outlook on life.
- Poor health tends to interfere with everything else in life: family harmony, work schedules, and relationships.
- Regular exercise and a healthy diet produce greater mental clarity, a higher energy level, and a more youthful appearance.[31]

Jones states that good health is something you must *choose* to have. She says, "Regardless of the lifestyle you've lived until now, you can, at any moment, choose differently."[32] If your breakfast is currently five cups of coffee and a danish, you can choose to change your diet. If you are spending thirty to forty hours a week sitting in front of a TV set, you can choose to spend that time in a different way. Your current level of health is the result of many choices made in the past. Later in this chapter we discuss ways to form new habits that will help you achieve vibrant health.

Education and Training It is sometimes easy to take for granted the time and energy required to earn a high school diploma, a certificate of completion in a technical field, a college degree, or some other form of recognition of achievement in education and training. We should view these achievements as important nonfinancial assets.

Throughout life we can continue to acquire this type of resource. With few exceptions, every job requires involvement in some form of continuing educa-tion. American Honda Motor Company, for example, offers a wide range of technical courses for auto technicians. Those persons who complete all the re-quired courses can earn the Master Technician Award. The recipients of this award enjoy not only a sense of pride but also more job security. Employees in the fields of insurance, real estate, travel services, health services, and numer-ous other areas can earn a professional designation that indicates they were willing to study long hours and complete examinations to be more competent in their work. Secretaries, for example, can earn the Certified Professional Sec-retary designation. In the insurance industry, the Certified Life Underwriter designation is an important professional achievement.

It is never too late to return to the classroom and acquire a nonfinancial asset that may enhance your life. Bobbi Erb, business manager for one of Beech Air-craft Corporation's product lines, started with the company as a billing clerk. When she began studying accounting at night, she let her supervisor know she wanted more responsibility. The company gave her more responsibilities and some promotions that were contingent on her completing the degree.[33]

Leisure Time Leisure time can provide us with the opportunity to relax, get rid of work-related stress, get some exercise, spend time with family and friends, or simply read a good book. Many people think they want more leisure time, but when it is available, they do not know what to do. Some people even feel guilty when they are not working. In her book *Downshifting,* Amy Saltzman talks about the problems Americans have with leisure time:

> The fact is, leisure today has something of a negative connotation. Having too much leisure implies we are wasting time and not working hard enough to get ahead. With so little time and so much of it devoted to professional pursuits, spending a Saturday afternoon on the front porch reading a book, talking to the neighbors or writing a letter to a friend is out of the question.[34]

If you are working for someone who is on the fast track, someone who may have given up all or most of his or her leisure time, you may be pressured to work at the same pace. If your boss is constantly trying to meet impossible deadlines and deal with last-minute rushes, you may feel the need to give up time for recreation or family. If this happens, try to identify the consequences of being overworked. Look at the situation from all points of view. If you refuse to work longer hours, what will be the consequences in terms of your relationship with the boss? Your relationship with other employees? Your future with the organization?[35] You have choices, but they may be difficult ones. If it looks like the pressure to work longer hours will never end, you may want to begin searching for another job.

What should you do if you are offered a promotion and you know the new position will require working longer hours? In a society that values getting ahead, saying no is not easy. Some organizations do not look favorably on an employee who puts personal or family considerations ahead of career choices. Turning down a promotion may damage your career with the organization. But accepting a position that you are not suited for or a position you do not want may actually make you a less valuable employee. If you are an excellent technician and love your work, should you accept a promotion to a management position? If you are an outstanding salesperson, will you be happy (and effective) in the role of sales manager? Study the consequences of the promotion in terms of how it will influence all aspects of your life.

If you want more leisure time, then you must establish your priorities and set your goals. This may mean saying no to endless requests to work overtime or rejecting a promotion. Achieving success does not always require seven-day workweeks and time away from family and friends. Lee Iacocca says, "Except for periods of real crisis I've never worked on Friday night, Saturday, or Sunday."[36] He takes pride in his ability to control his work schedule: "If you want to make good use of your time, you've got to know what's most important and then give it all you've got."[37]

Healthy Spirituality   A discussion of nonfinancial resources would not be complete without an introduction to healthy spirituality. To become a "whole" or "total" person requires movement beyond the concrete, material aspects of life to the spiritual side of the human experience. Healthy spirituality can bring a higher degree of harmony and wholeness to our lives and move us beyond self-centeredness.

   Spirituality can be defined as an inner attitude that emphasizes energy, creative choice, and a powerful force for living. It frees us to become positive, caring human beings.[38] An understanding of the many aspects of spirituality can give us an expanded vision of what it means to be human. Although spirituality is often associated with religion, it should be viewed in broader terms. Robert Coles, of Harvard Medical School, likes a definition of spirituality given to him by an eleven-year-old girl:

> I think you're spiritual if you can escape from yourself a little and think of what's good for everyone, not just you, and if you can reach out and be a good person — I mean live like a good person. You're not spiritual if you just talk spiritual and there's no action. You're a fake if that's what you do.[39]

   The words of this young girl remind us that one dimension of spirituality involves showing concern and compassion for others. It means turning away from rigid individualism and investing some time and energy in helping others. It means rolling up our sleeves and getting involved. We can enhance our spirituality through various forms of volunteer work. We might follow the example of Elliot Hoffman, cofounder of Just Desserts Inc., a San Francisco gourmet bakery. He turned a vacant lot next to his bakery into a large organic garden to be tended by the homeless and by parolees from the San Francisco County Jail. The gardeners sell the produce and share the proceeds.[40] Of course, you can display caring behaviors in less dramatic ways. Helping a stranded motorist or simply letting an elderly shopper move ahead of you in line can be a step in the right direction. By making these connections, you not only nourish your own sense of self-worth but also build the self-esteem of those you help.[41]

   Spirituality is present in people who have a zest for life and are enthusiastic about experiencing its richness. Visiting an art gallery, listening to a concert, or walking near the ocean can stimulate healthy spirituality.

   Healthy spirituality can often serve as a stabilizing force in our lives. The various twelve-step programs (Alcoholics Anonymous is one example) emphasize the need for a spiritual connection. "Working the steps" means, among other things, turning life over to a higher power. This spiritual connection seems to give hope to persons who feel a sense of loneliness and isolation. Although the spiritual component of twelve-step programs has not been fully explained by the scientific community, it is viewed as an important part of the healing process.

For many people, a commitment to a specific religion is an important dimension of their spirituality. Active membership in a religious group provides an opportunity to clarify their spiritual values and achieve spiritual direction. Although most people find this a positive psychological experience, a few develop an unhealthy form of spirituality. Leo Booth, in his book *When God Becomes a Drug: Breaking the Chains of Religious Addiction and Abuse,* states that it is possible to develop an addiction to religion. This may take the form of compulsive quoting of scriptural texts or an obsession with a particular religious practice. Religious beliefs are used by the addict to escape feelings of loneliness and low self-worth.[42]

Healthy spirituality can be a positive, enlightening force in our lives. It can grow during quiet times when we reflect on the meaning of life, meditate, pray, or enjoy nature during a long walk in the woods. We are more apt to experience healthy spirituality when we avoid self-pity and self-criticism and stay connected to others. Spirituality, according to William Sloane Coffin, has little to do with perfectionism. He says, "A spiritual person tries less to be godly than to be deeply human."[43]

Where does corporate America stand in terms of healthy spirituality? A few companies, such as AT&T, Du Pont, and Whirlpool Corporation, are taking a close look at personal growth experiences that emphasize mental and spiritual enrichment. These companies realize that almost everything in the organization is interconnected so it makes sense to emphasize harmony. Jim Channon, a consultant to these three companies, feels that a modern organization should acquire the ability to incorporate spiritual values into its culture. Jack Welch, General Electric chair, seems to agree when he says he wants his employees to feel rewarded "in both the pocketbook and the soul."[44]

As more companies accept the whole person in the workplace, healthy spirituality will grow in importance. Hyler Bracey, consultant and author of *Managing from the Heart,* said, "We used to check our feelings, health, sexuality, spirituality and family problems at the door of the workplace. We've matured enough to get beyond that. The unspeakable is now acceptable."[45]

Total Person Insight

"Take time for nurturing your wellness. If you don't take time for wellness, you are going to have to make time for sickness."

SUSAN SMITH JONES

Author and fitness instructor

DEVELOPING A HEALTHY LIFESTYLE

Earlier in this chapter we noted that a healthy lifestyle can provide a higher energy level, a greater sense of self-confidence, and generally a more positive outlook on life. People who maintain good health usually have more endurance, spend less time feeling tired or ill, and miss less work than persons who are not physically fit. Good health is receiving greater attention today because many Americans are investing more time and energy in their work. They are being asked to work longer hours and do more in less time. Good health can help combat stress and tension at work and at home.

There is another important reason to adopt a healthy lifestyle. The cost of health care is steadily increasing. The old saying "I can't afford to get sick" will be on the minds of many workers in the next decade.

The first step toward adopting a healthy lifestyle is to become well informed—to read, study, and learn what can be done to maintain your current level of health or improve your health. In this section we offer guidelines that form the framework for a good diet and a good exercise program. The second step is to determine what changes you need to make in your lifestyle and then make those changes. For many people, step one does not automatically lead to step two. Present-day Americans have access to more information about nutrition and exercise than any previous generation, but many have refused to give up poor eating habits and adopt an exercise program. When Ruth Lahmayer was hired to help IBM managers improve their eating habits, she discovered that they "don't focus on their diet because they're so focused on their jobs."[46]

Guidelines for a Healthy Diet

Eating the right foods can improve your health, boost your energy level, and in some cases extend your life. The link between health and diet is quite clear. Although we do not know enough about nutrition to identify the "ideal diet" for every person (food needs differ depending on age, body size, gender, phys-

ical activity, and other conditions), we can rely on dietary guidelines that are
suitable for most Americans.[47]

Eat a Variety of Foods   Eating a variety of foods is important because you
need more than forty different nutrients for good health: vitamins and minerals, amino acids (from proteins), essential fatty acids (from fats and oils), and
sources of energy (calories from carbohydrates, fats, and proteins).[48] If you eat
a variety of foods, you are more likely to maintain a well-balanced diet because
most foods contain more than one nutrient (see Figure 9.2).

Cut Down on Fatty Foods   The foods that are popular with many Americans
are relatively high in fat, especially saturated fat, which contributes to high
blood cholesterol levels. Many fast-food restaurant items are high in fat because
it gives menu items the flavor people often seek when eating out (see Table
9.1). Heart disease and certain kinds of cancer are by-products of a fatty diet.

FIGURE 9.2

Recommended Food
Groups and Amounts
Necessary for a
Healthy Diet

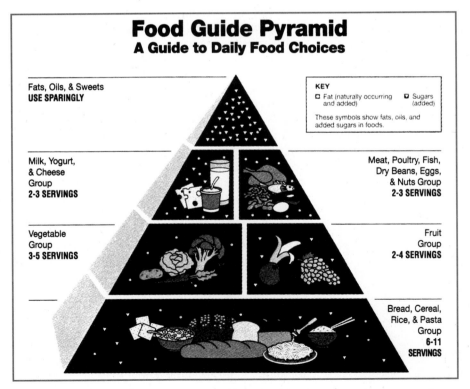

Source: U.S. Department of Agriculture/U.S. Department of Health and Human Services.

Although diet is the most important factor in lowering cholesterol, exercise can help. About ninety minutes of aerobic exercise per week along with dietary changes has been found to lower total cholesterol.

Eat Foods with Adequate Starch and Fiber   Foods high in starch, such as breads made with whole grains, dry beans and peas, and potatoes, contain many essential nutrients. Many starches also add dietary fiber to your diet. A growing number of scientists believe that high-fiber diets can help reduce the odds of getting cancer of the colon. Some cereals and most fruits and vegetables are good sources of fiber. The National Research Council recommends eating six or more servings of fruits and vegetables as well as six servings of breads or cereals each day to obtain the necessary amounts of fiber.[49]

Maintain Desirable Weight   A growing number of Americans are overweight and the problem seems to be getting worse. In 1992–93 the National Institutes of Health found that the average weight of adults, ages 25 to 30, was 171 pounds. In 1985–86, the average weight was 161 pounds for people in that age group.[50] The ten-pound weight gain over the seven-year period appears to be due to consumption of more calories and a decline in physical activity. Being overweight is associated with increases in blood pressure, blood sugar, cholesterol, and blood fats (triglycerides). To lose weight you must take in fewer calories than you burn. To do this you must either choose foods with fewer calories, become more active, or both.[51] Ideally, you should combine a low-calorie diet with appropriate exercise. Also, control overeating by eating slowly, taking smaller portions, and avoiding "seconds."

Avoid Too Much Sodium   A common by-product of excess sodium is high blood pressure. In the United States, where sodium-rich diets are very common, about one in four adults has elevated blood pressure. In populations with low sodium intakes, high blood pressure is very uncommon.[52] The recommended daily intake of sodium is 1,100 to 3,300 milligrams. It is difficult to avoid too much sodium in our diets because it is present in so many of the foods we eat and the beverages we drink. In fact, most of the sodium we consume comes from processed foods, not from the salt shakers on our tables.

If You Drink Alcohol, Do So in Moderation   Alcoholic beverages are high in calories and low in nutrients and cause serious health risks when used in excess. When alcohol is consumed in excess of one or two drinks per day, there tends to be a strong relationship between alcohol intake and high blood pressure. Excessive alcohol consumption has been linked to liver damage and certain types of cancer.[53]

TABLE 9.1

Fast-Food Restaurant Choices

	Fat (grams)	Sodium (milligrams)	Cholesterol (milligrams)	Calories
Unhealthy Choices				
Wendy's Big Classic Hamburger	33	1,085	80	570
Taco Bell's Taco Salad	61	910	80	905
Burger King's Double Whopper with Cheese	61	1,245	194	935
Hardee's Big Country Breakfast with Sausage	57	1,980	340	850
McDonalds's Quarter Pounder with Cheese	28	1,090	115	510
Healthier Choices				
Wendy's Grilled Chicken Fillet	3	330	55	100
Taco Bell's Soft Taco	12	554	32	225
Burger King's Hamburger	11	505	37	272
Hardee's Chicken 'n Pasta Salad	3	380	55	230
McDonalds's McLean Deluxe	10	670	60	320

Sources: "Nutrition Now—Eat Right at a Fast-Food Restaurant," by Denise Webb, RED-BOOK, July 1991 and A User's Guide to Fast-Food Dining, Fortune, March 11, 1991, p. 70. Copyright © 1991 by Time, Inc. All rights reserved. Reprinted by permission of Denise Webb and Fortune Magazine.

With the help of these healthy diet guidelines, you can develop your own plan for achieving a healthful diet. Keep in mind that good nutrition is a balancing act. You want to select foods with enough vitamins, minerals, protein, and fiber but avoid too much fat and sodium. You want to consume enough calories to maintain the energy level required in your life but avoid weight gain. Prior to developing your own diet plan, consider getting advice from a medical doctor or someone with expertise in nutrition.

Improving Your Physical Fitness

In terms of exercise, people often choose one of two extreme positions. Some adopt the point of view that only high-intensity activities (marathon running, high-impact aerobics) increase physical fitness. These people believe in the "no-pain, no-gain" fitness approach. The other extreme position is to become a "couch potato" and avoid all forms of exercise. Both positions should be avoided.

Physical fitness can be defined as the ability to perform daily tasks vigorously with enough energy left over to enjoy leisure activities. It is the ability to endure difficult and stressful experiences and still carry on. Physical fitness involves the performance of the lungs, heart, and muscles. Physical fitness can also have a positive influence on mental alertness and emotional stability.[54] Research indicates that we can achieve and maintain physical fitness with a moderate exercise program. For most people, a program that involves regular physical activity at least three times a week and includes sustained physical exertion for twenty to thirty minutes is adequate.[55] This modest investment of time and energy will give you a longer and healthier life.

You do not need to become an obsessive fitness fanatic to achieve lifesaving benefits from exercise. Start slowly with an activity you feel you will enjoy, such as those that follow.

Walking   In recent years, walking has become the nation's leading form of exercise. It is a safe, inexpensive way to make your heart stronger, decrease body fat, and give your mood an "uplift." When you feel tense, unable to think clearly, or depressed, take a walk. The calories burned per mile during a brisk walk are 100 (about the same as running), and you will use more than half the body's 650 muscles.[56]

Swimming   Many people swim for fitness and fun. If you swim at the proper intensity for at least twenty to thirty minutes, three times a week, you will develop a stronger heart and increase your resistance to fatigue. Swimming will also help you control your weight and reduce your muscle tension and stress level. You can burn from 150 to 400 calories during a half-hour swim.[57]

Jogging   Some people begin a walking program and then start jogging. Jogging will usually get your heart rate up to the prescribed level quicker than walking. But jogging without proper conditioning and warmups can put too much stress on your joints and may result in injuries. Some people do their jogging on a treadmill.

Walking, swimming, and jogging provide examples of aerobic exercise. When we engage in aerobic exercise, the body is required to improve its ability to handle oxygen.[58] These exercises strengthen the heart, burn up calories, increase stamina, and help release tension. Other examples of aerobic exercise are running, cross-country skiing, rope skipping, skating, rowing, and bicycling.

Some people find it easier to stay with an exercise program that includes a variety of fitness activities, such as swimming, walking, and weight training. This approach helps exercise the whole body and avoid the boredom that sometimes comes with the same exercise.[59]

If you are younger than thirty-five and in good health, you probably do not need to see a doctor before beginning an exercise program. If you are older than thirty-five and have been inactive for several years, consult your doctor before engaging in vigorous exercise.[60]

PLANNING FOR CHANGES IN YOUR LIFE

Throughout this book we have emphasized the concept that you can control your own behavior. In fact, during these turbulent times changes in your behavior may be one of the few things under your control. If making changes in your life seems to be a logical course of action at this point, then it is time to do some planning. The starting point is to clearly identify the personal growth goals that can make a difference in your life. What are some behaviors you can adopt (or alter) that will make an important positive change in your life? Once you have identified these behaviors, you can set goals and do what is necessary to achieve them. At the end of Chapter 1, you were encouraged to complete the self-assessment exercise at the end of each chapter. If you completed these exercises, then you no doubt gained awareness of your strengths and a better understanding of those abilities you want to improve.

The Power of Habits

Before we discuss specific goal-setting methods, let us take a look at the powerful influence of habits. Some habits, like taking a long walk three or four times a week, can have a positive influence on our well-being. Simply saying, "Thank you" when someone does a favor or pays a compliment can be a habit. Other habits, such as smoking, never saying no to requests for your time, feeling jealousy, or constantly engaging in self-criticism, are negative forces in our lives. Stephen Covey, author of *The Seven Habits of Highly Effective People*, makes this observation: "Habits are powerful factors in our lives. Because they are consistent, often unconscious patterns, they constantly, daily, express our character and produce our effectiveness . . . or ineffectiveness."[61]

Breaking deeply embedded habits, such as impatience, procrastination, or criticism of others, can take a tremendous amount of effort. The influences supporting the habit, the actual root causes, are often repressed in the subconscious mind and forgotten.[62] How do you break a negative habit or form a positive habit? The process involves five steps.

Motivation Once you are aware of the need to change, you must develop the willingness or desire to change. Habits can be learned and unlearned, but changing them requires a major commitment.[63] Most of us will not make changes just because others say we should. We must decide for ourselves why we need to change and what benefits we will gain. A positive attitude toward the change is what motivates us to take action.

Knowledge Once you clearly understand the benefits of breaking a habit, or forming a new one, you must acquire the knowledge you need to change. Seek information, ask for advice, or learn from the experiences of others. This may involve finding a mentor, joining a group, or gathering sufficient material and teaching yourself. For example, suppose you decide you need to lose weight. Your first step might be to visit a bookstore and buy one or two books on weight-reduction practices. Let us assume the books help, but you discover that reading is not enough. Your next step might be to talk with others who share the same goal. You might join a support group or just get together with two or three others who also want to lose weight. You might choose to see a counselor or an expert in nutrition if the process of change seems too difficult. In the process of acquiring information, you are actually gaining a better understanding of the habit you want to learn or unlearn.

Practice Information is only as useful as you make it. This means that you must *practice* what you have learned to change your behavior. If you are a shy person, does this mean you need to volunteer to make a speech in front of several hundred people? The answer is no. Although there is always the rare individual who makes a major change seemingly overnight, most people find that the best and surest way to develop a new behavior is to do it gradually. This is particularly true if you feel a lot of anxiety about changing. Take your time. Allow yourself to ease into your new behavior until you feel comfortable with it. Breaking negative habits can give you more freedom in your life. And as you break old habits, or form new ones, your self-confidence increases.

Feedback Whenever you can, ask for feedback as you attempt to change a habit. You will find that your progress will be much faster than if you use only the trial-and-error method. Everyone has blind spots, particularly when trying out something new. You will often need to rely on the feedback of others to tell you when you are off course or when you have really changed — sometimes you are too close to the process to tell.

Reinforcement When you see yourself exhibiting the type of behavior you have worked to develop — or when someone mentions that you have changed — reward yourself! The rewards can be simple, inexpensive ones — treating yourself to a movie, a bouquet of flowers, a favorite meal, or a special event. This type of reinforcement is vital when you are trying to improve old behaviors or develop new ones. Do not postpone rewarding yourself until the goal is reached. Intermediate success is just as important as the final result.

The Goal-Setting Process

Many years ago J. C. Penney, founder of the large retail chain, made a strong statement regarding the value of having goals: "Give me a stock clerk with a goal, and I will give you a man who will make history. Give me a man without a goal, and I will give you a stock clerk."[64] Penney recognized that it is goals that give direction to our lives. Goals provide a focus for our energy.

Many people avoid setting goals because they do not understand the importance of this self-improvement method. Others do not know how to set goals. Setting and achieving goals can contribute to our overall effectiveness. As we make and keep commitments to ourselves, we begin to establish an inner integrity that gives us the awareness of self-control. With the awareness of self-control comes the strength to accept more of the responsibility for our own lives.[65]

Goals should be an integral part of your plan to break old habits or form new ones. At this point in your life, goal setting may not be easy because you may be faced with unlimited goal-setting possibilities. This can almost become an excuse for doing nothing. After all, where do you begin? We hope that reading the previous chapters in this book, completing the self-assessment exercises, and reviewing the material in this chapter will help you narrow the possibilities.

The goal-setting process requires that you be clear about what you want to accomplish. If your goal is too general or vague, progress toward achieving that goal will be difficult to observe. Goals such as "I want to be a success" or "I desire good health" are much too general. The more specific the goal, the more easily you will be able to achieve it.[66]

A very important step in the goal-setting process is to put the goal in writing. Kazuo Wada, chair of the retail giant Yaohan International Group, strongly recommends written goals. He says, "If you write down a goal, it becomes part of your consciousness."[67] His approach is to put his goals in writing again and again until he achieves them. Although the power of written goals is widely recognized, many people do not put their goals in writing. A written goal, reviewed daily, is much more likely to be achieved. Achieving your goals will usually require hard work and effort over a period of time. The process of achieving your goals, however, can be very rewarding.

THE CHOICE IS YOURS

Are you ready to develop a life plan for effective human relations? We hope the answer is yes. One of the positive aspects of personal planning is that you are making your own choices. You decide what kind of person you want to be and then set your own standards and goals. The results can mean not only career advancement and financial benefits but also the development of strong, satisfying relationships with others. These relationships may be the key to future opportunities, and you in turn may be able to help others achieve their goals.

In the opening chapter of this text, we talked about the total person approach to human relations. By now, we hope you realize that you are someone special! You have a unique combination of talents, attitudes, values, goals, needs, and motivation—all in a state of development. You can decide to tap your potential to become a successful, productive human being, however *you* understand those terms. We hope this book helps you develop your human relations skills and become what you want to be. You can turn the theories, concepts, and guidelines presented here into a plan of action for your own life and career. We wish you the best!

Summary

The traditional definitions of success that most of us know are too confining. They view success almost entirely in terms of measurable job achievements. These definitions leave out the intangible successes to be had in private and in professional life.

Many people today are discovering that true success is a combination of achievements. Achieving right livelihood is one important dimension of success. Right livelihood is work consciously chosen, done with full awareness and care, and leading to enlightenment. Right livelihood is based on conscious choice. Although right livelihood recognizes that work is a vehicle for self-expression, it is a concept that places money in a secondary position. People who choose right livelihood are more apt to have high self-esteem, to be self-disciplined, and to have established meaningful goals.

A person's nonfinancial resources make one of the biggest contributions to a happy and fulfilling life. Each of us has four nonfinancial resources that can enrich our lives: physical and mental health, education and training (intellectual growth), leisure time (time for family, socializing, recreation), and healthy spirituality. These nonfinancial resources can be acquired throughout our lives.

Many Americans are working to achieve healthy lifestyles. Healthy lifestyles can give us a higher energy level, a greater sense of self-confidence, and generally a more positive outlook. People who maintain good health usually have more endurance, spend less time feeling tired or ill, and miss less work than persons who are not physically fit.

Planning for changes in your life often requires breaking negative habits or forming positive habits. The process of breaking habits and forming new ones involves five steps: motivation, knowledge, practice, feedback, and reinforcement. Goal setting is also an integral part of a successful plan to make changes.

Unspecified or vague goals are harder to reach and contribute less than they could to a productive, enriching life.

Career Corner

Q. I work for a large company and have a terrific job. Because of downsizing, all of us in the office are working sixty-hour weeks to get the work done. I take work home and do the work four people used to do. By the end of the week my mind is numb, my productivity is down, and I am exhausted. This not only is hard on my family but is bad for the company. It seems that if the work can't be handled during a normal workweek, then we need to hire more people to do the job. What do you suggest?

A. If you can get another job with no trouble, do it! If you feel lucky to have your job, then let your boss know that you need help. Gather your colleagues together and present your case. Set limits at work and quit taking work home. Perhaps this will allow you to be more productive at work. Don't accept an unreasonable amount of work because you are afraid you will be laid off. A job that is causing you to burn out is not worth it.

Key Terms

right livelihood   spirituality
nonfinancial resources   physical fitness

Review Questions

1. What have been the traditional criteria used to measure success? What are some of the reasons we need a new model for success in our society?
2. Explain the reasons many Americans have experienced a decline in leisure time.
3. What does the term *right livelihood* mean? What are the common characteristics of right livelihood?
4. What is the meaning of the *work-and-spend cycle*?
5. List and describe the four nonfinancial resources.
6. M. Scott Peck in the Total Person Insight says most people make decisions with little awareness of what they are doing. Do you agree or disagree with his point of view?
7. What are the major reasons we should adopt a healthy lifestyle?
8. List and describe the guidelines for a healthy diet.
9. Provide a brief description of physical fitness. Why is physical fitness so important in the life of a typical worker?
10. What are the five steps involved in breaking a negative habit or forming a positive habit?

Application Exercises

1. In recent years, it has become popular for organizations to develop a mission statement that reflects their philosophy and objectives. The Lotus Operating Principles prepared by Lotus Development Corp. (Chapter 6) provides an example of a mission statement. Prepare a personal mission statement that reflects your goals and aspirations for a successful life. Your mission statement should cover the roles of financial and nonfinancial resources in your life.

2. Throughout this chapter you were encouraged to take control of your life and establish your own definition of success. This chapter has a strong "all development is self-development" theme. Can we really control our own destinies? Can we always make our own choices? Mike Hernacki, author of the book *The Ultimate Secret of Getting Absolutely Everything You Want,* says yes:

> To get what you want, you must recognize something that at first may be difficult, even painful to look at. You must recognize that *you alone* are the source of all the conditions and situations in your life. You must recognize that whatever your world looks like right now, you alone have caused it to look that way. The state of your health, your finances, your personal relationships, your professional life—all of it is *your* doing, yours and no one else's.[68]

Do you agree with this viewpoint? Take a position in favor of or in opposition to his statement. Prepare a short one- or two-paragraph statement that expresses your views.

Self-Assessment Exercise

For each of the following statements, circle the number from 1 to 5 that best represents your response: (1) strongly disagree (never do this); (2) disagree (rarely do this); (3) moderately agree (sometimes do this); (4) agree (frequently do this); (5) strongly agree (almost always do this).

a. I try to maintain balance in my life by avoiding addiction to work and by engaging in leisure-time activities.　1　2　3　4　5

b. I envision my existence in a larger context and view healthy spirituality as a positive, enlightening force in my life.　1　2　3　4　5

c. I avoid rigid individualism (self-centered behavior) by investing time and energy in helping others.　1　2　3　4　5

d. I seek advice and counsel from friends, coworkers, and professionals in order to cope with life's problems.　1　2　3　4　5

e. I stay connected with family and friends   1   2   3   4   5
   and monitor the development of my
   nonfinancial resources carefully.

f. I have established well-thought-out, realistic   1   2   3   4   5
   goals for my life, and these goals are tied
   to my values.

Select an appropriate attitude or skill you would like to improve. Write
your goal in the space provided.

GOAL: _____

_____

_____

Case Problem   ## It's a Matter of Choice

As one of the top-ranking women builders in the nation, Julia Stasch insists
that women be given the same chance as men to succeed or fail on the
job. Her company has completed over $775 million worth of projects since
1990, and it employs about three times as many construction women as the
industry average. Stasch's professional career spans jobs such as being a Vista
volunteer on a Native American tribal reservation, a high school history
teacher, a secretary, and now the president of Stein & Co., a major Chicago
development firm. Along the way she and her husband, a professor at Loyola
University, made the conscious decision not to have any children. "I wouldn't
be where I am today if I'd made the decision to have a family," Stasch says.

Many men seeking a more nontraditional role are placing their relationship
with their children on a par with, or even above, their career goals. They may
delay career advancement while their children are young to be able to spend
more time with them. Magazine editor Robert Barker chose to cut his workweek and paycheck by two-fifths to share child-care responsibilities for his
infant daughter with his working wife. He joined the slower-paced "daddy-
track." After one year, the announcement of his wife's second pregnancy, and
a reorganization at work, he returned to his job full time only to find his career
goals and mind-set had been permanently altered. When offered a promotion,
he turned it down, knowing he wanted to be able to spend more time with his
family.

Newspaper editor Mary Newsom discovered a richer life after the birth of
her daughter and during her subsequent maternity leave. She found time in
the grocery store to speak to strangers who stopped to admire her baby and
she spent leisurely afternoons with neighbors and their infants. As she began to
acknowledge this slower pace, she admitted, "Not once did I hear a droning

deep in my head, the insistent buzz of tasks undone. . . . Time had become a sweetly flowing river, not the downhill rapids I once knew. . . . Only because I hadn't poured the last ounce of my spirit into my job was I able to make those simple connections with people."

Questions

1. How do you feel about the choices each of these individuals made? Do you believe you would feel the same way if you were placed in similar situations?
2. Under what circumstances would you say no to professional demands in favor of family demands?
3. Discuss the comment Mary Newsom made about pouring your last ounce of spirit into your job. How might this degree of dedication affect your human relationships at home and at work?

Notes

Chapter 1

1. Kenneth Labich, "Is Herb Kelleher America's Best CEO?" *Fortune,* May 2, 1994, p. 50.
2. Robert Levering and Milton Moskowitz, *The 100 Best Companies to Work for in America* (New York: Currency-Doubleday, 1993), p. 414.
3. Perry Pascarella, *The New Achievers* (New York: Free Press, 1984), p. x.
4. John A. Byrne, "The Pain of Downsizing," *Business Week,* May 9, 1994, pp. 60–69.
5. Jaclyn Fierman, "The Contingency Work Force," *Fortune,* January 24, 1994, pp. 30–34.
6. Karl Albrecht and Ron Zemke, *Service America* (Homewood, Ill.: Dow Jones–Irwin, 1985), p. 31.
7. Stephen B. Shepard, "Defining the Q-Word," *Business Week* (Quality Edition), 1991, p. 4.
8. "Questing for the Best," *Business Week* (Quality Edition), 1991, p. 8.
9. Alan Deutschman, "How H-P Continues to Grow and Grow," *Fortune,* May 2, 1994, p. 100.
10. Lynn Summers and Ben Rosen, "Mavericks Ride Again," *Training & Development,* May 1994, pp. 119–124.
11. Bob Filipczak, "It's Just a Job — Generation X at Work," *Training,* April 1994, pp. 21–27.
12. Frank Rose, "A New Age for Business?" *Fortune,* October 8, 1990, p. 162.
13. Marilyn Loden and Judy B. Rosener, *Workforce America!* (Homewood, Ill.: Business One Irwin, 1991), p. 23.
14. "Miles Traveled, More to Go," *Business Week/Quality,* 1991, p. 71.
15. Keith Davis, *Human Behavior at Work* (New York: McGraw-Hill, 1982), p. 12.
16. Teri Lammers Prior, "If I Were President . . . ," *Inc.,* April 1995, pp. 56–60.
17. Lisa Genasc, "The Best Place for Moms to Work," *Roanoke Times,* September 17, 1995, p. G-2.
18. Rebecca Wells Windinwood, "World Class Under Glass," *Destinations,* September 1990, pp. 14, 15; Robert Levering and Milton Moskowitz, *The 100 Best Companies to Work for in America* (New York: Plume, 1994), p. 234.
19. "Who Wins and Why," *Inc.,* April 1987, p. 103.
20. Laurie Hays, "Gerstner Is Struggling as He Tries to Change Ingrained IBM Culture," *Wall Street Journal,* May 13, 1994, p. 1.
21. Taken from a Ford Motor Company wallet card titled "Company Mission, Values, and Guiding Principles."
22. *Ibid.*
23. Alice G. Sargent, *The Androgynous Manager* (New York: AMACOM, 1980), p. viii (introduction by Elsa Porter).
24. D. R. Hampton, C. E. Summer, and R. A. Webber, *Organizational Behavior and the Practice of Management* (Glenview, Ill.: Scott, Foresman, 1973), p. 215.
25. J. David McCracken and Ana E. Falcon-Emmanuelli, "A Theoretical Basis for Work Values Research in Vocational Education," *Journal of Vocational and Training Education,* Spring 94, p. 7.
26. Betsy Jacobson and Beverly Kaye, "Balancing Act," *Training & Development,* February 1993, p. 26.
27. Roy W. Walters, "Improving Man/Machine Interface for Greater Productivity," *BNAC Communicator,* Summer 1982, p. 13.
28. Rochelle Sharpe, "Work Week," *Wall Street Journal,* September 26, 1995, p. A-1.
29. Jacobson and Kaye, "Balancing Act," pp. 24–26.
30. Sue Shellenbarger, "Dad Takes Home a Tough Day at Work," *Wall Street Journal,* June 29, 1994, p. B-3.
31. Rochelle Sharpe, "Labor Letter," *Wall Street Journal,* September 13, 1994, p. 1.
32. Sue Shellenbarger, "Keeping Workers by Reaching Out to Them," *Wall Street Journal,* June 1, 1994, p. B-1.
33. Levering and Moskowitz, *The 100 Best Companies to Work for in America,* p. 211.
34. Salvador Minuchin and Michael P. Nichols, *Family Healing* (New York: Free Press, 1993), pp. 35–47.
35. For a detailed examination of the Hawthorne criticisms and the legacy of the Hawthorne research, see David A. Whitsett and Lyle Yorks, *From Management Theory to Business Sense* (New York: American Management Associations, 1983).
36. Thomas J. Peters and Robert H. Waterman, Jr., *In Search of Excellence: Lessons from America's Best-Run Companies* (New York: Harper & Row, 1982), p. 14.
37. John R. Diekman, *Human Connections* (Englewood Cliffs, N.J.: Prentice-Hall, 1982), p. xii.
38. Stephen R. Covey, *The Seven Habits of Highly Effective People* (New York: Simon & Schuster, 1989), pp. 66–67.
39. John A. Byrne, "Wharton Rewrites the Book on B-Schools," *Business Week,* May 13, 1991, p. 43.

40. Robert Bolton and Dorothy Grover Bolton, *Social Style/Management Style* (New York: American Management Associations, 1984), p. 4.

41. "William Ouchi on Trust," *Training and Development Journal*, December 1982, p. 71.

Chapter 2

1. Robert Levering and Milton Moskowitz, *The 100 Best Companies to Work for in America* (New York: Currency-Doubleday, 1993), p. 419.

2. *Ibid.*, p. 420.

3. *Ibid.*, p. 421.

4. "Effective Listening Skills," *Women in Business*, March-April 1994, p. 28.

5. John Stewart and Gary D'Angelo, *Together — Communicating Interpersonally* (New York: Random House, 1988), p. 5.

6. "Keep in Touch," *Inc.*, October 1989, p. 131.

7. Stewart and D'Angelo, *Together — Communicating Interpersonally*, p. 14.

8. "Tom Chappell — Minister of Commerce," *Business Ethics*, January-February 1994, p. 18.

9. "Sunny Side Up," *Inc.*, January 1990, p. 104.

10. Ronald Henkoff, "Make Your Office More Productive," *Fortune*, February 25, 1991, p. 73.

11. Sy Lazarus, *Loud and Clear* (New York: AMACOM, 1974), p. 3.

12. Brian Hickey, "Throwing the Book at Legalese," *TWA Ambassador*, June 1990, p. 86.

13. "A Learner's Guide to Corpo-Babble," *Business Week*, March 7, 1994, pp. 41–42.

14. Roger E. Axtell, ed., *Do's and Taboos Around the World*, compiled by Parker Pen Company, 3rd ed. (New York: John Wiley & Sons, 1993), p. 155.

15. Judith C. Tingley, *Genderflex: Men and Women Speaking Each Other's Language at Work* (New York: AMACOM, 1994), p. 10.

16. Deborah Tannen, *You Just Don't Understand* (New York: Ballantine Books, 1991), p. 42.

17. Tingley, *Genderflex*, p. 33.

18. Allan Pease, *Signals: How to Use Body Language for Power, Success and Love* (New York: Bantam, 1984), p. 15.

19. Albert E. Scheflen, *Body Language and Social Order* (Englewood Cliffs, N.J.: Prentice-Hall, 1972), pp. xii—xiii.

20. "Server Posture Affects How We Tip," *The Menninger Letter*, November 1993, p. 5.

21. Janet G. Elsea, *The Four Minute Sell* (New York: Simon & Schuster, 1984), p. 34.

22. Leslie Smith, "Don't Ignore Body Langage," *Executive Female*, November-December, 1993, p. 54.

23. "The Anatomy of a Message," *Ford's Insider*, 1981, pp. 4, 9.

24. Axtell, *Do's and Taboos Around the World*, p. 46.

25. *Ibid.*, p. 47.

26. *Ibid.*, p. 49.

27. Cheryl Hamilton, *Communicating for Results* (Belmont, Calif.: Wadsworth, 1990), p. 48.

28. Susan Mundale, "Why More CEO's Are Mandating Listening and Writing Training," *Training/HRD*, October 1980, pp. 40–41.

29. Camille Wright Miller, "Working It Out," *Roanoke Times & World-News*, May 8, 1994, p. F4.

30. Thomas Koziol, "Listening . . . A Lost Skill?" *Hot Buttoneer*, August 1984, p. 1.

31. C. Glenn Pearce, "How Effective Are We as Listeners?" *Training & Development*, April 1993, pp. 79–80.

32. Tom Winninger, "Selling from the Subconscious," *American Salesman*, November 1981, p. 17.

33. Joseph A. DeVito, *The Interpersonal Communication Book*, 4th ed. (New York: Harper & Row, 1986), p. 52.

34. Donna Deepose, "Listen Your Way to Better Management," *Supervisory Management*, May 1993, pp. 7–8.

35. C. Glenn Pearce, "Learning How to Listen Empathically," *Supervisory Management*, September 1991, p. 11.

36. *Ibid.*

37. James G. Carr, "Dare to Share," *Pace*, June 1988, p. 22.

38. Hendrie Weisinger and Norman Lobsenz, *Nobody's Perfect — How to Give Criticism and Get Results* (Los Angeles: Stratford Press, 1981), p. 39.

39. Charlene Marmer Solomon, "Global Operations Demand That HR Rethink Diversity," *Personnel Journal*, July 1994, p. 44.

40. Jeremy Main, "How 21 Men Got Global in 35 Days," *Fortune*, November 6, 1989, p. 71.

41. M. Strangelove, "The Essential Internet: The Birth of Virtual Culture and Global Community," *Online Access*, August 6, 1993, pp. 28–30.

42. "Businesses Being Built Without Bricks, Mortar," *Springfield News-Leader*, April 28, 1994, p. 1B.

43. Diane Lewis, "Modem Can Link, or Chain, Worker to Office," *Boston Sunday Globe*, July 18, 1993, p. 12.

44. Ginger Trumfio, "Liberty, Equality, E-mail!" *Sales & Marketing Management*, March 1994, p. 38.

Chapter 3

1. Ron Zemke, "Custom Service as a Performing Art," *Training*, March 1993, p. 40.

2. Robert Levering and Milton Moskowitz, *The 100 Best Companies to Work for in America*, (New York: Currency-Doubleday, 1993), p. 398.

3. Alex Taylor, III, "Bla Car, Bad Book," *Fortune*, November 29, 1993, p. 17.

4. "A Matter of Attitude," *Royal Bank Letter*, May-June 1994, p. 2.

5. Jerome Kagan, *Psychology: An Introduction* (New York: Harcourt Brace Jovanovich, 1984), p. 558.
6. Wayne F. Cascio, *Costing Human Resources* (Boston: PWS-Kent Publishing, 1991), p. 130.
7. *Ibid.,* p. 131.
8. Marilyn Vos Savant, "Ask Marilyn," *Parade Magazine,* July 8, 1990, p. 22.
9. Bernie S. Siegel, *Love, Medicine and Miracles* (New York: Harper & Row, 1986), p. 26.
10. Myrna Lewis, "How Your Attitude Affects Your Health," *New Choices,* March 1994, p. 92.
11. Kagan, *Psychology,* p. 548.
12. "Tailored Health Plans Take Off," *Fortune,* June 27, 1994, p. 12.
13. Denis Waitley, *The Positive Parent* (Cedar Falls, Iowa: Advanced Learning, 1987), p. 16.
14. Barbara A. Meyer, "Role Modeling: Rewards and Responsibilities," *Delta Kappa Gamma Bulletin,* Winter 1982, p. 48.
15. Dennis T. Jaffee and Cynthia D. Scott, "Bridging Your Workers' Motivation Gap," *Nation's Business,* March 1989, p. 30.
16. William F. Schoell and Joseph P. Guiltinan, *Marketing,* 5th ed. (Boston: Allyn and Bacon, 1992), pp. 166–167; William M. Pride and O. C. Ferrell, *Marketing,* 6th ed. (Boston: Houghton Mifflin, 1989), p. 39.
17. Michael R. Quinlan, "How Does Service Drive the Service Company?" *Harvard Business Review,* November-December 1991, p. 156.
18. Levering and Moskowitz, *The 100 Best Companies,* pp. 102–106.
19. Jennifer J. Laabs, "Ben & Jerry's Caring Capitalism," *Personnel Journal,* November 1992, pp. 51–52.
20. Shawn Cavenee, "Spiritual Doctor Sets Up Shop," *Collegiate Times,* February 20, 1990, p. A-6.
21. Charles C. Manz and Henry P. Sims, Jr., *Super-Leadership* (New York: Prentice-Hall, 1989), pp. 13–23.
22. Anthony P. Carnevale, Leila J. Gainer, and Ann S. Meltzer, *Workplace Basics Training Manual* (San Francisco: Jossey-Bass, 1990), p. 3.
23. David Holzman, "When Workers Run the Show," *Working Woman,* August 1993, p. 74.
24. "Managing Diversity," *Inc.,* January 1993, p. 33.
25. Martin Seligman, *Learned Optimism* (New York: Alfred A. Knopf, 1991), p. 4.
26. *Ibid.,* pp. 218–219, 233.
27. Phil Catalfo, "Buckminster Fuller — the 50-Year Experiment," audiotape (San Francisco: New Dimensions Foundation, 1988).
28. James Allen, *As a Man Thinketh* (New York: Keenan Press, 1910).
29. Robert F. Mager, *Developing Attitudes Toward Learning* (Belmont, Calif.: Fearon-Pitman, 1968), p. 47.
30. Quoted in Nancy W. Collins, Susan K. Gilbert, and Susan Nycum, *Women Leading: Making Tough Choices on the Fast Track* (Lexington, Mass.: Stephen Greene Press, 1988), p. 1.
31. John Naisbitt and Patricia Aburdene, *Re-Inventing the Corporation* (New York: Warner Books, 1983), p. 88.

Chapter 4

1. L. B. Gschwandtner, "Creating a Champion," *Personal Selling Power,* March 1992, pp. 57–60.
2. Nathaniel Branden, *The Six Pillars of Self-Esteem* (New York: Bantam, 1994), p. xv.
3. Branden, *The Six Pillars of Self-Esteem,* pp. 26–27.
4. California State Department of Education, *Toward a State of Esteem,* Sacramento Department of Education, January 1990, p. 19.
5. Quoted in A. H. Maslow, "A Theory of Human Motivation," in *Psychological Foundations of Organizational Behavior,* edited by Barry M. Stow (Santa Monica, Calif.: Goodyear Publishing, 1977), pp. 7–8.
6. Wayne Weiten and Margaret Lloyd, *Psychology Applied to Modern Life* (Pacific Grove, Calif.: Brooks/Cole Publishing, 1994), p. 51.
7. Richard Laliberte, "Self-Esteem Workshop," *Self,* May 1994, p. 201.
8. Branden, *The Six Pillars of Self-Esteem,* p. 39.
9. Laliberte, "Self-Esteem Workshop," p. 201.
10. Nathaniel Branden, *The Psychology of Self-Esteem* (New York: Bantam Books, 1969), p. 109.
11. Amy Bjork Harris and Thomas A. Harris, *Staying OK* (New York: Harper & Row, 1985), p. 24.
12. Sue Baugh, "Cool Path to the Top," *NABW Journal,* January-February 1982, pp. 28–30.
13. "The New American Body," *University of California at Berkeley Wellness Letter,* December 1993, p. 1.
14. Margaret Henning and Ann Jardim, *The Managerial Woman* (New York: Anchor Books, 1977), pp. 106–107.
15. From Suzanne Dolezal, "He Teaches Students Self-Esteem," *Detroit Free Press,* December 5, 1985. Reprinted by permission.
16. Emmett E. Miller, *The Healing Power of Happiness* (Emmaus, Pa.: Rodale Press, 1989), pp. 12–13.
17. Amy Saltzman, *Downshifting* (New York: HarperCollins, 1990), pp. 15–16.
18. Miller, *The Healing Power of Happiness,* pp. 12–13.
19. Richard Ringer, David Balkin, and R. Wayne Boss, "Matching the Feedback to the Person," *Executive Female,* November-December 1993, p. 11.
20. Judith Briles, *Woman to Woman: From Sabotage to Support* (Far Hills, N.J.: New Horizon Press, 1987), p. 77.

21. Milton Layden, "Whipping Your Worst Enemy on the Job: Hostility," *Nation's Business,* October 1978, pp. 87–90.

22. Julia Flynn, "Julia Stasch Raises the Roof for Feminism," *Business Week,* January 25, 1993, p. 102.

23. Lee Iacocca, with William Novak, *Iacocca* (New York: Bantam Books, 1984), p. 137.

24. Robert Conklin, *How to Get People to Do Things* (Chicago: Contemporary Books, 1979), p. 69.

25. Gloria Steinem, *Revolution from Within — A Book of Self-Esteem* (Boston: Little, Brown, 1993), pp. 318–319.

26. "Self-Efficacy," *University of California at Berkeley Wellness Letter,* May 1987, p. 1.

27. J. Sterling Livingston, "Pygmalion in Management," *Harvard Business Review,* July-August 1969, p. 83.

28. Bernie S. Siegel, *Love, Medicine, and Miracles* (New York: Harper & Row, 1986), p. 43.

29. "Productivity and the Self-Fulfilling Prophecy: The Pygmalion Effect" (Carlsbad, Calif.: CRM Films, video).

30. Branden, *The Six Pillars of Self-Esteem,* p. 33.

31. California State Department of Education, *Toward a State of Esteem,* pp. 23–24.

32. Anita Shreve, "Careers and the Lure of Motherhood," *New York Times Magazine,* November 21, 1982, pp. 38–43, 46–52, 56.

33. Robert J. Kriegel, with Louis Platier, *"If It Ain't Broke . . . Break It!",* produced by Barr Audio, Irwindale, Calif., 1992, audiocassette.

34. Cheri Burns, "The Extra Edge," *Savvy,* December 1982, p. 42.

35. Shakti Gawain, *Creative Visualization* (San Rafael, Calif.: Whatever Publishing, 1978), p. 14.

36. Bob Colacello, "Diane Von Furstenberg: I Don't Believe in Fairy Tales," *Parade Magazine,* August 30, 1987, p. 5.

37. Rhonda Brandt, personal conversations with Dr. Denis Waitley, 1982–1988.

38. Shad Helmstetter, *What to Say When You Talk to Your Self* (New York: Pocket Books), 1982, p. 72.

39. Julia Flynn Siler, "The Corporate Woman: Is She Really Different?" *Business Week,* June 25, 1990, p. 14.

40. Sheila Ostrander and Lynn Schroeder, *Superlearning* (New York: Dell Publishing, 1979), pp. 87–109.

41. Roy J. Blitzer, Colleen Petersen, and Linda Rogers, "How to Build Self-Esteem," *Training & Development,* February 1993, pp. 58–60.

Chapter 5

1. Kevin Helliker, "Smile: That Cranky Shopper May Be a Store Spy," *Wall Street Journal,* November 30, 1994, p. B-1.

2. Julia H. Martin and Donna J. Tolson, "Changing Job Skills in Virginia: The Employer's View," *Newsletter* (University of Virginia), January 1986, p. 2.

3. Stephen R. Covey, *The 7 Habits of Highly Effective People* (New York: Simon & Schuster, 1989), pp. 22 and 34.

4. Susan Bixler, *Professional Presence* (New York: G. P. Putnam's Sons, 1991), p. 16.

5. "Author: Success Pivots on First Impressions," *San Jose Mercury News,* November 8, 1992, p. 2 PC.

6. Zick Rubin, "The Rise and Fall of First Impressions — How People Are Perceived," in *Interpersonal Communication in Action,* ed. Bobby R. Patton and Kim Fiffen II (New York: Harper & Row, 1977), p. 150.

7. Leonard Zunin and Natalie Zunin, *Contact — The First Four Minutes* (New York: Ballantine Books, 1972), p. 5.

8. Connie Brown Glaser and Barbara Steinberg Smalley, "Four Minutes That Get You Hired," *Reader's Digest,* August 1993, p. 130.

9. "Postal Polish: Improved Image Is Aim of Efforts at Postal Service," *Roanoke Times & World-News,* January 1, 1989, p. D-1.

10. Zunin and Zunin, *Contact,* p. 17.

11. James Gray, Jr., *The Winning Image* (New York: American Management Associations, 1982), pp. 3–5.

12. Gray, *The Winning Image,* p. 6.

13. Robert L. Simison, "GM Is Spending $25 Million to Teach Good Olds Guys to Be Even Friendlier," *Wall Street Journal,* May 11, 1994, p. B-5.

14. John T. Molloy, *Dress for Success* (New York: Peter H. Wyden, 1975); and John T. Molloy, *The Woman's Dress for Success Book* (New York: Warner Books, 1977).

15. Susan Bixler, *Professional Presence,* p. 141.

16. David Woodruff, "Talk About Life in the Fast Lane," *Business Week,* October 17, 1994, p. 160.

17. Michael Solmon, "Standard Issue," *Psychology Today,* December 1987, pp. 30–31.

18. "Workers Voice Needs," *Roanoke Times & World-News,* January 1, 1989, p. D-1.

19. Dave Knesel, "Image Consulting — A Well-Dressed Step Up the Corporate Ladder," *Pace,* July-August 1981, p. 74.

20. Haidee Allerton, "Working Life," *Training & Development,* April 1993, p. 96.

21. Bill Saporito, "Unsuit Yourself — Management Goes Informal," *Fortune,* September 20, 1993, p. 118.

22. Teri Agins, "Between Suits and Jeans: The Corporate Casual Look," *Wall Street Journal,* January 21, 1994, p. B-1.

23. Janet G. Elsea, *The Four-Minute Sell* (New York: Simon & Schuster, 1984), p. 34.

24. Susan Bixler, *The Professional Image* (New York: Perigee Books, 1984), p. 217.

25. Bixler, *The Professional Image,* p. 219.

26. Martha Sherrill Dailey, "The Way We Sound," *Roanoke Times & World-News,* May 8, 1988, p. 1.
27. Adapted from Zunin and Zunin, *Contact,* pp. 102–108.
28. Amy Gamerman, "Lunch with Letitia: Our Reporter Minds Her Manners," *Wall Street Journal,* March 3, 1994, p. A-14.
29. Barbara Lazear Ascher, "Mind and Manners," *Self,* May 1994, p. 129.
30. Jacqueline Thompson, *Image Impact* (New York: Ace Books, 1981), p. 8.
31. Bob Greene, "Why Must We Say Things Like . . . and . . . ?" *Roanoke Times & World-News,* April 27, 1980, p. 7.
32. Ann C. Humphries, "Errors Steal Power from Power Lunch," *San Jose Mercury News,* November 4, 1990, p. 2.
33. Ann Marie Sabath, "Meeting Etiquette: Agendas and More," *DECA Dimensions,* January-February 1994, p. 8.
34. Susan Bixler, "Your Professional Presence," *Training Dimensions,* Vol. 9, No. 1, 1994, p. 1.
35. Letitia Baldrige, *Letitia Baldrige's Complete Guide to Executive Manners* (New York: Rawson Associates, 1985), p. 13.
36. "Careers, Lies, and Videotape," *Training & Development,* July 1993, p. 11.

Chapter 6

1. Dennis Levine, "The Inside Story of an Inside Trader," *Fortune,* May 21, 1990, p. 82.
2. "The Strength of Character," *Royal Bank Letter* (Royal Bank of Canada) May-June 1988, p. 1.
3. "Practicing What You Preach," *The Pryor Report,* Vol. 10, No. 1a.
4. Stephen R. Covey, *The 7 Habits of Highly Effective People* (New York: Simon and Schuster, 1989), p. 92.
5. Joseph Josephson and Ednah Josephson, *Character Counts Wallet Card,* Josephson Institute of Ethics (Marina del Ray, Calif., 1994).
6. Warren H. Schmidt and Barry Z. Posner, *Managerial Values and Expectations* (New York: AMACOM, 1982), pp. 12–14.
7. J. David McCracken and Ana E. Falcon-Emmanuelli, "A Theoretical Basis for Work Values Research in Vocational Education," *Journal of Vocational and Technical Education,* Spring 1994, p. 4.
8. Tom Pickens, "Ethics: Easy as A-B-C?" *Creative Living,* Vol. 22, No. 4, p. 8.
9. "Put First Things First," *Inc.,* December 1987, p. 168.
10. Chris Lee and Ron Zemke, "The Search for Spirit in the Workplace," *Training,* June 1993, p. 21.
11. Stanley M. Elam, Lowell C. Rose, and Alec M. Gallup, "The 26th Annual Phi Delta Kappa/Gallup Poll of the Public's Attitudes Toward the Public Schools," *Phi Delta Kappan,* September 1994, p. 49.
12. Sonia L. Nazario, "Schoolteachers Say It's Wrongheaded to Try to Teach Students What's Right," *Wall Street Journal,* April 6, 1990, p. B-1.
13. Andrew Stark, "What's the Matter with Business Ethics," *Harvard Business Review,* May-June 1993, p. 38.
14. William J. Bennett, *The Index of Leading Cultural Indicators: Facts and Figures on the State of American Society* (New York: Simon & Schuster, 1994), p. 103.
15. Morris Massey, *The People Puzzle* (Reston, Va.: Reston Publishing, 1979).
16. Quoted in Will Lorey, "Values System Analysis Theory," *Training/HRD,* January 1981, pp. 38–39.
17. "Newsbreakers," *Inc.,* October 1990, p. 25.
18. Jeffrey Leib, "Competition Spurs DU Changes," *Denver Post,* November 5, 1989, p. 1.
19. Joan E. Rigdon, "Some Workers Gripe Bosses Are Ordering Too Much Overtime," *Wall Street Journal,* September 29, 1994, pp. A-1, A-6.
20. "Time — Top Priority for American Workers," *Destinations,* June 1991, p. 19.
21. Charles M. Kelly, "Confrontation Insurance," *Training/HRD,* August 1981, pp. 91–94.
22. H. B. Karp and Bob Abramms, "Doing the Right Thing," *Training and Development,* August 1992, p. 38.
23. Sidney B. Simon, Leland W. Howe, and Howard Kirschenbaum, *Values Clarification* (New York: Hart Publishing, 1972), p. 15.
24. Marian Wright Edelman, *The Measure of Our Success* (Boston: Allyn and Bacon, 1992), pp. 502–503.
25. Charles Siler, "Body Shop Marches to Its Own Drummer," *Advertising Age,* October 10, 1994, p. 4.
26. Eric D. Randall, "Money No Longer Tops for MBAs," *USA Today,* May 25, 1994, p. 5-B.
27. Dawn Anfuso, "Soul-searching Sustains Values at Lotus Development," *Personnel Journal,* June 1994, pp. 54–61.
28. Betsy Weisendanger, "Doing the Right Thing," *Sales & Marketing Management,* March 1991, p. 82.
29. M. Scott Peck, *The Road Less Traveled* (New York: Simon & Schuster, 1978), p. 19.
30. Michael H. Mescon and Timothy S. Mescon, "And Then Some . . . ," *Sky,* August 1989, p. 92.
31. George Kegley, "Broker with a Difference: A. G. Edwards, Chairman," *Roanoke Times & World-News,* April 13, 1990, p. B-6.
32. Quoted in "Values Added," *Inc.,* January 1986, p. 31.
33. Krystal Miller, "Former Honda Executives Plead Guilty to Charges Tied to Bribes From Dealers," *Wall Street Journal,* March 15, 1994, p. A-4.
34. Peter J. Howe and Judy Rakowsky, "Illegal Gifts by Hancock Detailed," *Boston Globe,* March 23, 1994, pp. 1, 10.

35. Richard Behar, "Skimming the Cream," *Time,* August 2, 1993, p. 49.

36. Andrew Stark, "What's the Matter with Business Ethics?" *Harvard Business Review,* May-June 1993, p. 38.

37. "Tom Chappell — Minister of Commerce," *Business Ethics,* January-February 1994, p. 17.

38. Weisendanger, "Doing the Right Thing," p. 82.

39. "Ukrop's Corporate Values," Ukrop's Super Markets, Inc., Richmond, Va.

40. Joshua Hyatt, "How to Hire Employees," *Inc.,* March 1990, p. 2.

41. Claudia H. Deutsch, "You Want This Job? Pass the Integrity Test," *San Jose Mercury News,* February 25, 1990, p. 2.

42. "Honesty Tests: The Defense Rests," *Training,* May 1991, p. 12.

43. Robert McGarvey, "Doing the Right Thing," *Training,* July 1993, pp. 35, 36.

44. Phillip Barnhart, "The Ethics Game," *Training,* June 1993, pp. 65, 66.

45. John Bussey and James McGregor, "What, Why, and How," *Wall Street Journal,* December 19, 1993, p. R-19.

46. Chris Hill and Toby Hanlon, "26 Simple Ways to Change How You Feel," *Prevention,* August 1993, p. 126.

Chapter 7

1. R. Roosevelt Thomas, Jr., "From Affirmative Action to Affirming Diversity," *Harvard Business Review,* March-April 1990, p. 107.

2. "The Immigrants: How They're Helping to Revitalize the U.S. Economy," *Business Week,* July 13, 1992, p. 116.

3. Marilyn Loden and Judy B. Rosener, *Workforce America!* (Homewood, Ill.: Business One Irwin, 1991), p. 18.

4. Loden and Rosener, *Workforce America!* p. 121.

5. Loden and Rosener, *Workforce America!* p. 21.

6. Loden and Rosener, *Workforce America!* p. 52.

7. "Vicious Bigotry: Jewish Women Face Ugly Stereotypes Labeling Them Princesses," *Roanoke Times & World-News,* September 3, 1987, p. A-4.

8. Karen Shepherd, "Why Stereotypes Hurt," *Management World,* January 1985, pp. 41, 44.

9. Charles M. Kelly, "Confrontation Insurance," *Training/HRD,* August 1981, pp. 91–94.

10. Lewis Brown Griggs and Lente-Louise Louw, *Valuing Diversity* (New York: McGraw-Hill, 1995) pp. 3–4, 150–151.

11. "Working Women Feel Cheated," *Roanoke News and World Report,* October 15, 1994, p. A-3.

12. "A Special News Report About Life on the Job — and Trends Taking Shape There," *Wall Street Journal,* November 22, 1994, p. 16.

13. Susan Garland, "Throwing Stones at the Glass Ceiling," *Business Week,* August 19, 1991, p. 29.

14. "Woman Wins Bias Suit Against Texaco," *New York Times,* September 28, 1991, p. L-25.

15. "Fifty-Something," *Training & Development,* May 1994, p. 143.

16. Griggs and Louw, *Valuing Diversity,* p. 17.

17. "The Job Market Beckons Retirees," *AARP News Bulletin,* January 1987, p. 2.

18. Sam Fulwood, III, "Black Still Isn't the Color of Money," *Venture,* March 1988, p. 32.

19. Griggs and Louw, *Valuing Diversity,* p. 16.

20. Griggs and Louw, *Valuing Diversity,* p. 16.

21. "Hispanics: Just Another Immigrant Story?" *Fortune,* November 21, 1988, p. 188.

22. Griggs and Louw, *Valuing Diversity,* p. 16.

23. Griggs and Louw, *Valuing Diversity,* p. 17.

24. Anthony Ramirez, "America's Super Minority," *Fortune,* November 24, 1986, p. 148.

25. Deborah L. Jacobs, "The Americans with Disabilities Act," *Your Company* (Milwaukee, Wisc.: Northwestern Mutual Life Insurance Company), Summer 1994, p. 10.

26. "Ordinary People," *American Demographics,* August 1987, p. 10.

27. "Everybody Wins at Red Lobster," *Training,* December 1990, pp. 32–33.

28. Thomas A. Stewart, "Gay in Corporate America," *Fortune,* December 16, 1991, p. 44.

29. Jay H. Lucas and Mark G. Kaplan, "Unlocking the Corporate Closet," *Training & Development,* January 1994, pp. 36–37.

30. Stewart, "Gay in Corporate America," p. 50.

31. U.S. Commission on Civil Rights, *Promises and Perceptions: Federal Efforts to Eliminate Employment Discrimination Through Affirmative Action* (Washington, D.C.: U.S. Government Printing Office, October 1981), p. 17.

32. "Appearance Bias in Workplace Is Widespread and Usually Illegal," *BNAC Communicator,* Spring-Summer 1994, p. 20.

33. Loden and Rosener, *Workforce America!* p. 12.

34. Thomas, "From Affirmative Action to Affirming Diversity," p. 110.

35. Melissa A. Berman, "Talking Through the Glass Wall," *Across the Board,* July-August 1988, p. 26.

36. Kathy Seal, "Know Thy Neighbor," *American Way,* August 15, 1991, p. 36.

37. Thomas, "From Affirmative Action to Affirming Diversity," p. 113.

38. Faye Rice, "How to Make Diversity Pay," *Fortune,* August 8, 1994, p. 86.

39. Rice, "How to Make Diversity Pay," p. 82.
40. Rice, "How to Make Diversity Pay," p. 84.
41. Rice, "How to Make Diversity Pay," p. 82.
42. Rice, "How to Make Diversity Pay," p. 84.
43. "Twelve Companies That Do the Right Thing," p. 59.
44. Rice, "How to Make Diversity Pay," p. 84.
45. "The Daily Experience of Genuine Workplace Diversity," *Harvard Business Review,* March-April 1990, p. 115.
46. Walter Guzzardi, "A Fresh View of Affirmative Action," *Fortune,* September 23, 1991, p. 210.
47. Jim Schachter, "Facing Bias in a Diverse Work Place," *Los Angeles Times,* April 24, 1988, p. F-9.

Chapter 8

1. Rensis Likert and Jane Gibson Likert, *New Ways of Managing Conflict* (New York: McGraw-Hill, 1976), pp. 7–8.
2. Gordon Lippitt, "Managing Conflict in Today's Organizations," *Training and Development Journal,* July 1982, pp. 67–74.
3. Julie Gravelle, "Conflicts Among Workers Found to Hurt Bottom Line," *Roanoke Times & World-News,* July 4, 1993, p. B-2.
4. "Study Finds Most Workers Unhappy in Their Firms," *Chicago Tribune,* December 13, 1982, pp. 1–2.
5. "Surviving the Office Jerk Takes Patience," *Springfield News-Leader,* November 6, 1994, p. 2E.
6. Edward Glassman, "Selling Your Ideas to Management," *Supervisory Management,* October 1991, p. 9.
7. "Assertiveness: More Than a Forceful Attitude," *Supervisory Management,* February 1994, p. 3.
8. Stephen Ash, "How to Make Assertiveness Work for You," *Supervisory Management,* p. 8.
9. Stephen R. Covey, *The Seven Habits of Highly Effective People* (New York: Simon & Schuster, 1989), p. 237.
10. Covey, *The Seven Habits of Highly Effective People,* p. 237.
11. Alan Filley, *Interpersonal Conflict Resolution* (Glenview, Ill.: Scott, Foresman, 1975), pp. 60–69.
12. Lippitt, "Managing Conflict in Today's Organizations," p. 70.
13. Willard Gaylin, *Feelings* (New York: Ballantine Books, 1979), p. 1.
14. John Selby, *Conscious Healing* (New York: Bantam Books, 1989), p. 32.
15. Selby, *Conscious Healing,* p. 32.
16. Douglas A. Bernstein, Edward J. Roy, Thomas K. Srull, and Christopher D. Wickens, *Psychology,* 2d ed. (Boston: Houghton Mifflin, 1991), p. 52.
17. Bernstein and others, *Psychology,* p. 52.
18. William C. Menninger and Harry Levinson, *Human Understanding in Industry* (Chicago: Science Research Associates, 1956), p. 29.
19. Joan Borysenko, *Guilt Is the Teacher, Love Is the Lesson* (New York: Warner Books, 1990), p. 70.
20. Donella H. Meadows, "We Are, to Our Harm, What We Watch," *Roanoke Times & World-News,* October 16, 1994, p. G-3.
21. "Schools Hit by Epidemic of Violence," *Roanoke Times & World-News,* January 6, 1994, p. A-1.
22. Stanley M. Elam, Lowell C. Rose, and Alec M. Gallup, "The 26th Annual Phi Delta Kappa/Gallup Poll of the Public's Attitudes Toward the Public Schools," *Phi Delta Kappan,* September 1994, pp. 41–43.
23. Data published by Handgun Control, Inc.
24. "Youth Violence Reflects Culture," *Menninger Letter,* October 1993, p. 6.
25. Kimes Gustin, *Anger, Rage, and Resentment* (West Caldwell, N.J.: St. Ives' Press, 1994), p. 1.
26. Helen Hall Clinard, *Winning Ways to Succeed with People* (Houston: Gulf Publishing, 1985), p. 82.
27. Susan Bixler, *Professional Presence* (New York: G. P. Putnam's Sons, 1991), pp. 190–191.
28. Rolland S. Parker, *Emotional Common Sense* (New York: Barnes & Noble Books, 1973), pp. 80–81.
29. Jane Brody, "Turning Anger into Useful Force," *Roanoke Times & World-News,* November 30, 1993, p. E-1.
30. Gustin, *Anger, Rage, and Resentment,* p. 37.
31. Les Giblin, *How to Have Confidence and Power in Dealing with People* (Englewood Cliffs, N.J.: Prentice-Hall, 1956), p. 37.
32. Gustin, *Anger, Rage, and Resentment,* p. 42.
33. Joan Borysenko, *Minding the Body, Mending the Mind* (New York: Bantam Books, 1987), p. 163.
34. Selby, *Conscious Healing,* p. 32.
35. Walton C. Boshear and Karl G. Albrecht, *Understanding People: Models and Concepts* (San Diego: University Associates, 1977), pp. 41–46.
36. Chris Hill and Toby Hanlon, "Twenty-Six Simple Ways to Change How You Feel," *Prevention,* August 1993, p. 63.
37. William J. Crockett, "Our Two Worlds," *Training & Development,* May 1982, p. 60.
38. Borysenko, *Minding the Body, Mending the Mind,* p. 169.
39. Ellen Safier, "Our Experts Answer Your Questions," *Menninger Letter,* May 1993, p. 8.
40. Leo F. Buscaglia, *Loving Each Other* (Thorofare, N.J.: Slack, 1984), p. 160.
41. Sam Keen, *Fire in the Belly: On Being a Man* (New York: Bantam Books, 1991), p. 242.

Chapter 9

1. Joshua Hyatt, "Mapping the Entrepreneurial Mind," *Inc.,* August 1991, pp. 26–31.

2. Hyatt, "Mapping the Entrepreneurial Mind," p. 31.

3. Brian O'Reilly, "Preparing for Leaner Times," *Fortune,* January 27, 1992, pp. 46–47.

4. Amy Saltzman, *Downshifting: Reinventing Success on a Slower Track* (New York: Harper Collins, 1991), p. 16.

5. Joseph Weber, "Farewell, Fast Track," *Business Week,* December 10, 1990, pp. 192–200.

6. Robert Kuttner, "No Time to Smell the Roses Anymore," *New York Times Book Review,* February 2, 1992, pp. 1, 21.

7. Amanda Bennett, "Broken Bonds," *Wall Street Journal,* December 8, 1989, p. R-21.

8. Bennett, "Broken Bonds," p. R-21.

9. Lynn Lannon, "Giving Back: The Secret of Creating Success," *Training and Development Journal,* April 1990, p. 58.

10. Robert McGarvey, "Softening the Blow," *U.S. Air,* September 1991, p. 18.

11. Kuttner, "No Time to Smell the Roses Anymore," p. 21.

12. "U.S. Workers Suffer from a Time-Off Gap," *Business Week,* August 12, 1991, p. 16.

13. "When Success Fails to Make You Happy," *Working Smart,* September 1991, p. 1.

14. Lee Iacocca, *Iacocca* (New York: Bantam Books, 1984), pp. 30–31.

15. Interview conducted on February 8, 1992.

16. Pam Black, "Jump-Starts for Stalled Careers," *Business Week,* July 1, 1991.

17. Marsha Sinetar, *Do What You Love . . . The Money Will Follow* (New York: Dell, 1987), p. 11.

18. Sinetar, *Do What You Love . . . ,* pp. 11–12.

19. Michael Phillips, *The Seven Laws of Money* (Menlo Park, Calif.: Word Wheel and Random House, 1974), p. 9.

20. Sinetar, *Do What You Love . . . ,* pp. 14–15.

21. John Naisbitt and Patricia Aburdene, *Re-Inventing the Corporation* (New York: Warner Books, 1985), p. 5.

22. Sinetar, *Do What You Love . . . ,* p. 15.

23. Sinetar, p. 19.

24. Sinetar, p. 16.

25. Melvyn Kinder, *Going Nowhere Fast* (New York: Prentice-Hall, 1990), p. 76.

26. Michael Toms, "Money: The Third Side of the Coin" (Interview with Joe Dominguez and Vicki Robin), *New Dimensions,* May-June 1991, p. 9.

27. Interview with Juliet B. Schor, author of *The Overworked American,* aired on Public Radio, February 3, 1992.

28. Brian O'Reilly, "Preparing for Leaner Times," *Fortune,* January 27, 1992, pp. 40–47.

29. *Money Management* (Blacksburg: Virginia Cooperative Extension, 1990), pp. 1–5.

30. Toms, "Money: The Third Side of the Coin," (Interview), p. 7.

31. Susan Smith Jones, "Choose to Be Healthy and Celebrate Life," *New Realities,* September-October 1988, pp. 17–19.

32. Smith Jones, "Choose to Be Healthy and Celebrate Life," p. 18.

33. Guy Boulton, "Those Who've Made It Share Secrets of Success," *San Jose Mercury News,* November 17, 1991, p. PC-1.

34. Saltzman, *Downshifting,* p. 23.

35. Jay T. Knippen, Thad B. Green, and Kurt Sutton, "Asking Not to Be Overworked," *Supervisory Management,* February 1992, p. 6.

36. Iacocca, *Iacocca,* p. 20.

37. Iacocca, *Iacocca,* p. 20.

38. Leo Booth, "When God Becomes a Drug," *Common Boundary,* September-October 1991, p. 30.

39. "Making the Spiritual Connection," *Lears,* December 1989, p. 72.

40. Brenton R. Schlender, "The Values We Will Need," *Fortune,* January 27, 1992, p. 77.

41. Pythia Peay, "Creative Altruism," *Common Boundary,* July-August 1991, p. 37.

42. Booth, "When God Becomes a Drug," pp. 26–27.

43. "Making the Spiritual Connection," p. 75.

44. Frank Rose, "A New Age for Business?" *Fortune,* October 8, 1990, pp. 155–164.

45. Chris Lee and Ron Zemke, "The Search for Spirit in the Workplace," *Training,* June 1993, p. 25.

46. Russell Mitchell, "Sure, You're Busy. That's No Reason Not to Eat Right," *Business Week,* October 9, 1989, p. 122.

47. *Dietary Guidelines for Americans,* 2nd ed. (Washington, D.C.: U.S. Department of Health and Human Services, 1985), pp. 3–21.

48. *Dietary Guidelines for Americans,* p. 6.

49. "The Straight Facts About Fiber," *AICR Newsletter,* Fall 1990, p. 4.

50. "Weight of Average Young U.S. Adult Rose 10 Pounds in Seven-Year Period," *Wall Street Journal,* March 18, 1994, p. 5B.

51. *Dietary Guidelines for Americans,* p. 9.

52. *Dietary Guidelines for Americans,* p. 21.

53. *Dietary Guidelines for Americans,* p. 23.

54. *Fitness Fundamentals* (Washington, D.C.: Department of Health and Human Services, 1988), pp. 2–3.

55. "One Small Step . . . ," *University of California at Berkeley Wellness Letter,* January 1991, p. 1; Kenneth Blanchard, D. W. Edington, and Marjorie Blanchard, *The One Minute Manager Gets Fit* (New York: Morrow, 1986), p. 36.

56. Jane E. Brody, "Enjoy the Health Benefits of Walking," *Roanoke Times & World-News,* March 18, 1991, p. E-4.

57. "An Exercise Program You Can Stick With," *Johns Hopkins Medical Letter,* August 1990, p. 7.

58. Robert A. Gleser, *The Healthmark Program for Life* (New York: McGraw-Hill, 1988), p. 147.

59. Gleser, *The Healthmark Program for Life,* p. 143.

60. *Fitness Fundamentals,* p. 2.

61. Stephen R. Covey, *The Seven Habits of Highly Effective People* (New York: Simon & Schuster, 1989), p. 46.

62. James Fadiman, *Be All That You Are* (Seattle: Westlake Press, 1986), p. 25.

63. Fadiman, *Be All That You Are,* p. 27.

64. Robert McGarvey, "Getting Your Goals," *U.S. Air,* July 1989, p. 28.

65. Covey, *The Seven Habits of Highly Effective People,* p. 92.

66. Fadiman, *Be All That You Are,* p. 45.

67. Pete Engardio and Peter Finch, "Kazuo Wada's Answered Prayers," *Business Week,* August 26, 1991, p. 66.

68. Mike Hernacki, *The Ultimate Secret of Getting Absolutely Everything You Want* (New York: Berkley Books, 1988), p. 35.

Credits

Chapter 1

Case Problem: Rochelle Sharpe, "Being Family Friendly Doesn't Mean Promoting Women," *Wall Street Journal,* March 29, 1994, p. B-1; Sue Shellenbarger, "Work and Family," *Wall Street Journal,* June 1, 1994, p. B-1; "Working Mother Lists Best," *Roanoke Times & World-News,* September 14, 1994, p. B-8; Sue Shellenbarger, "'Best' List for Working Mothers Shows New Faces: Midwest Firms, Oil Giants," *Wall Street Journal,* September 16, 1993, p. A-8.

Chapter 2

Case Problem: Rick Atkinson, "Mercedes Workers Polish Their Y'Alls and Howdies," *The Denver Post,* February 27, 1994, p. 3H; Jack Yamaguchi, "Eagles Are Landing in Japan," *Road & Track,* July 1994, p. 24; "White House Watch," *The New Republic,* October 25, 1993, p. 48; Atkinson, "Mercedes Workers Polish Their Y'Alls and Howdies," p. 3H.

Chapter 3

Case Problem: Robert Levering and Milton Moskowitz, *Thee 100 Best Companies to Work for in America* (New York: Currency-Doubleday, 1993), pp. 270–272.

Chapter 4

Case Problem: California Assembly Bill No. 3659; *Toward a State of Esteem,* California State Department of Education, 1990, p. 37; Gloria Steinem, *Revolution from Within: A Book of Self-Esteem* (Boston: Little, Brown, 1992), pp. 26–31.

Chapter 5

Case Problem: "Don't Ignore Dressing for Success," *Supervisory Management,* September 1994, p. 5; Susan Bixler, "Your Professional Presence," *Training Dimensions,* Vol. 9, No. 1, 1994, p. 1.

Chapter 6

Case Problem: "Paying Employees to Work Elsewhere," *Inc.,* February 1993, p. 29; "Interview with Tom Chappell," *Business Ethics,* January-February 1994, pp. 16–18; Milton Moskowitz, "Business Prophets," *Common Boundary,* March-April 1994, pp. 55–58; "Profiles in Marketing: Katie Shisler," *Sales & Marketing Management,* March 1993, p. 12.

Chapter 7

Case Problem: David Zuckerman, "Serving Up Apologies," *Sales & Marketing Management,* October 1993, pp. 133–135; Benjamin A. Holden, "Denny's Chain Settles Suits by Minorities," *Wall Street Journal,* May 24, 1994, p. A-3; Stephen Labaton, "Civil Rights Milestone," *Denver Post,* May 25, 1994, p. 2-A; "The Stiff Price of Bias: $35,000 a Customer," *U.S. News & World Report,* June 6, 1994, p. 14; "Denny's: The Stain That Isn't Coming Out," *Business Week,* June 28, 1993, pp. 98–99; "What To Do When Race Charges Fly," *Fortune,* July 12, 1993, p. 95.

Chapter 8

Case Problem: Ellen Goodman, "Many U.S. Workers Are Drowning in Overtime Gravy," *Roanoke Times & World-News,* October 11, 1994, p. A7; Gary Cross, "Overtime Costing Dearly," *Roanoke Times & World-News,* October 19, 1994, p. A11; "G.M. Strike Spotlights New Labor Grievance; Forced OT," *Roanoke Times & World-News,* September 30, 1994, p. A9; Joan E. Rigdon, "Some Workers Gripe Bosses Are Ordering Too Much Overtime," *Wall Street Journal,* September 29, 1994, pp. A-1 and A-6; "Rumble in Buick City," *Business Week,* October 10, 1994, p. 42.

Chapter 9

Case Problem: Julia Flynn, "Julia Stasch Raises the Roof for Feminism," *Business Week,* January 25, 1993, p. 102; Robert Barker, "One Man and a Little Lady," *Business Week,* April 15, 1991, p. 91; Mary Newson, "The Time of Our Lives," *Roanoke Times & World-News, Extra,* January 11, 1993, p. 4.

Career Corner Credits

Chapter 1: Louis S. Richman, "How to Get Ahead in America," *Fortune,* May 16, 1994, pp. 46–54; Ronald Henkoff, "Winning the New Career Game," *Fortune,* July 12, 1993, pp. 46–49.

Chapter 2: Joan E. Rigdon, "Even When They Ask, Bosses Don't Want Your Complaints," *Wall Street Journal*, August 10, 1994, p. B-1.

Chapter 4: Maxwell Maltz, *Psycho-Cybernetics* (New York: Pocket Books, 1972) pp. 6–7.

Chapter 5: "How Much Can Employer Dictate Your Lifestyle?" *San Jose Mercury News*, May 2, 1993, pp. 1 PC and 2 PC; Susan Barciela, "Looks and Dress Still Count, Though the Lawyers Might Argue," *Roanoke Times & World-News*, June 19, 1993, p. D2; Susan Bixler, "Your Professional Presence," *Training Dimensions*, Vol. 9, No. 1, 1994, p. 1.

Chapter 6: Andrew W. Singer, "Can a Company Be Too Ethical?" *Across the Board*, April 1993, pp. 17–22.

Chapter 7: "Good Customer Phone Form," *Training & Development*, December 1992, p. 9.

Chapter 8: Sue Shellenbarger and Carol Hymowitz, "As Population Ages, Older Workers Clash with Younger Bosses," *Wall Street Journal*, June 3, 1994, pp. A-1 and A-5.

Total Person Insight Credits

Chapter 1:

p. 12: William Raspberry, "Topmost Priority: Jobs," *Washington Post*, (n.d.) 1977; **p. 8:** Marsha Sinetar, *Do What You Love . . . The Money Will Follow* (New York: Dell, 1989); **p. 16:** James Baughman quote from Frank Rose, "A New Age for Business?", *Fortune*, October 8, 1990, p. 162.

Chapter 2

p. 30: Paul R. Timm, "The Way We Word," in *Effective Communications on the Job*, ed. William K. Fallon (New York: AMACOM, 1981), p. 74; **p. 42:** Gerry Mitchell quote from "Listen, Listen, Listen," *Business Week*, September 14, 1987, p. 108.

Chapter 3

p. 58: Denis Waitley, *The Winning Generation: The Self-Esteem Training Program for Youth* (Cedar Falls, Iowa: Advanced Learning, Inc., 1987), p. 18; **p. 70:** Pamela R. Johnson and Claudia Rawlins, "Daydreams and Dialogues: Key to Motivation," *Supervisory Management*, January 1991, p. 2.

Chapter 4

p. 82: Nathaniel Branden, *The Six Pillars of Self-Esteem* (New York: Bantam, 1994), p. 19; **p. 95:** Nathaniel Branden, *The Six Pillars of Self-Esteem* (New York: Bantam, 1994), p. 105.

Chapter 5

p. 112: Janet G. Elsea, *The Four-Minute Sell* (New York: Simon & Schuster, 1984), p. 34; **p. 121:** Judith Martin, "Low Income Is Not Low-Class," *Roanoke Times & World-News*, March 13, 1988, p. E-10.

Chapter 6

p. 141: Dan Rice and Craig Dreilinger, "Rights and Wrongs of Ethics Training," *Training and Development Journal*, May 1990, p. 105.

Chapter 7

p. 154: Jack Pluckhan quote from Beau Bauman, *The Most Important Thing I've Learned in Life* (New York: Simon & Schuster, 1994), p. 150; **p. 169:** Lewis Brown Griggs and Lente-Louise Louw, *Valuing Diversity: New Tools for a New Reality* (New York: McGraw-Hill, Inc., 1995), p. 9; **p. 162:** George Tunick, "Re-educating Chauvinists," *Executive Female*, January/February 1995, p. 82.

Chapter 8

p. 183: Gordon Lippett quote from "Managing Conflict in Today's Organizations," *Training and Development*, July 1982, p. 3; **p. 192:** Roger Fisher and William Ury, *Getting to Yes* (New York: Penguin Books, 1981), p. 4; **p. 201:** Kimes Gustin, *Anger, Rage, and Resentment* (West Caldwell, N.Y.: St. Ives' Press, 1994), p. 13; **p. 206:** Joan Borysenko, *Minding the Body, Mending the Mind* (New York: Bantam Books, 1987), p. 169.

Chapter 9

p. 214: Amy Saltzman, *Downshifting: Reinventing Success on a Slower Track* (New York: Harper Collins Publishers, 1990), p. 15; **p. 218:** Hugh Prather poem from *Notes to Myself*, Copyright © 1970 by Real People Press. Used by permission of Bantam Books, a division of Bantam Doubleday Dell Publishing Group, Inc.; **p. 223:** M. Scott Peck, *The Road Less Traveled* (New York: Simon & Schuster, 1978), p. 285; **p. 228:** Fred Huyghue, "Merging Spirituality with Work," *Business Ethics*, July/August 1994, p. 27; **p. 229:** Susan Smith Jones, "Choose to Be Healthy and Celebrate Life," *New Realities*, September/October 1988, p. 17.

Name Index

Subject Index